OFF THE BEATEN PATH® SERIES

Arkansas

FIFTH EDITION

BRINGING RIVERS TO LIFE

American Rivers

FOUNDED 1973

www.americanrivers.org

by Patti DeLano

Revised and updated by
Diana Lambdin Meyer

The
Globe
Pequot
Press

Guilford, Connecticut

The prices and rates listed in this guidebook were confirmed at press time. We recommend, however, that you call establishments before traveling to obtain current information.

Cover and text design by Laura Augustine
Cover photo by Dave Bartruff
Maps created by Equator Graphics © The Globe Pequot Press
Text illustrations by Cathy Johnson

ISBN 0-7627-1032-2
ISSN 1537-0550

Manufactured in the United States of America
Fifth Edition/First Printing

Acknowledgments

This book is dedicated to my great-grandfather, Ransom Lambdin, who settled in Grant County Arkansas on Christmas Eve 1885, where he homesteaded 160 acres, much of which remains in the Lambdin family today. This book is also dedicated to my grandfather, John Lambdin, who taught me the value of spinning a good yarn.

—Diana Lambdin Meyer

Finding offbeat places in Arkansas often means following directions like "You know where that big ole tree used to be?" or, "Hang a left there, you know, by that red barn?"

So I owe a lot to friends like Barbara and John Glover, and Art and Terry Hapke, who offered hospitality and help from their homes in Arkansas and spent endless hours helping me find places as common as antiques shops and as remote as an elephant farm. My mom and dad, Sally and John Randazzo, also endured mountain roads and odd places, with the sense of humor I love them for, as we wandered around the state.

This fifth edition is in memory of my husband, Bob, who had an instinct for finding unique eating places and unlikely shortcuts not shown on any map (even when he had never been there before). Serendipitous travel with him to odd places was always fun. Going it alone will not be the same.

—Patti DeLano

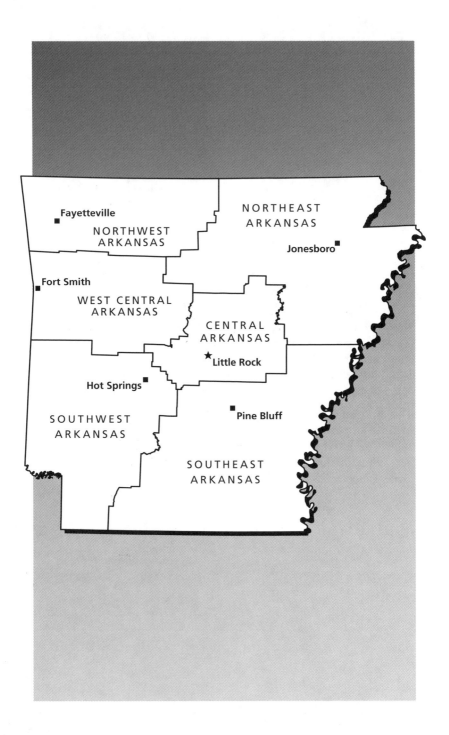

Fayetteville

NORTHWEST
ARKANSAS

NORTHEAST
ARKANSAS

Jonesboro

Fort Smith

WEST CENTRAL
ARKANSAS

CENTRAL
ARKANSAS

★ Little Rock

Hot Springs

Pine Bluff

SOUTHWEST
ARKANSAS

SOUTHEAST
ARKANSAS

Contents

Introduction

Arkansas is the perfect vacationland: 60-foot waterfalls and quiet sandbars seen only from a canoe or wooded hiking trail. Add trout streams and hunting lodges—nature at its best for people who want to be outdoors—plus golf courses, racetracks, and the big-city fun of fine restaurants, and you have the vacation choice of millions in the nation's heartland.

Thousands of artists and craftspeople have settled in the Ozarks. Vineyards and wineries dot the Arkansas River Valley, and an elephant breeding farm lies hidden in the foothills. You will find the friendliness of the Old South, hardy spirit of the Southwest, and practicality of the Midwest in the people here.

This undiscovered wonderland, far from any ocean, may be one of the most beautiful states on the continent. It has more designated National Scenic Byways than any other state in the nation. But Arkansas is more than just the beauty of stair-step waterfalls or Class V rapids in a canoe. It offers wine country, good Cajun food, old cotton plantations, and the only bordello on the National Register of Historic Places. If that's too much excitement for you, there's a Benedictine monastery where you can retreat, search your soul, and start over.

The climate boasts four distinct seasons—but with Gulf air creating the moderate temperatures of the southern United States. Spring comes early, attracting visitors from bordering states not so lucky in the weather game. Unlike its northern neighbors, Arkansas has a long, long spring filled with pleasant days perfect for outdoor activities.

Golfers, fishermen, hikers, and canoeists flock here. So do people who have retired from the rat race and do all their racing now on whitewater rapids or at the greyhound or horse track. Arkansans are serious about outdoor activities. No wimps can be found on the 225-mile Ouachita Trail, which allows hikers to follow the ridges and valleys from Pinnacle Mountain State Park to Queen Wilhelmina State Lodge and into Oklahoma.

Yes, it's hot as the dickens in August, but as the muscadine grapes (known as scuppernongs) ripen to a reddish brown, the nights begin to cool. In late September the black-gum trees change from glossy green to shining crimson—suddenly and completely—standing out from the green of the other, more hesitant trees. Then other colors begin as casual blushes of yellow and red and spread from north to south during October to finish in a blaze of color. Fall colors are dazzling, and the endless days of perfect weather and bright blue skies make this about the best time of year.

Winters are characterized by brief cold snaps and a splash of clean snow, with crisp nights, bright stars, and crystal ice formations in the gleaming winter sun—followed quickly by warmer days. Mistletoe and five kinds of holly grow throughout the state, making hunting in the December woods popular.

Because this book is filled with listings of small crafts shops, mom-and-pop restaurants, bed-and-breakfasts in beautiful old homes, and log cabins tucked in sleepy hollers and mountain foothills, it is wise to call ahead and double-check before making a long drive to a particular place. When something disappears, something else pops up in its place; getting off the beaten path in this state is always interesting. If something is gone or some other fascinating place has sprung up, let the publisher know about it so we can include it in the next update of this book.

The tourist information centers will give you a free road map, or you can call (800) NATURAL and get a vacation guide for the area you are visiting. Internet users can e-mail admin@RoomsPlus.com for a list of some bed-and-breakfasts in the state or log on to www.bbonline.com/ar/ for others. Bring your camera or your sketch pad and find the best Mother Nature has to offer. That's why they call it the Natural State.

Arkansas at a Glance

Arkansas: The Natural State. Arkansas means "South Wind," the name of the Quapaw Indian tribe the French Jesuits met. It was spelled and pronounced many different ways, but the pronunciation Ar-kan-saw was settled on by the legislature in 1881. The state flag is a blue-bordered white diamond on a rectangular field of red; the border contains twenty-five stars, the diamond has four.

Capital: Little Rock

Motto: The People Rule

Earliest Inhabitants: Pre-Columbian bluff dwellers about A.D. 500. They used a weapon similar to the Aztec *atlatl*—a throwing stick—to hunt buffalo and deer.

Earliest Explorers: Hernando de Soto crossed the Mississippi near Sunflower Landing, June 29, 1541. The first permanent white settlement was founded by René Robert Cavelier, sieur de la Salle, who took

INTRODUCTION

formal possession for Louis XIV of France in 1763. It became part of the Louisiana Purchase in 1803.

Geography: One-fourth of Arkansas is covered by standing timber. There are at least 210 species of trees, the oak group being the largest with forty-three types.

Lowest Elevation: 54'

Highest Elevation: 2,723'

Land Area: 53,187 square miles (ranked 27th in the U.S.)

Population: 2,673,400

Statehood: June 15, 1836 (25th state; entered as a slave state)

State Bird: Mockingbird

State Tree: Short-leaf pine

State Flower: Apple blossom

State Mammal: White-tailed deer

State Gemstone: Diamond

State Beverage: Milk

State Instrument: Fiddle

Average Annual Precipitation: Ranges from 45 inches in the mountains to 55 inches in the Delta.

Major Newspapers: *Arkansas Democrat Gazette, Arkansas Times, Little Rock Free Press* (Little Rock); *The Benton County Daily Record* (Bentonville); *Gurdon Times, Herald Leader* (Siloam Springs); *The Hutchinson News, Morning News of Northwest Arkansas* (Springdale); *Nevada County Picayune* (Prescott); *Northwest Arkansas Times* (Fayetteville)

Travel Information: Call (800) NATURAL for brochures, (800) 828–8974 for Arkansas Department of Parks and Tourism, or log on to the Web site at www.arkansas.com.

Northeast Arkansas

Things don't change much in the Ozarks—dogwoods, redbuds, and wild plum bloom in the spring; wildflowers color the meadows of summer; and thousands of acres of autumn forest splash color over the hills where the clear-running streams and rivers still sparkle in the sun. The colors of the Ozarks shift like a kaleidoscope, but things in the Ozarks don't change much.

The pace is slower here. The people are friendly. In a place that did not have a paved highway until after the Second World War, a culture emerged unique in the country. In fact, many people here insist that the Ozarks should have constituted its own state instead of meandering across two state lines.

Four beautifully different seasons bring vacationers to the Ozarks year-round. Hikers follow trails up grades to towering bluffs that cast soft shadows on the waters and offer views of pristine valleys. Gentle wildlife hide in the forest, and the scenes change with light and shadow.

These gentle, timeworn hills roll across the horizon without jagged peaks or sharp edges. A palette of colors—pale-pink anemone in the early spring, soft shades of green in summer, blazing gold and crimson in fall, gray-green rock faces and clean white snow in winter—splash the canvas of cobalt-blue sky.

> **Trivia**
>
> The word Arkansas *comes from* Kansas, *"people of the south wind" or "downstream people." But spelling the state name has never been easy. Explorers used* Arkansoa, Arkancas, *and* Arkensa *to name a few. Not everyone agreed on the pronunciation—was it Ar-KANSAS or AR-kan-saw? The legislature settled on* ar-kan-saw *in 1881.*

Spring slips into the state early—while snow still clings to the rest of the heartland—and woods burst with the glory of dogwoods, redbuds, jonquils, sarvis, and wild azaleas before summer's rich green canopy shades the trails of the quiet foothills.

Bed-and-breakfast inns are not too common in Arkansas, and many of them are hidden in the woods. They are all worth searching out, so

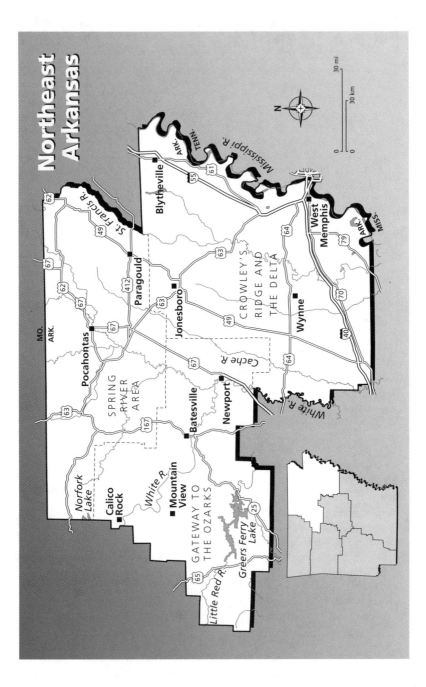

Northeast Arkansas

30 mi
30 km

N

MO.
ARK.

62

67

62

67

63

49

St. Francis R.

412

Paragould

63

67

67

Cache R.

Pocahontas

SPRING
RIVER
AREA

167

Batesville

Newport

White R.

Jonesboro

63

49

64

64

CROWLEY'S
RIDGE AND
THE DELTA

Wynne

40

70

79

West
Memphis

64

63

55

61

Blytheville

TENN.

ARK.

Mississippi R.

ARK.
MISS.

Norfork
Lake

Calico
Rock

White R.

Mountain
View

GATEWAY TO
THE OZARKS

Greers Ferry
Lake

25

65

Little Red R.

BEST ATTRACTIONS IN NORTHEAST ARKANSAS

Caves Court Motel,
Cave City; (870) 283–5010

Pearls Unique, Newport;
(800) 637–3233

Ironworks, Mountain View;
(870) 269–IRON

*McSpadden's Dulcimer
Shop,* Mountain View;
(870) 269–4313

Ozark Folk Center,
Mountain View;
(870) 269–3851

Blanchard Spring Cave,
Fifty-Six; (870) 757–2211

Happy Lonesome Cabins,
Calico Rock; (870) 297–8899

Nature Scent, Heber Springs;
(501) 362–2449

Anderson House, Heber
Springs; (501) 362–5266

Captain's House, Heber
Springs; (501) 362–3963

Antiques Warehouse,
Botkinburg; (501) 745–5842

many of them are included here. Arkansas and Ozarks Bed and Breakfast is a referral service for a number of the B&Bs. Call Ken or Lynn Griffin at (800) 233–2777.

Gateway to the Ozarks

Batesville calls itself the "Gateway to the Ozarks"; it is a logical place for us to start. The town was founded in 1822 where the Southwest Trail met the White River crossing. (Some folks decided not to cross and stayed.) It is Arkansas's oldest existing city. It is now the home of Lyon's College, and there is always something interesting going on in this college town. The annual Ozark Scottish Festival, held in the spring, features competitions in bagpiping, drumming, dancing, and athletics at the college campus; the Batesville Air Festival, held each autumn, has thirty hot-air balloons in the air daily, along with antique and rare aircraft. The **Old Independence Regional Museum** opened in 1998 in the old National Guard Armory at Ninth and Vine in Batesville. Visitors walk into a 12,500-square-foot Works Progress Administration building made of native stone. The museum represents a twelve-county area and is a genealogist's dream with a climate-controlled archival vault to store rare and fragile documents, photographs, and fabrics. The large 2,680-square-foot gallery houses major exhibits with a comfortable study area for researchers. Call (870) 793–2121 for more information. Hours are 9:00 A.M. to 4:30 P.M. Tuesday through Saturday. If you have a sweet tooth, head downtown to *Arkansaw Traveller Gourmet Foods.* In this little storefront shop, you can watch Donice and Charles Woodward make molded chocolate candies—offered in white, dark, and diet chocolate—as well as jam, jelly, butters, roasted pecans and peanut or pecan brittle, all available to taste. The shop is located at 1368 Neeley, Batesville 72501 call or fax (870) 793–7936 for information. Hours are from 10:00 A.M. to 5:00 P.M. weekdays and until 2:00 P.M. on Saturday. Their Web site is www.arktraveller.com.

The Cave Courts Motel is the oldest operating motor court in the state and also the oldest tourist attraction, according to the State Historical Society.

Newark is a restored 1880s community situated between Jacksonport and Batesville on Highway 69. It was an old railroad town built where the Ozark Mountains meet the flatlands of the Arkansas Delta. Native son Bill Freeze has undertaken a personal crusade to bring the good times back to this railroad town. His father's mercantile store opened in 1922 and operated until 1979. When it was to be demolished, Bill bought it back and began restoring it along with other buildings downtown. It now houses **Yesterday's Gifts,** at 109 East Front Street, Newark 72562, which is open from 9:00 A.M. to 5:00 P.M. every day but Sunday when it doesn't open until noon. Call (870) 799–8676 for more information. His enthusiasm included having a mural depicting life in the 1800s painted on a large building next to the park. Now you will find antiques shops, restaurants, a restored 1907 barbershop, and plenty of other interesting things on the main street. Bill also runs **The Nut House,** on Highway 122, where he sells pecans from his family's grove on the White River, plus candy, antiques, and other good things. It is open from 8:00 A.M. to 5:00 P.M. every day (870–799–3244). **Country Girl's Antiques** (870–799–3100) is on Highway 122, next to the elementary school, and is open from 9:00 A.M. to 5:00 P.M. Wednesday through Sunday.

If you are traveling north from Batesville on Highway 167, you will want to visit one of the most unusual motor courts in the state, maybe even the country. **Crystal River Cave Courts Motel,** at 206 North Main, Cave City 72521, is the love of Dan and Irma Carrigan, who drove to Evening Shade to look at a bed-and-breakfast for sale there. It was too new, they thought. They wanted something they could fix up. Well, they found it in **Cave City.** The motel was covered in weeds, brambles, and scrub brush. The entrance was blocked by the growth. It was a disaster. Underneath the property was the huge multiroom cavern from which the town got its name. The motel had been vacant for many years and was not even for sale. The Carrigans tracked down the owner in another state and bought the property.

The motel was originally built in 1932 by a man with a love of rocks. He collected thousands of small crystals, geodes, and quartz to set in the walls to decorate the building. There are crystals in the form of crosses, faces, animals, and just about anything else your imagination can dream up. In fact, interpretations of the symbolism are much of the charm of the place. Sharp rocks jut out along the eaves, creating a castle effect. The downspouts are curved rocks that catch the water and direct it away

NORTHEAST ARKANSAS

from the building. The house is very large and the Carrigans have put several years of work into it. Behind the house is the entrance to the cave.

Lou and Becky Carrigan, Dan and Irma's daughters, have become the tour guides, and for a $4.00 fee ($2.00 for children) they will lead you into the cave opening and share the many legends surrounding it. The cave's opening is a courtyard for the motor court. A large rock formation that looks like an Osage Indian head guards the entrance. Legends and stories about the cave abound.

It is said that a bloody Osage Indian massacre happened here, and that the burial site of the chief of the fourteen murdered Osage is just inside the cave. The largest room in the cave is 100 feet underground and measures 10 feet high by 80 feet wide. There are at least five chambers, and the underground Crystal River flows through them. The depth of the river fluctuates with that of the Mississippi River, which is nearly 100 miles away. Several people have lost their lives to the swift current of the dark river. The original owner took a boat and a mile of rope into the cave and did not find the end before he ran out of rope.

Best Annual Events in Northeast Arkansas

Lights on the Ridge, *Jonesboro; Christmas season; (870) 932–6691*

Loose Caboose Festival, *Paragould; third weekend in May; (870) 236–7684*

Portfest, *Newport; first Friday and Saturday in June on the banks of the White River; (870) 523–3618*

Tuckerman's Hometown Days, *Tuckerman; on Mother's Day weekend, May; (870) 349–5313*

White River Water Carnival, *Batesville; July; (870) 793–2378*

World Championship Cardboard Boat Festival, *Greers Ferry Lake, Heber Springs; fourth weekend in July; (800) 77–HEBER*

Although the town has been known as the home of the "sweetest watermelons in the world" for the last few years, instead of the caves for which it was named, now that the motel is open, people in town have reclaimed its fame, and the interesting motor court has once again become a main attraction. Rates are $25 ($35 for a room with kitchenette). For more information call the Carrigan residence at (870) 283–5010, because there is no motel office.

From Batesville the White River flows southeast to the town of ***Jacksonport. Jacksonport State Park and Museum,*** 3 miles north on Highway 69, is the permanent home of *Mary Woods Number 2,* a refurbished, upriver packet stern-wheeler moored at the park; it's authentically outfitted with furnishings typical of the late 1800s, the heyday of the steamboat era. Capable of speeds up to 20 miles per hour, the steamer braved snags, sandbars, shoals, and boiler explosions; life expectancy of a riverboat was only about five years. More than 117 steamers were lost on the Arkansas River before 1872, and the White River offered some of the greatest challenges for riverboat crews. But the smaller packet steamers could move in only 3 feet of water and would venture up the smaller rivers, at least during the rainy season.

Jacksonport was a riverboat town until the end. After city leaders refused right-of-way to the railroad in 1872, the population began to decline; in 1891 the county seat was moved, and the stores, saloons, and wharves disappeared.

The *Mary Woods* and courthouse are always closed on Monday, but Jackson State Park also has twenty Class A campsites, a barrier-free bathhouse/rest room, a tree-shaded picnic area within a stone's throw of the river beach, a covered pavilion to rent for large gatherings, a gift shop, and the twenty-eight-acre wildlife conservation area called the Tunstall Riverwalk. There is a boat ramp for access to the White River. But a word of caution: According to the locals, in the murky waters where the White River and Black River join, a creature called the "White River Monster"—known as "Whitey"—has been sighted. (I'm not making this up.) Sightings of this elusive monster date to when Native Americans lived in this county. The most recent "reliable" (chamber of commerce quotes, not mine) sightings were in 1937 and the 1970s. So positive there is a White River Monster, the state legislature proclaimed this section of the White River to be a "White River Monster Refuge." (Hey, if the Arkansas legislature says it's true, it must be.) And now that the Loch Ness Monster has been declared a sham, this could be the only monster left in the world, so be careful not to hurt it. There is an admission charge. Call (870) 523–2143 for information.

Highway 67 follows the White River south to **Newport,** where since the turn of the century, the White and the Black Rivers that converge near Newport have yielded delicately tinted natural pearls that are highly valued, becoming heirlooms for families lucky enough to find them. In fact the Royal Crown of England has a lustrous White River pearl in it.

Pearls Unique is the place to find these rare beauties. The freshwater pearls are found in mussels in the cold river waters and, because of channeling, dredging, and pollution, are becoming rare. They come in all sizes, from the tiny ones to large collectors' pearls, and range in price from $5.00 to $50,000. The pearls are not just round; they come in shapes carrying such romantic names as *angel wings, rosebud, snail,* and *popcorn.* Customers have the option of selecting from loose pearls and having a setting custom-designed or finding a piece already made.

Mary Woods Number 2

Manager Phyllis Holmes has studied pearls most of her life and will explain how the value of the pearls is determined—by size, luster, shape, and color. Colors can be in shades of peach, apricot, rose, lavender, bronze, silver, gold, cream, white, or even blue and green. The shop has some very rare collectors' baroques, including a large white snail shape. Pearls Unique is located at 1902–D McLain, Newport 72112, in Pratt Square. Hours are from about 8:00 A.M. to 4:30 P.M. and tours are conducted from 9:00 A.M. to 4:00 P.M., but call ahead to make an appointment: (870) 523–3638 or (800) 637–3233. You can also send a fax: (810) 523–3639, E-mail: pearls@ipa.net, or visit their Web site: pearlsunique.com.

Arkansas is the only state to produce both pearls and diamonds. (Did you know the best way to clean pearls is to use Woolite and water, rinse, and air dry?)

The **Bob E. Jackson Memorial Museum of Funeral Service** is on 1900 Malcolm Avenue, Newport 72112. A horse-drawn, glass-sided funeral coach and a vintage 1880 family buggy are the highlights of this unusual funeral service collection. An 850-pound bronze casket, manufactured in 1927, is on display (needs *big* pallbearers!). It is one of only five made—three were used for burials—the other is on display in Texas. This unique museum has toe-clincher and glass-sealer caskets (ask about them) and home embalming tools. A "must-see" museum, if you like this kind of thing. If you are just along for the ride, the museum also includes a small chapel and an extensive collection of Mr. Jackson's World War II memorabilia. Call (870) 523–5822 for times; ask for Jan Marris.

The **Jimmy Dunham Family Music Hall** is the place where gospel music fans can congregate. It is located in the Balch community, fifteen miles east of Newport, and the Dunham family and special guests perform every other week in the old Baptist church. The performances are free; call (870) 523–6044 for times.

Elvis once played the **King of Clubs** on Highway 67 North just north of Swifton, which celebrated its fiftieth anniversary in 2001. Owners Evelyn and Bob King can tell you about the Elvis era, when performers such as Johnny Cash, Roy Orbison, Jerry Lee Lewis, and Conway Twitty also played there. In fact, one night both Elvis and Cash performed. Sonny Burgess, another rock and roll pioneer, still performs at the club. Hours are Monday to Friday 9:00 A.M. to 1:00 P.M., Saturday 9:00 A.M. to midnight. Closed Sunday (870–458–9280).

Other interesting places to search out in Newport include **Virginia Arnett's Doll Museum** on 2001–B Eastern Avenue, Newport 72112 with more than 5,000 dolls of all kinds, including a complete set of *Gone with the Wind* characters. Dolls of all kinds line the walls and are displayed at tiny card tables, sewing machines, and in high chairs and buggies. Call (870) 523–2194 for museum information.

The local airbase/industrial park on Highway 18 is the home of **Newport Raceway Drag Strip** if you are thrilled by the roar of drag racing. Races are held every weekend. The Holmes Building at the corner of Front and Hazel Streets is the location of Sam Walton's first Ben Franklin store. A bronze plaque honors this spot. The **Old Iron Mountain Railroad Depot,** at 425 Front Street, Newport 72112, has been restored and is open to the public. Railroad and train memorabilia bring railroad history to life here. Call (870) 523–8078.

Travel northwest from Newport on Highway 14 as it flows along the curve of the White River; the scene changes as mountains pop up, trees line the highway, and cattle graze on the rolling hills and valleys. The drive to **Mountain View** is an event in itself. For a drive through some lovely Ozark countryside, travel north on Highway 69, then east on Highway 58. You can also stay on Highway 69, turning east on Highway 9, a twisting two-laner from Melbourne along a ridge with a view of White River Valley. No matter how you do it, the last 30 miles scribble through hills with rocky streams and spectacular vistas. All roads lead to Mountain View, so it becomes the center point from which directions to other attractions in the area begin.

Free Saturday musicals held in the Mountain View town square have been a tradition for some thirty years, and "pickin' and grinnin'" goes on well into the night, as local strummers gather by the court-house and folks bring lawn chairs to get comfort-able on balmy evenings. Folk music lovers by the thousands come into town to hear the fiddles and dulcimers sing. Favorite son Dick Powell, crooner

Trivia
Doll collecting is the second most popular hobby in this country (stamp collecting is number one).

and leading man of the forties and fifties, was born here. Mountain View also has the annual **Bean Fest.** More than thirty huge iron kettles of pinto beans, along with cornbread and onions, are cooked and served free to everyone. The tall tale–telling contest (and they get taller every year) is part of the event called "The Big Blowout." But the highlight is the Great Outhouse Race—each privy is decorated and, after the musket shot, pushed along the course with the driver sitting on the seat inside. The coveted gold, silver, or bronze toilet seat trophies and cash prizes for best-decorated comfort station and best-dressed driver are awarded on the courthouse steps. This is not the only outhouse race in the state, but it is, citizens here will tell you, the only one fueled by beans.

Courthouse Square is the heart of the community, and most of the shops there have no address; in fact, there are only a few street names. Highways become streets, streets become highways, and the names are interchangeable. Ask directions, and the people who live in Mountain View will just point or say it's near some other place on the square. If you walk around the square, you will find everything sooner or later. It is illegal to buy liquor and impossible to find a good restaurant meal, but good music is easy to find.

Woods Pharmacy, at 301 West Main Street, Mountain View 72560, has an early 1900s restored antique soda fountain that serves deli sandwiches and old-fashioned ice-cream treats. Remember thick, rich milk shakes and malts, phosphates, hand-dipped ice cream, and fresh limeade and lemonade? They are still here, just 1 block west of Courthouse Square. Hours are 8:00 A.M. to 5:00 P.M. Monday through Saturday. Call (870) 269–8304 for more information.

A number of B&Bs are clustered near the square. The **Wildflower Bed and Breakfast on the Square,** (100 Washington Street, Mountain View 72560) on the northeast corner of the square across from the old jailhouse, is owned by Lou Anne Rhodes and calls itself a "vintage guest house." This B&B, located at the corner of Peabody and Washington Streets, has seven rooms all with private baths. Named to the National Register of Historic Places, this old hotel was built for traveling salesmen in 1918. In 1998 the B&B went through extensive renovation, and the old innkeeper's apartment upstairs became a spacious three-room suite, with a sleeping loft with two twin beds in addition to the main bedroom. It has a kitchenette and living room area and is fine for a family or group. Rooms range from $67 to $99, including a hearty buffet breakfast served in the sunny parlor dining area. Lots of games, puzzles, and reading materials are available for the guests. But here is the real reason to stay here: The **Wildflower Porch Band** plays on the wraparound porch at some time every weekend and many guests are regulars because of the band. The B&B's location is perfect for guests who come to hear the old country tunes picked by impromptu gatherings of musicians. Call (870) 269–4383 or (800) 591–4879 for reservations. The inn also has a Web site: www.bbonline.com/ar/wildflower.

Lou Anne recommends several places in town, including **Corner Stone Gifts,** located at 101 North Peabody Street, Mountain View 72560. Corner Stone is owned by Lou Anne's friend Debbie Verilla and is located in the building that used to be home to the busiest Chevrolet dealership in the entire state. The store carries an eclectic selection of sophisticated gifts. Call (870) 269–8826 for more information.

Tommy's Pizza specializes in handmade pizza and won second place in the state for best pizza. Call (870) 269–FAST to place your order. Tommy is also famous for his Memphis-style barbeque and ribs, and because Lou Anne is from Memphis, these are her favorite. You can't miss Tommy's bright purple building, 4 blocks west of the square off Highway 66 West. He is open seven days a week from 3:00 P.M. until whenever—7:00, 8:00, or 9:00 P.M., depending on how many people are still there. If it's too crowded inside, and the weather is nice, eat on the picnic tables outside.

Another Lou Anne favorite is **Bar None Bar-B-Q,** at 303 West Main Street, Mountain View 72560 (870–269–2200). Jimmy and Karen Shields are from Texas and know how to do a brisket, pork loin, ribs, or steaks.

Peabody Street crosses Main at the south end of the square, and just past the post office is where **Ozark Country Inn Bed and Breakfast** sits in the shade of old maple trees. Many of the musicians you will hear on the square stay here. It was built in the early 1900s. Maple trees surround the second-story porch where people pick and play well into the night when the weather is warm. Because the inn is only steps away from Courthouse Square, where good music making and jiggin' can be enjoyed almost every night, it is often booked up. Bring your fiddle and join in. Don and Sissy Jones invite you to enjoy their hospitality. Call (870) 269–8699 or (800) 379–8699. The inn also has a Web site: www.globalriver.com/ozarkcountryinn. Rooms at the inn—located at 219 South Peabody Street on Highway 9 South, Mountain View 72560—are $59 and up, all with private baths. An old-fashioned breakfast is served at 8:00 A.M.

The **Stone County Ironworks** is a historic building on Courthouse Square. It has a complete line of hand-forged iron from the ironworks. Owner David Mathews has recently opened the upstairs with more crafts, decorative accessories, and goodies of all kinds. Hours are seasonal and different almost every day: Opening at 9:00 A.M. daily, the shop stays open until 5:00 P.M. on Monday, 6:00 P.M. on Tuesday and Wednesday, 7:00 P.M. on Thursday, and 9:00 P.M. on Friday and Saturday. Sunday hours are from noon to 5:00 P.M. Winter hours are Monday through Saturday from 9:00 A.M. to 5:00 P.M.; call (870) 269–IRON or (800) 380–IRON for the exact closing time, or see their Web site: www.STONEIRON.com. Their address is 17430 U.S. Highway 66, Mountain View 72560.

The Inn at Mountain View, just off Courthouse Square at 307 Washington Street, Mountain View 72560, dates to 1886 and features a porch that is great for sitting and rocking. A large stone fireplace in the living room warms guests on cool autumn nights. Owners Scott and Cheryl Poole keep up many of the traditions of the famous old inn, while adding great new ideas. The antiques and handmade quilts are still there, and Cheryl continues to fill the inn with fresh flowers. Guests can enjoy "cookies by Lucas," along with spiced cider or iced tea, depending on the weather, on the wide front porch. (Lucas is the Poole's young son who has taken over his grandmother's cookie recipes and made them his own.) At 8:30 A.M., Scott, the breakfast chef, whips up Belgian waffles or his biscuits and sausage gravy, while telling tall tales to guests around the kitchen table. Telephones and television are not available, but Internet access and a big screen TV are available for corporate meetings. The restored inn is air conditioned, and large minisuites will range in price from $63 to $98 for two. All have private baths. Call (870) 269–4200.

Scott and Cheryl are musicians who play on the square every weekend. Scott plays guitar and banjo; Cheryl plays the fiddle. They guarantee music not only on the porch, but in the parlor, too.

A popular activity while enjoying music on the square is to take a

Mountain View

My late husband, Bob, and I have had a home in the Missouri Ozarks for a number of years, so when we drove into the Ozark Mountains of Arkansas we expected to find picture-perfect hills covered with the deep russet of fall. We also knew there would be the real Ozarks behind the gift shops and antiques shops—the Scotch-Irish people who came to the hills and hollows of the Ozarks from Appalachia and were cut off from the world for several generations until highways brought the world to them in the 1930s.

We certainly didn't expect to fall in love with an unlikely little town called Mountain View, a town full of musicians who come down out of the hills at night to play folk music in the square and on porches of the simple bed-and-breakfasts and hotels. This is a town where the biggest event is the annual outhouse race, fueled by a huge pot of beans cooking on the square.

I was looking for interesting places— places off the beaten path—to write about and discovered that a great deal of Arkansas is off the beaten path. This patch of ancient mountains is the oldest in the country, worn away by thousands of years of storms and wind. They have never been accessible, and that is why the folk music here is unlike music anywhere else. It is music crooned by a mother to a babe in her arms. It is music plunked on old instruments by grinning fathers while children tap time with bare toes. It is music drifting from the mud-chinked log cabins like the smoke rising from the chimney. It is music to warm your heart the way the fire warms the dirt-floored room inside.

There might even be a still bubbling in the woods out back. Such are the surprises of the Ozarks—always changing, always the same. Mountain View is a slice of that life waiting for folks fleeing the urban rat race to taste.

buggy ride around town. Starting about 7:00 P.M. on Friday and Saturday nights, March through October, folks from the *OK Trading Post* bring their horses and buggies to the square. The cost is $3.00 for adults and $2.00 for children. You can also book trail rides and hay rides through the Trading Post by calling (870) 585–2217.

Also east of the square, but on Sylamore Road (which is also Highway 9), is where Lynn McSpadden and his team of craftspeople make dulcimers at *McSpadden's Dulcimer Shop.* The shop is filled with local artists' crafts—pottery, wood carvings—all natural items. You can watch through the glass wall as five woodworkers make Mountain Dulcimers (that's the kind that goes on your lap). If you ask, someone will play one and give you a quick lesson. They'll have you playing "Mary Had a Little Lamb" in no time. Prices here are quite reasonable—from $180 with a case, music, and instructions to $1,000 for a custom-carved beauty. The shop is open from March through October; hours are Monday through Saturday from 9:00 A.M. until 5:00 P.M.; call (870) 269–4313 for information. There is a Web site at www.mcspaddendulcimers.com, or you can e-mail mcspadden@mvtel.net.

The Ozark Rocker and Wood Company is across the street from the courthouse. Arlene Duncan carries hand-crafted rocking chairs by local crafters and distributes other Arkansas-made crafts. The company offers regular-sized rockers made from oak, ash, walnut, and cedar. There also have double and triple rockers, slider rockers, and rockers with hand-carved backs. In addition to the furniture, they carry handmade wooden spoons, rolling pins, brooms, and pottery.

All the wood furniture is made by families who have been crafting rockers for more than sixty years. One of the largest selection of oak rockers in the country is here. Ozark Rocker is also the home of "The Giant Rocker" (makes you feel like Lily Tomlin's Edith Ann and is a great photo opportunity), a hand-turned monster rocker waiting on the front porch of the shop at 116 West Main Street, Mountain View 72560. They've recently added dining room and bedroom furniture made of red cedar. Summer hours are from 9:00 A.M. until 7:00 P.M. Monday through Thursday, until 10:30 P.M. on Friday, and until 11:00 P.M. on Saturday. Sunday hours are from 10:00 A.M. until 6:00 P.M. There is a Web site at www.ozarkrocker.com. You can e-mail the shop at sales@ozarkrocker.com.

Arkansas Craft Gallery, 104 East Main Street, Mountain View 72560, showcases the best artists from all over the state. Linda VonTrump, executive director, says that more than 300 artists are members of the guild, and they have been sending top-quality, handmade crafts here for more than twenty years. The guild also has the largest selection of pottery in the state, as well as five styles of working spinning wheels, furniture, wooden bowls, and candles. Works from seven glass artists, five basket makers, two broom makers, and thirty jewelry makers are likewise available. Each month the gallery highlights a different artist. Several guild shops dot the state. This one is open from 9:30 A.M. to 5:00 P.M. every day (and from 9:00 A.M. to 5:30 P.M. during daylight savings time). The shop is closed on Sunday in January and February. Call Linda at (870) 269–3897 or e-mail her at arkcraftguild@mvtel.net. You'll find a Web site at: www.arkansascraftguild.org.

Two miles north of Mountain View on Highway 5/9/14 is the *Jimmy Driftwood Barn and Folk Museum.* If you don't know who Jimmy Driftwood is, you will by the time you leave Mountain View. He built the barn for the Rackensack Folklore Society, a loose-knit group of locals who are dedicated to preserving the folk music of the hills. It is operated by the University of Central Arkansas. Driftwood has been called this country's finest folk balladeer, although he started his career quite by accident at age fifty, when he wrote "The Battle of New Orleans" for his sixth-grade American history class and it became an instant success. Jimmy died in July 1988, but his style of music lives on here. The barn welcomes folk musicians and the public to free Friday and Sunday musicals at 7:30 P.M. throughout the year. Other programs and activities are offered at various times during the week. Call (870) 269–8042 for information.

Don and Suzie Mellon had the Mellon Patch business in a converted chicken house in Mountain View. It was built around a wooden train whistle, musical spoons, wooden trains, and other wooden items, which they sold wholesale. Their dream was to build a new workshop and retail store on property they owned near the Jimmy Driftwood Barn. The dream has become an old country store, "the kind of place you like to pull into" when traveling across Arkansas, according to Don.

The white clapboard building, now called *Mellon's Country Store,* has tall narrow windows. A 35-foot tower is out front with a circa 1930 aeromotor windmill. A 1924 vintage gas pump with Don's pride and joy—a 1939 Ford—parked in front of it will certainly stop traffic.

Inside there are hanging hams, barrels of hard candy, and the scent of coffee being ground. You can buy sausage grinders, cast-iron pots, horseshoes (and mule shoes), and washboards. Felt hats are displayed on an old hatbox dresser, and lots of vintage musical instruments—

banjos, fiddles, and guitars—are all over the place. In fact, Don will sit a spell on the porch with you and do some pickin' if you've a mind to. Or you can have an RC Cola and a Moon Pie and listen to Don, a toy maker by trade, tell about his own handmade wooden toys—all of which are checked out by his own grandchildren—of which he is justifiably proud. "Our motto is, 'If they can't break it, then we'll make it.'" he says. Aisles are crowded with reminders of a time when metal trademark signs for Coke, Hershey, Lipton, and Nehi were common. You can have homemade jellies, chow-chow, smoked hams, and stone-ground corn meal or browse among antiques, curiosities, marbles, iron skillets, books, and handmade crafts. This is the place to see hats from the Clearwater Hat Company (see p. 17), too.

Mellon's Country Store is 2 miles north of Mountain View on Highway 9 at the windmill. Seasonal hours are April through October, 9:00 A.M. to 5:00 P.M. daily; in March, November, and December, 9:00 A.M. to 5:00 P.M. Friday, Saturday, and Sunday. It is closed in January and February. Call (870) 269–3354 for information.

If you don't want to stay in town and listen to all the music, or if you just want a good night's sleep before you hit the Ozark Folk Center, then check out *Country Oaks Bed & Breakfast,* located just 1 mile from town off Highway 9 south of Mountain View (on the road to Shirley). Here you can have the feeling of yesterday and the comfort of today. Antiques, lace curtains, claw-foot bathtubs, and marble showers create ambience at this lush hideaway on sixty-nine acres. It has its own six-acre lake, with a path for morning strolls, and is surrounded by majestic oak trees. Queen-size beds, fireplaces, and ceiling fans give you all the modern comforts, as does an upstairs sitting room with television and free snacks and beverages. A full gourmet breakfast, prepared by innkeepers Carole and Jerry Weber, is served in the dining room each morning. Three rooms are available, all with showers. This is a new house but done in Victorian style, so there is a porch with rockers. (Adults only, which makes it even more quiet.) A second building offers five more guest rooms and a meeting room for corporate groups. Rooms run from $85 to $100. Call (870) 269–2704 for information and reservations. You can e-mail them at countryoaks@mvtel.net or go to their Web site: www.bbonline.com/ar/countryoaks.

What brings people to the Mountain View area, though, is the *Ozark Folk Center,* north of town off Highway 5/9/14 on Folk Center Road. Built to maintain the unique folk traditions of the Ozarks, the center preserves almost-forgotten arts and music of the hill people who lived on the hillsides and hollers of the mountains. Artists like Dutch Wigman, who makes bowed psalteries; Terri Bruhin, a weaver who makes lace-weave table linens and rag rugs (more about her later); and Owen Rein, a master chair maker who creates white-oak rockers with drawknife and bending forms, or "jigs," to curve the green wood to the measurements of the person planning to use it, show their skills at the center. This show-case for hill-life traditions was founded by descendants of the river val-ley pioneers to preserve the lore and crafts that were quickly disappearing. Twenty-five "cabin crafts," practiced in rustic shops scat-tered across an Ozark hilltop, and a heritage herb garden are open daily from 10:00 A.M. to 5:00 P.M. May through October. If you have never experienced the sweet scent of cedar from a cooper's shop or the sharp tang of coal smoke from a blacksmith's forge, this is your chance to travel back to simpler times. The park renews a time when plain materials like white-oak sheaves or apples became baskets and dolls and when com-mon farm implements such as saw blades and buckets became musical instruments. Music is made here with such instruments as the bowed psaltery, dulcimer, pickin' bow, and spoons, as well as fiddles, banjos, and guitars. Concerts are presented Monday through Saturday at 7:30 P.M. in the center's 1,000-seat auditorium. Sunday-night gospel concerts are held once or twice a month through the season. Call (870) 269–3851 for a schedule. Admission to the crafts demonstrations or music perfor-mances is $8.00 for adults, $5.00 for children 6–12. Combination tickets are $13.50 adults, $7.25 children.

The century-old Shannon Cabin at the center is open to visitors. It has a stone fireplace, homemade furniture, front and rear porches, and a sleeping loft typical of the rural log homes of the past. Scheduled for demolition, it was brought to the center from Happy Hollow in Stone County. Tina Marie Wilcox, Ozark Folk Center herbalist, did the land-scaping, planting an assortment of homestead flowers, herbs, and bushes around the cabin, the way a pioneer woman might have done.

Although the *Ozark Folk Center Restaurant and Dry Creek Lodge* is located in the middle of the state park, innkeeper June Burroughs takes care of you as though you were her personal guest. The octagonal cabins are built from native cedar and scattered around the grounds. Three slid-ing glass doors let in the breeze and a wide view of the trees outside, and the dining room serves traditional southern cooking—beans and ham, greens, and cornbread. Call (870) 269–3871 or (800) 264–FOLK for room reservations, or visit the center's Web site at www.ozarkfolkcenter.com.

An underground stream flows into *Blanchard Springs Caverns,* which is just 14 miles north of Mountain View off Highway 5/9/14 at the town of Sylamore (where Highway 5/9/14 splits), then east on Highway 14.

The water emerges as Sylamore Creek, winding its way through the Ozark National Forest to the White River. It is an important part of the cavern; 216 feet beneath the lush green of the Ozark National Forest lies the underground world of massive stalactites and towering sandstone columns, sculpted by water and time and home to blind salamanders and albino crayfish. This is a living cave because the continuous water supply keeps the formations growing. The uppermost caverns consist of two huge rooms, the Cathedral Room and the Coral Room, which are large enough to hold several football fields each. The explored part of the lower section, where the river flows, is almost 5 miles long.

The Dripstone Trail passes through the uppermost part of the caverns for ⁷/₁₀ mile with stone curbs or handrails. Every type of calcite formation can be found in the limestone caves—stalactites, stalagmites, hollow soda straws, massive flowstones, and giant columns in colors ranging from snow-white to dark brown because of the varied minerals found in the deposits.

The Discovery Trail—discovered when someone fell through a hole in the floor—is 1²/₁₀ miles long and has more than 600 steps that take you deeper into the caverns, where there are water-carved passages, a cave stream, and the natural entrance. One spot looks as though billions of diamonds had spilled into the cavern, the crystals sparkling in the lights. The skeletal remains of a Native American who explored the cave more than a thousand years ago were found next to a bundle of reeds—perhaps used to make torches—but no one knew much about the cave until it was explored in 1956. It has been open to the public only since 1973. You might want to wear a long-sleeved shirt or maybe even a sweater when exploring the cave because it's a constant 58 degrees in the cave, and with the humidity near 100 percent, dampness adds to the chill.

Blanchard Springs is in the town of *Fifty-Six* (870–757–2211). Hours are 10:00 A.M. to 4:00 P.M. daily April through October, and Wednesday to Sunday November through March. Admission is $9.00 adults, $4.50 seniors, $5.00 children 6–15. There is a $3.00 per car day-use charge for the picnic areas with a spring-fed stream for swimming (complete with bathhouse); camping facilities are $10 per night with a five-night minimum. From Mountain View take Highway 14 west to Fifty-Six. Granted these caverns are a well-known tourist spot, but they are among the most beautiful caves in the world. It would be a shame to miss them.

The **Clearwater Hat Company** owners, Kay and Bob Burton, are believed to be the only makers of historical fur-felt hats in the country.

They work in **Newtana,** west of Mountain View on Clearwater Road. The Burtons searched the Smithsonian archives to study hats worn in Europe and America from 1750 to 1900 and now can produce anything from the French-Indian War period to the 1920s. Reenactors are the couple's best customers. Colonial hats, worn by men like Thomas Jefferson and George Washington, had three corners turned up to show off the powdered wigs stylish then. Civil War hats include the "hardee" hat: one side of the brim turned up with a plume. All are made with fur felt just as they were 200 years ago. Even most of the equipment used in the factory predates 1920. Crowns and brims are hand shaped after the bodies of the hats are steamed, sized, and shaped. But mercury nitrate is no longer used, as was done in the old days, so there are no "mad hatters" here. Kay tells the story of the day the beautiful Porsche pulled up to the shop (which is so far off the beaten path as to be a challenge to find), bringing everyone out of the shop. The driver stepped out of the little car with this book and a satellite operated GPS (ground positioning system) in his hand. Ah, the wonders of electronics! And speaking of electronics, their Web site is www.clearwaterhats.com, and their e-mail address is burton@mvtel.net. Or call (870) 746–4324 to order a catalog. You can also see the hats at Mellon's Country Store.

Traveling west on Highway 66 from Mountain View leads to **Timbo,** the hometown of Jimmy Driftwood. Here **Ozark Mountain Trail Rides** invites you to take your horse on vacation in the Ozark Mountains. Talk about getting off the beaten path—Bob Roper has the way to do it: a weeklong camp-out with guides to take you through some Ozark wilderness that can't be seen by car. Most of the trail is old logging roads crossing Roasting Ear Creek and other streams. Bring your favorite steed to the permanent camp on Roasting Ear Creek between Mountain View and Leslie, where each day begins and ends at the campsite, which has electricity and a bathhouse; all you need is your horse and sleeping gear. Meals are served in a screened dining room, and you can buy hay and sweet feed for your mount. The end of the trail for riders is not the end of the fun, though. The campsite has a dance floor and live music. Dancing until midnight is part of the fun, and on Thursday night an auctioneer begins his chant to sell anything you have to sell. The rides are in April, June, and October, and advance reservations are necessary; call (870) 746–4300. The weeklong trail rides cost $160 for adults, with prices ranging down from $130 for children under twelve, $95 for children under six, and $45 for children under three. To find the place, turn off Highway 66 to Highway 263 North at Timbo and watch for the sign.

Brad and Dad's Drive-In in Timbo advertises itself as having the best burgers in town. Never mind that it's the only place to eat in town, the food is pretty good. Brad Folks and his dad now run the gas station across the street, and their friend David Shellstrom runs the drive-in in their name. David keeps the business open seven days a week, but you may have to call him to find out specific hours. Call (870) 746–4733.

On top of Fox Mountain is the small, small town of ***Fox*** (two grocery stores and a post office) on Highway 263 just south of Timbo. Fox is about an hour's drive from Mountain View, with two ways to get there. One is to travel on scenic Highway 66 to Highway 263, but this route has a terror of a hairpin turn onto Highway 263 that you might find exciting if you are an Ozark Mountain Daredevil driver. Or try Highway 9 south to Highway 263. This is a more pastoral drive along a road of soft hills lined with old barns. There are about five artists living in the area; some work at the Ozark Folk Center, others don't, and they are a challenge to find.

Fox Mountain Pottery is the home shop of Joe and Terri Bruhin, the weaver you met at the Ozark Folk Center. Joe is a potter whose pride and joy is a Noborigama-type, three-chambered, climbing natural-draft-wood-fired kiln ("I don't think there's another one like it in the state," remarks Terri). Here he creates one-of-a-kind stoneware and porcelain pottery, everything from traditional casseroles and mugs to large urns that stand 2 feet tall. The kiln reaches temperatures of 2,500 degrees, so the resulting high-fired pottery is good in the oven, microwave, or kitchens on Mercury or Venus. It's pottery meant to be used, as well as being original artwork. To find the shop once you're in Fox, turn onto the dirt road next to the post office and begin the trek into the hills. Call Joe for directions at (870) 363–4264. Be warned. Joe has an attitude, some have said, and can be pretty snarly if you don't call first.

Joe can also direct you to the other craftspeople around Fox—a silversmith, a needlepoint artist, a woodworker who makes fishing lures, and a couple who do woodworking and weaving. Terri Bruhin can usually be found at the Ozark Folk Center in the weavers' shop, where she weaves contemporary and traditional lace-weave table linens, breadbasket liners, and such. She also makes rag rugs and contemporary clothing.

Calico Rock is a pretty little town of about 1,000 people, located on the bluffs of the White River exactly halfway between Mountain Home and Mountain View on Highway 5. The many colors of the sheer vertical cliffs along the river make it easy to see how the town got its name—steamship captains used to say, "Stop by them calico rocks," because it was the northernmost accessible port for steamboats in the spring of the year—and the name stuck. There's a view of the river from Main Street, and the old buildings, made of the colored rock and brick, reflect the 1920s and 1930s, when the railroad and sawmills that had made the town led to its destruction: A passing locomotive sparked a fire on a warehouse roof, and Main Street was destroyed. The town was rebuilt, however, and now the buildings are filled with crafts, collectibles, and antiques shops.

This small-town shopping area has the *Family Shoe and Dry Goods Store* at 104 Main Street, Calico Rock 72519, which has been run by Billie and Jim Clinkingbeard since 1947. You can shop for some new jeans or a dress for church (and have the hem adjusted). This one-stop shop also has a bright soda fountain next door, where you can have a malt and a smoked turkey sandwich, a simple dip of wild blackberry ice cream, or a banana split.

In 1903 a hardware store was built on the corner of Main Street's west side across from the railroad tracks. Now the building is the home of *River Bend Market,* a part craft, part antiques store.

Mills can still be seen in the older part of town, and wood homes of the 1920s and 1930s perch on the river bluffs. The 1923 *River View Hotel* at 100 Rodman Avenue is 1 block from the Main Street of Calico Rock. The white cement block hotel (not fancy but built for railroad workers who passed through the town in the 1920s when the woodmills were active) is now a B&B. This old-fashioned inn is filled with antiques and collectibles of the 1920s; it has iron beds in some rooms and oak mission furniture in others and overlooks the White River. Owner Sherry Sanford (a former professional actress who loves to entertain) has a quirky sense of humor. She serves complimentary Moon Pies and RC Colas to her guests ("There is nothing but *class* here," she says). In fact, her Web site is www.quirkyhotel.com. House dog Dingy takes care of leftovers and has gained considerable weight on the Moon Pies. There are eight rooms, five of which are two-bedroom suites—each with a private bath—some with tubs, others with showers. One has a kitchenette. This is called the Presidential Suite because there is a photo of President Bill Clinton with a couple of Sherry's children and a glass Bozo. ("Read that anyway you want to," she says, "I don't want anyone here who doesn't have a sense of humor.")

Prices range from $50 to $65 and include a huge breakfast of biscuits, sausage, fruit, sweet rolls, pork loin, bread pudding, or whatever else strikes the cook's fancy. Breakfast is served buffet-style in the small sunroom off the lobby. You can make reservations by calling (870) 297–8208. (People become regulars here, and Sherry discounts rooms $10 for every night after the first one.)

Nearby, **The Cedars Bed & Breakfast** is of Stockdale design in a rustic setting on 240 wooded acres. There are three guest rooms (one with a private bath) and a large great room with fireplace and entertainment center. Innkeepers Lynn and Ken Griffin serve a country breakfast in the dining room or on the deck each morning. The Griffins have added a sunroom and a swimming pool. Rooms are $50 to $85. The newest addition to the Cedars is the **Cabin at the Cedars.** This rustic log cabin in the woods sleeps four with the loft and hide-a-bed. Continental breakfast is left in the kitchen for you. The price of this romantic spot is $54 for two and $10 for each additional person. Call (870) 297–4197 for information and reservations.

Ken and Lynn also operate the **Arkansas and Ozarks Bed and Breakfast Reservation Service** (800–233–2777). They are quite knowledgeable about the area and good people to see first. Using this service is the fastest way to book rooms for a trip and much easier on your phone bill than calling every B&B along the route.

Probably the most romantic setting for a bed-and-breakfast is that owned by Carolyn and Christian Eck. The Ecks' two log cabins, called **Happy Lonesome Log Cabins,** are surrounded by the Ozark National Forest. These are 1½ miles from anywhere. In fact, after you reach the property, it is still ½ mile of woods to the cabins. Talk about a perfect location for a honeymoon hideaway! There are hiking trails and mountains to climb. Each cabin has a sleeping loft and a wood-burning stove, and both are unhosted for maximum privacy but provided with coffee and homemade fruit bread (the pumpkin bread is a favorite)— all for $65 for two, plus $10 for each additional person. The Happy Lonesome Cabins has a Web site at www.bbonline. com/ar/ hlcabins or e-mail the Ecks at cjeck@juno.com or hlcabins@centuryinter.net. Call (870) 297–8764.

Downtown Calico Rock has a number of interesting places worth checking out. Chris and Carolyn Eck's hardware store on the east side of Calico Rock's Main Street has an outdoor display of sturdy pieces of country furniture handmade by Walter and Martha Hagan. A gigantic rocking chair they built is every visitor's favorite photo. It's the kind of place where you can go in to buy just one screw, if that's all you need. What used to be Edith Floyd's grocery is now **Don Quixote's Calico Kitchen,** at 103 Main Street, Calico Rock 72519, owned by Gloria and

Bob Gushue. The bakeshop in front, where Gloria does all the baking, is filled with rye, whole wheat, and other interesting breads and pastries. A favorite is hummingbird cake. Ask Gloria about her bird collection, visible in the rustic, woodland decor of the restaurant. She started with placing one or two fabric birds in tree branches and now customers bring birds and nests to add to her collection from their travels all over the world. Bob is also an antiques dealer specializing in Tiffany glass (he is a registered Tiffany dealer). There are Tiffany pieces for sale in the restaurant along with other antiques, such as American Brilliant Cut Glass. Continental cuisine is their specialty—Northern Italian and French dishes dominate the menu, but he also makes a great Polish stew called *capusta* with sauerkraut and beans. The restaurant serves nothing but choice meats. Often, folks from Mountain View or other nearby towns will call ahead to order a meal, and Bob and the crew will begin work so lunch is ready when they arrive. That says something about the food, doesn't it? The bakery opens at 10:00 A.M., and lunch is served from 10:30 A.M. until 4:30 P.M. Dinner begins at 4:30 and continues until 9:00 P.M. Sunday hours are 11:00 A.M. to 4:00 P.M. Call (870) 297–8899 for reservations or visit their Web site at www.donquixotes.com.

Nearby is *Erma's Collectibles,* 107 Main Street, Calico Rock 72519, where Erma Goodsen has a neat assortment of old things to peruse. Hours are

See You at the Movies!

*I*f Calico Rock looks slightly familiar to you, it may be because you saw the movie **Boot Leggers** starring Kate Smith. It was shot in Calico Rock in 1973 and continues to air regularly on cable TV. The incredible scenery of the Ozarks and the charming personalities of towns like Calico Rock make Arkansas a popular state with Hollywood. In all, about seventy-five movies have been shot in the state, including the opening credits of **Gone with the Wind**—that's the Old Mill in North Little Rock. Other movies you may remember that were shot, at least in part, in Arkansas, include:

White Lightin'	1972
Crisis at Central High	1980
The Blue and the Gray	1981
A Soldier's Story	1983
Biloxi Blues	1987
Rosa Lee Goes Shopping	1988
Tuskegee Airman	1995
Sling Blade	1997

Plus, much of John Grisham's two movies, **The Client** and **The Firm,** were shot in West Memphis and other parts of eastern Arkansas. And all of the exteriors of the television show **Designing Women** are homes in Little Rock.

10:00 A.M. to 5:00 P.M. Monday through Saturday and sometimes on Sunday. Call (870) 297– 3722 for information.

Most of the businesses on Main Street are family-owned, which adds to the quaint personality of this town. One of those is **The Calico Clipper,** 115 Main, Calico Rock 72519, owned by Marty Marsee and her family since the 1920s. The shop contains the original barber's chair and pole from the 1920s. You can still get a great hair cut here for $5.00 and most of the time you don't need an appointment, but if you think you do, call (870) 297–4200. Marty opens her shop Tuesday through Saturday at 9:00 A.M. and closes at 4:00 P.M.

Greer Lake Area

As you pass through the intersection of Highways 16 and 25 just outside Heber Springs, you'll see **KC's Corner.** It's just a convenience store with a game room in back. Owner Rick Sanders keeps the outpost stocked with fresh seafood—lobster, shrimp, crab, or salmon—and Petit Jean meats for Heber residents. The store is open from 6:00 A.M. to 10:00 P.M. every day, year-round. Call (501) 362–7775 for information.

The Aromatique Factory, a multimillion-dollar business located on the outskirts of Heber Springs, started on a whim in 1982. Patti Upton created a pretty arrangement of pinecones and gum balls, brightened with green bay leaves, and gave it a Christmas scent with cinnamon, cloves, and such for her friend Sandra Horne's gift shop. The result, called "The Smell of Christmas," was a sellout hit. What started as a small business for the two women has grown into the Aromatique Factory, a corporation employing more than 400 persons on Highway 25 North in Heber Springs.

A showroom for the factory, called **Panache,** is filled with the lovely scents created here. Described as "A romantic shop," it is part of the factory complex and carries the decorative room fragrances sold only in upscale gift shops and the finest department stores. It's a treat just to walk into the little shop and be bathed in the delicate scents. Choosing among them is fun, too. Now there are fifteen scented mixtures of wood chips and botanicals, over a hundred ingredients in all, with scents romantically named "Smell of Spring"—a hyacinth-scented collection of bougainvillea; German statice in purple, pink, and white; bright-green bay leaves; and curled poplar in mauve—or "Gentleman's Quarters," made up of "rugged, exotic botanicals" with a masculine, outdoors scent. All combine colors and textures artfully and carry a delicate but definite scent. Prices range from $8.00 for a small cellophane bag to $125 for elegant holiday baskets. The shop is open from 9:30 A.M. to 5:00 P.M. Monday through Friday and on Saturday from 10:00 A.M. to 5:00 P.M. Call (501) 362–7919 for information or visit their Web site at www.aromatique.com..

Nature Scent, not to be outdone, has a three-room gift shop at the factory owned by Darrel and Martha Bufford at 1259 Wilburn Road, Heber Springs 72543, on Highway 110 near the Winckley Bridge. Thirty fragrances of potpourri, candles, and bath oils are displayed with shampoos and lotions. The most popular is the original mulberry potpourri. Hours are from 8:30 A.M. to 4:30 P.M. Monday through Friday. Call (501) 362–2449 for information or visit their Web site at www.naturescent.com.

The town of Sugar Loaf was founded in 1882 and became Heber Springs in 1910. *Heber Springs is* a tourist mecca, but it still keeps the small-town ambience of those earlier days. The *Gem Community Theater* at 117 West Main, Heber Springs 72543, has temporary exhibits, commu-

Morbid Curiosity

*O*kay, maybe this is not the kind of museum the kids will jump up and down about, but the **Olmstead Mortuary Museum** has a certain morbid pull to it. It is in the building that housed the Olmstead Funeral Home until the business required larger quarters. The circa 1910 stone building is on the National Register of Historic Places. Fire destroyed the original wood-frame undertaker shop built there in 1896. Thomas Dwight Olmstead is the grandson of Thomas Edward Olmstead, who arrived from Indiana in a covered wagon in 1896 and opened a funeral parlor. Over the years the paraphernalia became more and more interesting. The museum's centerpiece is a somber, black horse-drawn hearse, the finest of its kind. After that, the displays mainly appeal to a curiosity for things we never get to see. There is a home cosmetics kit used to make the deceased look less deceased and more "natural." Books on embalming and funeral directing that date back to the early 1900s line the shelves for your perusal. The funeral home's first electric Porti-Boy embalming machine (1938) looks like a giant blender. An 1896 grave tamper will give you the willies if you read any Edgar Allan Poe. Also here are the first sealed metal coffins, from about 1908, and an impressive and expensive-looking (you can take it with you) oversize casket made of cypress and covered with doeskin that was built in 1926 for someone who, for whatever reason, never had to use it. All in all, it is a very interesting museum, at 108 South Fourth Street, Heber Springs 72543. Open from 10:00 A.M. to 4:00 P.M. during the week. Call (501) 362–2422 for information.

nity theater, puppet theater and other presentations. The theater was built in the 1920s, and was fully renovated in 1998 to seat 200 people. Call (501) 362–7971 for information.

The Oak Tree Inn, atop Vinegar Hill at 1802 West Main Street (Highway 110 West), Heber Springs 72543, boasts four spacious rooms, each with a fireplace and whirlpool tub. Breakfast and dessert are served to guests. It is for nonsmoking adults only, and rooms range from $85 up. Owners are Steven and Kay Tinkle. You can reach them at (501) 362–7731 or via e-mail at oaktreeinn@arkansas.net. Preview the inn at its Web site: www.bbonline.com/ar/oaktree/.

Heber Springs is at the foot of Round Mountain and still has, downtown in Spring Park, the original spring for which it was named. Across the street from the park, the **Anderson House** is a historic country inn that has been here as long as the town—since 1882, when this was a spa and gave Hot Springs a run for its money. Terry and Amabilia Bryant bought and refurbished the old inn, which has fifteen rooms. The white, Williamsburg-style inn with its green shutters and tin roof (it's an interesting phenomenon that when it rains, everyone sleeps late) has beautiful rooms and large private bathrooms. Every other room was halved and made into large baths with showers and deep old tubs.

The inn's bedrooms open onto a wide front porch and upper balcony overlooking the tree-filled park. The rooms are furnished with country antiques, mostly oak with iron beds modernized to queen-size, each bed covered with a hand-stitched quilt. Lace curtains and pretty wallpaper give the place a turn-of-the-century feel. Breakfast of homemade coffee cake, muffins, and egg casserole is served buffet-style in the large parlor, which has a tall stone fireplace and hardwood floors. The inn, located at 201 East Main Street, Heber Springs 72543, has rooms at $68 to $98. Call Arkansas & Ozark Bed and Breakfast Reservation Service at (800) 233–2777 or Anderson House at (800) 264–5279 or (501) 362–5266 for reservations. You can check out the rooms online at www.yourinn.com.

Captain's House is a restaurant in a circa-1915 house at 603 West Quitman Street, Heber Springs 72543, only a half block off Highway 25 South. The restaurant's four rooms are done in a Victorian ship motif complete with Oriental rugs. Owners Janice and Jerry Nordquist purchased the restaurant after Jerry had been the chef for several years. Jerry specializes in healthy, low-fat dishes that emphasize the use of Arkansas products. Fresh fruit joins dishes like sesame-sauteed catfish or poached catfish—dishes unique in a state where catfish is usually

Anderson House

fried. The luncheon menu has sandwiches (including Jerry's favorite, a Reuben "done the right way") that come with a salad or the soup du jour. But this is no tearoom. The menu offers foods served at a captain's table—including steak and French fries. And the devastating desserts would please any sailor's palate: fresh fruit cobblers, European tortes with fresh raspberries, or lemon *vacherin* (a baked meringue) with mousse. Lunch is served Monday through Sunday from 11:00 A.M. to 2:00 P.M. Dinner is served Monday through Saturday from 5:00 to 9:00 P.M. Call (501) 362–3963 for information.

Betty Hazel found an old farmhouse built at the turn of the century and restored it to its original beauty. Now she shares it with guests. The ***Azalea Cottage Inn Bed and Breakfast*** is at 320 Sunny Meadow, Heber Springs 72543. There are four guest rooms, ranging in size from a small room on the main floor with a full-size bed to suites with fireplaces and Jacuzzi on the second floor. One of the main floor bedrooms has a Jacuzzi and queen-size bed. A very full breakfast of entrees such as eggs Benedict and fresh fruit and homemade bread, is served in the dining room or on the patio under the oak trees. Rooms range from $85 for the smaller room to $120 for the suites. Call (501) 362–1665 or e-mail azalea@arkansas.net. You can preview the rooms at the Azalea Web site: www.azaleacottageinn.com.

Cafe Klaser, at 106 West Second Street, Heber Springs 72543, is a favorite spot to eat. Billy Klaser is a five-star chef and makes a great tenderloin stuffed with rice and crawfish. It opens for lunch at 11:00 A.M. and stops serving at 2:00 P.M. Dinner is served at 5:00 until 8:30 P.M. Call (501) 206–0688.

North of Heber Springs you can visit the **William Carl Garner Visitors Center** between Memorial Day and Labor Day, and staff members will lead you through the dam and powerhouse located here. Nature trails, both easy and challenging, begin at the center, too. A U.S. Fish and Wildlife Service hatchery just north of the dam stocks the Little Red River and other cold waterways below dams in the region with more than a million trout each year. The center is open 7:30 A.M. to 3:30 P.M. daily March through November and is free. Call (501) 362–9067.

Jon's Pocket River Cottage is tucked into eight acres on the Little Red River off Highway 210 on the east side of Heber Springs. The cottage has 1,200 square feet, two bedrooms, and two bathrooms. There is a swing on the front porch and a grill for cooking out. Within walking distance is Ritchey Shoal, a great place for fly-fishing. The cottage is air-conditioned and has a washer and dryer. It is a great place to take the family (but no pets, please), and there is plenty of privacy. Owners Freddie and Jerry Quist say the cottage goes fast, and often people will rent it for the entire season. The cottage rents for $140 a night, with a two-night minimum. Once you get there, you won't want to leave. Curl

Traversing Big Creek

*T*he **Big Creek Natural Area,** 12 miles east of Heber Springs, embraces 3 ¹/₂ long, winding miles of Big Creek. Rocky streamside bluffs rise 200 feet above the creek, creating quiet and solitude. Within this natural area you will find a number of rare plants that prefer this cool, moist, and heavily shaded area. Wild pink azaleas and maidenhair fern adorn the area. You are asked to leave nothing but footprints and take nothing but photographs while walking the fairly rugged 2.4-mile trail. For more information, call (501) 324–9619.

up by the wood-burning fireplace on a fall night, and you will want it for the season, too. The cottage has a full kitchen and a deck near the river's edge. It accommodates four to six people and is wheelchair accessible. You can settle back in a hammock and enjoy the quiet. Call (501) 206–1242 for reservations or get more information, try the Web site at www.bbonline.com.

There are a couple of routes around Greers Ferry Lake by highway to the towns on the other side. Sugar Loaf Mountain is between Heber Springs and the town of Greers Ferry, too, but you need a boat to get to the mountain because it rises 560 feet in the middle of Greers Ferry Lake. The first National Nature Trail established by Congress climbs to the 1,001-foot summit. The trail is an easy climb and has spectacular bird's-eye views of the lake. (There is another Sugar Loaf Mountain, a landlocked mountain that shares its name with the one in Greers Ferry Lake. It is on Highway 110 and also has a foot trail to the summit for great views.)

Rex Harral's Shop at his home in **Wilburn,** at 710 Tyler Road, Wilburn 72719 (10 miles east of Heber Springs on Highway 110), is filled with hand-carved wooden objects that show the skill his hands have developed in the fifty years he has whittled. It isn't a hobby, it's his life's work. He fells the tres himself on his own land. Rex also makes carving tools. This creative man will make any tool he finds he needs. His berry-picking buckets, made from live bark when the sap is flowing, sell for $25. These are made exactly the way pioneers made them when they found a mess of berries in the woods. They simply stripped some bark from a nearby tree and made themselves a bucket. His wooden churns bring $125. There are bread bowls ($125), rolling pins and mixing bowls, blanket chests, candlesticks, carved ducks, and vases all made from basswood, ash, walnut, and oak.

Harral is a tale teller, too, so be ready to spend some time listening while you browse among the sweet-smelling carved pieces. Rex says he's there when he's there, but he works about six and a half days a week (he likes to have Sunday mornings to himself). So you can call ahead if you want to, at (501) 362–6569.

The drive from Heber to Fairfield Bay on Highway 16 is more scenic than the drive on Highway 92.

Longbow is unlike anything you have ever seen. Ben Pearson, legendary archer and member of the Archery Hall of Fame, the Bowhunter's Hall of Fame, the Arkansas Outdoor Sportsman's Hall of Fame, and the Sporting Goods Hall of Fame, bought these rugged original 400 acres in Prim after reading an ad in the *Wall Street Journal.* His son, Ben, Jr., has remodeled the cabin, and named Longbow after his dad's first bow, maintaining the canyon's natural beauty, while adding some modern conveniences.

The land is covered with sheer cliffs, enormous boulders, and a 30-foot waterfall. The cabin is an integral part of the landscape. Some of the interior walls are jagged cliffs, and a natural rock wall rises 20 feet from the living room floor and shows earthy colors from mineral deposits. There are skylights and a sleeping loft that lets you wake up at treetop level. The living room and full kitchen are wedged between two cave walls and overlook a waterfall cascading into a 6-foot-deep pool. Stone steps lead from the back door down to a patio at the pool's edge. A hammock is tucked under a rock overhang that shades it from direct sunlight.

The creek has bream, and you can see kingfishers, deer, and beaver. In the winter, bald eagles soar overhead. The property is now 1,400 acres, and a second cabin with a whirlpool tub has been built. Full of fossils, Indian spear points, and petroglyphs (rock carvings), this may be one of the most beautiful places in the state. This is a romantic getaway for adults, but small children need careful watching because of all the rocks and steps. Rates are $150 per night. Call (870) 948–2362 for information.

Ben continued his father's tradition when he built the ***Bushmaster,*** also in honor of a famous bow. The cabin is far enough from Longbow to ensure privacy, yet close enough that a family could rent both and share this remote canyon. In the Bushmaster cabin, aged rocks form two bathroom walls. The cabin is built directly over a rushing stream. Decks on two levels overlook a 250-million-year-old rock formation, which was once part of a massive river system that carved out the bluffs. The canyon changes dramatically with the seasons, from the lush green foliage of summer to bare-tree views of the frozen waterfall in winter. The rate is $150 for this cabin, too. Web site for Longbow and Bushmaster is www.longbowresort.com.

While you are in ***Prim,*** a hundred-year-old community with a population, last count, of eight, stop at ***Carlton's Diner.*** It's mostly a local hangout, but occasionally J. B. Hunt drops by to shake hands with folks (he was raised in Prim). People go there for really good hamburgers. Owners John and Joyce Carlton butcher their own beef and grind their own hamburger, which is hand patted and grilled. The dessert everyone orders is the blackberry cobbler made with hand-picked berries. The diner is also the town library, filled with books donated by locals. There are even bald eagles in the grove of trees across the way. The diner is open daily except Monday from 10:00 A.M. to 8:00 P.M. (or whenever everyone goes home).

The Carltons go to church on Sunday, so the diner doesn't open until 11:30 A.M. There is always a dinner special on Sunday and they stay open "until all the churches are over," which is usually about 3:00 P.M. Call them at (870) 948–2449.

The town of **Edgemont** on Highway 16 between Greers Ferry and Fair-

Mushrooming Town

*T*he little town of Shirley (population 350) is 10 miles northeast of Clinton on Highway 9. There's not much there anymore except for a nice little cafe for lunch. But there's something else going on in Shirley. A number of people grow a gourmet delicacy: shiitake mushrooms.

Growing shiitake here is the brainchild of Tom Kimmons, a professor at University of Missouri, before he retired to Shirley. It is not well known as a food crop in this country, but the shiitake contain all eight essential amino acids in better proportion than soybeans, meat, milk, or eggs. It contains a good blend of vitamins and minerals, including vitamins A, C, and D and niacin. As little as five grams of shiitake taken daily reduces serum cholesterol and blood pressure dramatically. They produce interferon and interleukin compounds, which strengthen the body's immune response to protect against cancer and virus infections, and produce a fat-absorbing compound that aids in weight reduction. A shiitake a day really can keep the doctor away, experts say.

Shiitake originated in the woodlands of China on oaklike shii trees. They have been used with acupuncture for the past 2,000. The Japanese discovered the full-bodied flavor of the delicacy and soon became the world's leading producer. Shiitake grow on white oak, which is abundant in this part of Arkansas—as is humidity. They are organically grown in logs. In early December, the planting begins. A high-speed drill creates a series of holes in the logs, and moist shiitake fungus is injected into the holes. To keep the fungus moist, the holes are sealed with cheese wax heated to 400° F. The logs are stacked in square crisscrossed piles—called crib stacks—covered with burlap, and left to sit in the shade for several months. The fungus requires care and must be taken inside if it is too hot or too cold, and uncovered and allowed to dry after a rain. Mushrooms are harvested in the fall, when the logs are flooded with water for twenty-four to seventy-two hours to fool the fungus into believing a rainstorm has occurred. About four days after white pinholes appear on the logs—early stage of mushrooms—it is picking time. Tours are available on Thursday or Friday mornings or by appointment. Call (501) 723–4443 for information.

For a lot more information about the health and medicinal properties of this organic treat, shiitake products and gifts, or how to grow these mushrooms, log on to www.shiitakecenter.com.

field Bay features the *Circa Collection,* a neat little antique jewelry store at 55 Stanfield Road, Edgemont 72044. The owner of this very elegant shop, Nancy Garot, displays estate jewelry, fine china and crystal, and sterling silver serving pieces. There are old Oriental vases and fine old eighteen-carat-gold, one-of-a-kind pieces for your selection. The shop is open by appointment only. Call (501) 723–4605 for an appointment.

Now head for the Historic Railroad Trail, a 2-mile round-trip excursion that starts at Highway 9 near the hardware store and runs along the historic Missouri and North Arkansas Railway. It goes by an Indian burial ground, and the end of the trail is at the old pioneer Cottrell-Wilson Cemetery.

Driving along Highway 65 is always interesting as several *emu farms* are in the area. Mina Hoskins owns one off Highway 65 on Highway 16 just 2 miles south of the Fairfield Bay entrance. You can see the birds from the highway, and it's fun to see them strutting around. But her son, Allen and his wife Margaret, managers of the ranch, would also love to have you stop in and see all the things that are made from the emu. Nothing is wasted; they "use everything but the beaks and toenails." Call (501) 723–4454 for more information.

Roberta Katz-Messenger is one of the finest stained-glass artists in Arkansas, having apprenticed with a European-trained stained-glass artist. Today her work appears in churches, homes, and office buildings around the state. Her studio, 3 miles west of Clinton on Highway 95 includes her work as well as that of potters, jewelers, and carvers from the region. Roberta welcomes guests by appointment anytime between 10:00 A.M. and 5:00 P.M. Monday through Saturday. You can talk to Roberta at (501) 745–4589 or e-mail her: pentacle@artelco.com. She can also direct you to some other interesting places in the area.

One of her favorite places is the *Therapeutic Massage at Garden Oaks* in the Lynch subdivision off Highway 65. Here Susan Fox will turn on mellow music, anoint you with aromatic oils, and relax away all of your aches. A sauna is available, too. Call (501) 745–6110 for an appointment.

Roberta says a good spot to stop for lunch in *Clinton* is *Chip's Court Street Cafe* at 107 North Court Street, Clinton 72031. This is what she calls "ethnic Ozark"—all mom's recipes—and where the locals all eat. Unfortunately, only breakfast and lunch are served here between 7:00 A.M. and 2:00 P.M. Monday through Friday. Call (501) 745–2163.

Going north from Clinton on Highway 65 will take you to places tucked out of sight (the backcountry keeps its secrets to itself unless you are in a canoe) or in plain view on the highway. The highway passes the *Antiques Warehouse* in *Botkinburg,* one of the largest antiques shops in the Ozarks and perhaps in the state, at Highway 65/110, and it's open seven days a week. Owner Don Keathley buys and restores European furniture, all of excellent quality and ready for the finest home. The back rooms also have unrestored pieces to browse among. Along with the furniture, there are decorator items of brass and silver, mirrors, and hundreds of stained-glass windows, and everything in the three warehouses and two showrooms dates from the 1860s to the 1880s. Hours are from 9:00 A.M. to 5:00 P.M. Monday through Saturday, and from noon to 5:00 P.M. on Sunday. The telephone number at the warehouse is (501) 745–5842. For more information—and a preview—e-mail the warehouse at antiquewarehouse@artelco.com or visit the Web site: www.antiquewarehouse.com.

Spring River Area

f you've headed north from Batesville on Highway 167, take Highways 62 and 63 to *Mammoth Spring,* so named because of its size, not because of any prehistoric elephant remains. Almost straddling the Arkansas/Missouri state line, it is the outlet of a subterranean river, and legend has it that the spring was found when an Indian chief dug a grave for his son, who had died searching for water during a drought. The Spring River is created by the flow from Mammoth Spring in the foothills; it is one of the largest natural water flows in the nation and, because of a constant release from the huge natural spring—nine million gallons each hour—has canoeing and trout fishing year-round.

The *Roseland Inn* in the Morris-Pace House in Mammoth Spring is on six lots of tree-shaded yard, surrounded by the original wrought-iron fence. There are leaded-glass windows, a carved oak mantel, and pocket doors decorating this 1906 Colonial Revival home at 570 Bethel Street, Mammoth Spring 72554. The owner and hostess is Jean Pace, formerly mayor of this sleepy little Ozark town, home to about 1,100 people; she is now president of its chamber of commerce. Jean lives in the house next door but fixes breakfast, late-afternoon dessert, and tea as part of the hospitality in the carefully restored, four-bedroom house. The first floor has a dining room, a double parlor, and a spring room where the original cistern still pumps water. The kitchen has what was surely, in 1908, a state-of-the-art zinc metal sink and original cabinets. A gazebo in the yard and a large porch across the front of the house have rockers for late-evening sitting. Rooms are $50 to $55; call

(870) 625–3378 for reservations. Roseland has a Web site that can be reached by clicking on lodgings at www.ozarks.com or E-mail at rose-land@ozarks.com. Jean takes most of the chamber of commerce calls at her house, so she is a good source of information.

There's plenty to do in Mammoth Spring during the spring, summer, and fall months. For example, every Thursday night square dancing takes place downtown, and every Friday night a free musical show, with a live band made up of local people, plays good country music. In fact, it's an open-mike arrangement, so if you want to get up there and show off your own banjo or fiddlin' skills, the crowd welcomes you. There's a two-step dance on Saturday night, also with a live band.

The town is country music crazy because of George D. Hay, the founder of the Grand Ole Opry. He traveled to the springs in the 1920s as a reporter with the Memphis *Commercial Appeal.* Invited to a hoedown, Hay was inspired by the local band that played well into the night and by the crowd that stayed up with it. "No one in the world has ever had more fun than those Ozark mountaineers did that night," Hay said. "It stuck with me until the idea became the Grand Ole Opry. . . . It's as fundamental as sunshine and rain, snow and wind and the light of the moon peeping though the trees. . . . [I]t'll be there long after you and I have passed out of this picture." And so it is. Every Labor Day weekend the town now has the Solemn Old Judge Days celebration to remember that enthusiasm—it's a regular hoedown with jig dancing and all. Then Saturday night the townsfolk get very serious about the flattop guitar and fiddle contest that anyone can enter; the winner is guaranteed a spot at Fanfare in Nashville—the Grand Masters' fiddle contest.

Mammoth Spring is known for its antiques shopping, and bargains are plentiful. *Michaels Antiques* is just one example. Owner Wayne Michaels has two floors of antiques and used furniture, situated at 304 Main Street, Mammoth Spring 72554. Hours are by chance or appointment. Call (870) 625–3254 for information. If you are looking for a place to eat, Wayne recommends *Fred's Fishhouse*—not just because it's the only place in town, but because it happens to be pretty darn good, too. You can get chicken or a burger, if fish isn't your thing. Fred's is just 1 block from Michaels at 204 Main Street, Mammoth Spring 72554. Call (870) 625–7551 for hours.

In the town of *Salem,* southwest of Mammoth Spring on Highway 9, music has always been a tradition. Every Saturday night instruments get tuned up and crowds gather to hear country, folk, and bluegrass music.

A tradition in the area is sponsored by the Ozark Mountain Music Makers at the *Music Barn,* 2 miles east of Salem on Highway 62/412. Here you can listen to more traditional country, bluegrass, and folk music and dance a little, if you like. Shows start at 7:00 P.M. Call (870) 895–3004 for a schedule.

Country music star David Lynn Jones has a recording studio at his home in Bexar, less than 20 miles from town, so you may see him on the streets of Salem when he is not touring.

Salem also has a farmers' market and trade days every Friday, Saturday, and Sunday, beginning around 7:00 in the morning and ending at dusk. The best one is the Christmas Market, copied from German towns, where you'll find warm drinks and Santa giving children rides on a hay wagon or tractor regardless of the weather.

The Spring River flows from Mammoth Spring to Hardy. On the banks of the Spring River, the historic village of **Hardy** is where professional artists have settled, and trout fishermen and canoes have filled the summertime river for more than a century. The main street is filled with turn-of-the-century storefronts that have been converted into a collection of antiques, crafts, and gift shops. Though the restored area is not big enough to tire you, it does hold more than fifty shops full of antiques, collectibles, and most unusual things in the 3 blocks of Main Street known as "Old Hardy Town."

The **Old Stone House Bed and Breakfast** is right on Main and School Streets, within easy walking distance of all shops. It is owned by Peggy Volland. The two-story, native-stone house has two large porches along the front and one side. A jumbo country rocker on the front porch overlooks a hedge of simplicity roses, and the side porch has white wicker furniture. Located at 511 Main Street, Hardy 72542, the establishment is just across the street from the Spring River, where you can always see rafts, canoes, or kayaks floating by. Three bedrooms and baths are on the second floor, where vaulted ceilings and ceiling fans move cool air; antiques grace both these and the three bedrooms and baths on the first floor. Guests can use the living room, and the Vollands have an extensive library of books, CDs, tapes, and board games. Coffee trays are brought to the rooms or to the side porch for early risers, and brunch is served about 9:00 A.M.—homemade granola and fresh fruit with homemade bread or muffins and fresh strawberry butter for the diet conscious and something really decadent like baked German apple pancakes for the rest of us. ("You don't have to eat it all," says Peggy.) Rooms are $79 to $95. Call (870) 856–2983 or (800) 514–2983 for reservations.

Nearby, Peggy has opened **Shaver Cottage,** a 1905 Victorian-influenced cottage that has two two-room suites with a television, VCR, refrigerator, and coffeemaker for honeymooners and other special occasions. The Rose Suite and the Victoria Suite are all done in antiques with "mood-setting fireplaces" (which means they look real but are not). The Rose has a two-person hot tub; the Victoria a single. There's a large yard with big, old trees, plus bikes to borrow for the 3-block trip to town. If that sounds like too much effort, there's a swing in the front yard for quiet contemplation. The Arbor Room is a single with bath for $95, and suites are $135 with a two-night minimum on weekends. Breakfast is brought up in a basket, and when you check in, a snack basket is sent up with you—also a choice of movies for the VCR. It's designed to be romantic, and it is. View their Web site at www.hardy-stonehouse.com.

Do you remember the 1958 BMW Isetta 300? If you ever saw one, you couldn't forget it because the entire front of the car opens up so you can climb inside. It only had a one-cylinder motor—about the size of a lawn mower engine—but ran really well. You can see a candy-apple red Isetta at the *Good Old Days Vintage Motorcar Museum* at 301 West Main Street, Hardy 72542. Keeper of the museum is Ernie Sutherland, and he makes sure that each of the museum's sixty cars is in perfect condition. There is almost every variation of the Ford Model T ("You can have any color you want as long as it's black"). The 1928 Ford Model A sedan still has World War II ration stickers on the windshield. There is a 1981 DeLorean and a 1946 Lincoln V-12 convertible. Some of the cars are for sale, so you might want to take your checkbook. There are motorcycles, bicycles, and even a rickshaw, and the walls are lined with car and tire company signs and gas pumps. There is even a gift shop where you can buy license plates and a multitude of reference manuals. Hours are 9:00 A.M.–5:00 P.M. Monday through Saturday. and 10:00 A.M. to 5:00 P.M. on Sunday. Admission is $5.00 adults, $2.50 children 12 and under. You can call (870) 856–4884 for more information.

The Hideaway Inn is just that, hidden away on 376 acres full of wildlife and birds. There's a fishing hole, picnic sites, and walking trails. There are queen-size beds in all three guest rooms, and one room has a private bath. Breakfast is served in the dining room. Rooms run from $60 to $75. You can call the innkeeper, Julia Baldridge, at (870) 966–4770 or (888) 966–4770 for information and reservations or check the Hideaway Web page: www.bbonline.com/ar/hideaway/.

Jeff and Debbie Kamps's *Flat Creek Dulcimer Shop* is at 644 Main Street, Hardy 72542. Jeff's mountain dulcimers are entirely handcrafted in the glass-front workshop, as are door harps and other crafts. But the dulcimers and dulcimer tapes are what bring folks in. The instruments are made of walnut and butternut and cost around $300, a price that includes a case and instruction book. Jeff's whole family plays the dulcimer. Hours are 9:00 A.M. to 5:00 P.M. six days a week, sometimes seven. Call (870) 856–2992 for more information.

Dale and Liane Maddox create **Hardy Pottery** at 200 East Main Street, Hardy 72542, and sell it along with hand-forged fireplace sets, white oak baskets, porch swings, wooden toys, hand-tied brooms, and a host of other craft items. The pottery is both functional—mugs, serving pieces, canisters—and decorative—lamps, vases. Dale works at the potter's wheel at the back of the shop, and visitors are invited to watch him there. Liane has a workshop at their home where she develops new designs. The shop is open from 9:00 A.M. to 5:00 P.M. Monday through Saturday; call (870) 856–3735 for information.

Hardy's Main Street is fun to explore. There's a music shop, featuring Asian and Indian instruments and a beautiful shop called **Southern Exposure** at 724 Main Street, Hardy 72542—one of the prettiest shops in town. Owned by David Hutchinson and Roy Whetstone, it's a gallery, actually, featuring large sculptures of deer and buffalo, among other things. There are fountains, and, well, you just must stop by and see it yourself. Hours are 9:00 A.M. to 5:00 P.M. seven days a week. Call (870) 856–3556.

Take Highway 167 south to **Evening Shade,** a town with more buildings on the National Register of Historic Places than any other city of its size. But of course that is not the reason you are driving to Evening Shade, is it? No. You want to take a photo of the city limits sign. And why is that? Well, because Burt Reynolds made the town famous with his television show of the same name, popular in the late 1980s, that's why.

There is a tribute to Burt Reynolds, for putting the town on the map, in the Burt Reynolds Gymnasium/Thompson Auditorium. The $750,000 gym/auditorium was built from the profits on sales of the *Evening Shade Cookbook,* which residents of the town and Reynolds combined to produce. In fact, Charlie Dell, who played Nub on the show, came to Evening Shade to marry actress Jennifer Williams at the local Methodist church.

So stop by and browse the crafts shops or have your photo taken standing next to the city limits sign, then have a cup of coffee or a piece of pie at the **Evening Shade Cafe** on Highway 167. There Cora Lou Davis will serve you from 10:30 A.M. until 8:00 P.M. every day except Sunday and Monday. On Sunday, Cora Lou opens for the church crowd from 11:00 A.M. to 2:00 P.M. And don't forget to buy a copy of the cookbook, which now has a second edition called, strangely enough, *Evening Shade Cookbook II.* Call (870) 266–3334 for more information.

Fayon Graddy makes a good sandwich at the deli counter in the back corner of her tiny store, **Graddy Grocery,** too (if you have a mind to eat and run).

The town of **Maynard** lies by the Missouri border, north and east of Hardy and Cherokee Village. If you pass through Maynard in September, you will become part of the **Pioneer Days Festival,** with its hour-long parade, dress revues, frontier games, and free musicals. This little town—population 381—swells to beyond 6,000 for the two-day event, which includes a crafts festival, a chicken and dumpling dinner, a gospel sing, and a bluegrass music festival in the park.

The **Maynard Pioneer Museum** is housed in a century-old log cabin not far from the business district of this small town. The museum is on Highway 328 and Spring Street, and a city park surrounds it. The cabin was to be demolished in 1979, but the citizens of Maynard took it apart log by log, numbered them, and reconstructed the cabin in the park. The inside depicts a typical rural home of the late 1800s, with handmade furnishings, old photos, tools, and heirloom needlework; a muzzle-loader rifle hangs over the fireplace. The museum, said to be one of the finest pioneer museums in the region, is open May through September from 10:00 A.M. to 4:00 P.M. Tuesday through Saturday and from 1:00 to 4:00 P.M. Sunday, though you can see the museum just about anytime by calling Bea Hearn at City Hall (870–647–2701). No admission is charged.

In **Pocahontas,** at the intersection of Highways 67 and 62, **The Living Farm Museum** is the only holistic farm museum west of the Mississippi River. Horse-drawn plows, harrows, disks, planters, threshers, hay rakes, and balers are among the implements demonstrated. Old hand

Natural History

The Rock Creek Natural Area is on the Ozarks' Salem Plateau, which extends from northern Boone County east to Pocahontas. Surface rocks are dolomite and limestone formed during the Ordovician Period 510 million years ago. Bubbling Spring Run is an upland headwater run and Rock Creek is the upland stream. The rare Riddell's Goldenrod and a species of skullcap, a member of the mint family, is restricted to the glades found here. You might also see a Spotted Sandpiper here, if you are lucky.

tools, kitchen equipment, antique tractors, and other farm vehicles—more than 800 items are on display, and another thousand are being readied. The equipment is actually used by the Good Earth Association to plant crops in the spring and harvest in the fall. Spectators can watch or even help in grinding corn and making bread and in grinding cane and making molasses the old-fashioned way.

The museum is a work in progress as things are added. Because it is an all-volunteer organization, the best way to see it in action is to contact Don Waterworth at (870) 892–9545. It is worth the trouble—hundreds of children come here for demonstrations and it is all free. You can fax Don at (870) 892–8329 or e-mail him at dwater@tcac.com.

Another museum in town is the *Bible In Oils Museum* at 901 Highway 62, Pochahontas 72455. This is Bud and Shirley Suhl's private collection of more than 140 oil paintings depicting scriptures of the Bible. Most of the works that fill the two floors are by European artists, but a few local artists have their work on display here also. These paintings are not for sale, but Bud and Shirley own the Thomas Kinkade Gallery across the street. The museum is open Monday through Saturday from 9:00 A.M. to 5:00 P.M. Call (870) 892–0441 for more information.

Near Maynard, Susan Reed and her husband grow wheat on their 400-acre farm outside of Walnut Ridge, south of Pocahontas on Highway 67. But at *Harvest Naturals,* Susan does more than just grow wheat: She weaves the stalks into beautiful designs. Her weavings, ranging from the usual sheaves (also called shocks) to wall hangings, house blessings, and useful items like napkin rings—some sixty different designs—are all originals. Her sister Sandy contributes dried floral arrangements to the creative selection. To see Susan's work, drive north 7 miles on Highway 67 to a bright blue building, turn right onto the gravel road, and go 1 mile to the first house. Call Susan first at (870) 892–3157.

Crowley's Ridge and the Delta

One of the surprises of this part of the Mississippi Delta is that it has hills. Rising abruptly above the Delta region is a narrow band of gently rolling hills known as Crowley's Ridge; stretching north to south, it breaks the flat plains and is one of the great oddities of the world. It extends nearly 210 miles from the northeast corner of the state to the Mississippi River at Helena and covers a half-million acres. This tree-blanketed hill was formed by wind and water over millions of years just prior to the Ice Age, when the Mississippi and Ohio Rivers cut vast trenches into the great plains of eastern Arkansas. The ridge was an island left when the two rivers retreated to the west. Crowley's Ridge Parkway, which stretches 200 miles through the Delta from St. Francis to Helena, was declared a National Scenic Byway in 1999.

The "highland" area of the ridge and the Ozark foothills, a region bounded by I–40 and Highway 167, contains a cluster of state parks, eleven of them to be exact, including two state museums and a memorial. Sixteen miles east of Crowley's Ridge State Park is downtown *Paragould.* But it's not called downtown anymore. The townsfolk decided that "uptown" sounded more, well, uptown than downtown, and so downtown Paragould is now called uptown Paragould. The pride of the town is a lighted mural of an old steam engine and depot. When driving on the Highway 412 overpass, you can look down into uptown Paragould.

The *Hamburger Station* at 110 East Main Street, Paragould 72450, is home of the famous "hum-burger" with grilled onion, a burger so good it was mentioned in *USA Today* as one of the best hamburgers in the country. Bert Daggett is the owner of this carryout-only spot located in an old train depot. Since its beginning in 1985, Hamburger Station has served sandwiches that rate high on the charts in this fast-food world: a roast turkey sandwich on a sesame-seed bun with bacon, cheese, lettuce, and tomato—and made from real turkey, roasted right there at the station. The roast beef sandwich is also made of "real beef," roasted in the station's oven. No pressed-meat, imitation stuff here. The station also makes great shakes and malts. Hours are from 10:00 A.M. to 7:00 P.M. Monday through Saturday; call (870) 239–9956 for information.

Discover writer Ernest Hemingway's Arkansas connection at the restored home and barn-studio where he penned portions of *A Farewell to Arms* and other famous works. The *Hemingway-Pfeiffer Museum and Educational Center* is at 1021 West Cherry Street, Piggott 72454. This is where Hemingway's second wife, Pauline, lived. Call (870) 598–3487 for more information or visit the Web site at hemingway. astate.edu.

Farther south along Crowley's Ridge on Highway 140 is the town of *Lepanto.* A town that didn't have a paved road until 1937, Lepanto now has a four-room living model of the Delta's heritage called *Museum Lepanto, USA* at the intersection of Berney and Main Streets. When the town was first founded, the only way into Lepanto was by boat on the Little River. Later the train came through, although it still took "all day to get out and another day to get back," according to Sue Chambers, the museum's director. This unique city shares the history of the Delta—the agricultural days, the Civil War and Indian conflicts, the Victorian era—

in a museum supported entirely by the annual Terrapin Derby, a turtle race held the first Saturday of October for more than sixty-five years. (Of course, a crafts fair, square dancing, and a parade are held, too.)

The people are proud of their history and show it in the town and the all-volunteer museum. The blacksmith shop, roofed with hand-hewn shingles, contains a huge iron anvil and all the tools and items created there, with a printed guide to identify and explain each one. A Victorian parlor, a general store full of supplies, and a doctor's office and barber-shop have been rebuilt there, too. Fossilized Delta mud, old tintype photos, an early printing press, and one of the first Maytag washing machines, made in 1902, offer a perspective on the changes that swept the Delta region over the years. A collection of artifacts shows the life of the Woodland Indians, who were native to the area. The museum is right on Main Street and is open on Saturday and Sunday from noon to 4:00 P.M., April 1 to November 1. As long as Sue is the director, however, she will open it anytime, year-round—just wander into the *Victorian Rose Antiques* shop (870–475–2568) at 244 Greenwood Avenue, Lepanto 72354, two doors down (two buildings full of glassware, china, and furniture) and the owner, Imogene Harris, will let you use the phone there to call Sue at 475–2591. Another manifestation of this town's pride is the mural at the four-way stop at Highway 140/135, depicting the town's Medal of Honor winner.

The *Hampson Museum State Park,* one of the state parks along Crowley's Ridge, features a most unusual museum, given to the state by James K. Hampson, a medical doctor with a successful practice who turned his boyhood fascination with arrowheads into the research and study of the physical remains of the early inhabitants of his family plantation, the Nodena, for whom the plantation is named. He and his family excavated, studied, and inventoried the mounds and subsurface remains of a complex civilization that lived on the meander bend of the Mississippi River in a fifteen-acre palisaded village from A.D. 1350 to 1700. The result is an educational facility devoted to the study of these, the state's earliest inhabitants, that exhibits artifacts from the Late Mississippian–Period culture. The Nodena people were farmers who developed a civilization of art, religion, political structure, and trading networks. The park is 5 miles east of I–55 at the junction of Highway 61 and Lake Drive. Admission is $2.25 for adults and $1.25 for children six to twelve years old. Hours are from 8:00 A.M. to 5:00 P.M. Monday through Saturday and from 1:00 to 5:00 P.M. on Sundays. Call (870) 655–8622 for more information.

Traveling south along the Mississippi from the Nodena site will take

Trivia

Arkansas' earliest inhabitants were the pre-Columbian bluff dwellers about A.D. 500. Burial remains indicate that the bluff dwellers planted corn, beans, pumpkins, sunflowers, and other plants. They used bows and arrows and a weapon similar to the Aztec atlatl—a throwing stick—to hunt deer and buffalo.

you through the ***Wapanocca National Wildlife Refuge,*** 5,500 acres 5 miles west of the Mississippi River. The heart of the refuge is the 600-acre Wapanocca Lake, a shallow old oxbow of the once-meandering Mississippi River. Surrounded by 1,200 acres of cypress and willow swamp, the other two-thirds of the refuge is equally divided between remnants of once-extensive bottomland hardwood forest and cropland of the refuge's farm unit. A Nature Drive to observe a variety of birds and wildlife in each habitat is offered, and more than 228 species of birds are known to pass through here.

Hungry? ***Colby O'Carroll's*** is a gourmet sandwich shop in ***Forrest City*** ("You create it, we make it!") that is famous for its eight-ounce burger with sauteed onions, mushrooms, bacon and cheese, and a special secret sauce. The Colby's Creation is a magnificent chef's salad with piles of ham, turkey, cheddar and Swiss cheese, chopped eggs, and crispy bacon. The burger and salad compete with all the other choices for sandwiches—and the selection will make you crazy if you hate to make decisions—with plenty of breads, together with toppings to adorn a variety of meats, cheeses, and vegetables. Do not miss this place. Colby O'Carroll's is located at 737 North Washington Street, Forrest City 72335. Hours are 6:00 A.M. to 10:00 P.M. Monday through Saturday and from 10:30 A.M. to 2:30 P.M. on Sunday. Call (870) 633–8811 for information.

Are you a real sportsman, not just a tourist? Then find the ***Pluck-a-Duck Goose Lodge*** in ***Wynne.*** This is prime duck-hunting country right in the middle of the Mississippi flyway with more than 15,000 acres of rice fields, flooded timber, and river blinds. Highly experienced guides take you to productive areas. Trained hunting dogs are provided, or you can bring your own dog. The comfortable lodge is famous for its outstanding meals prepared by Barbara Owens and accommodates up to twenty-six people. The day begins early with coffee and sweet rolls. After the morning hunt, you can return to the lodge for a country breakfast and a few hours of relaxation before heading out for the afternoon hunt. A big evening meal follows. The lodge is within minutes of the best hunting in the area. All you need to buy are shells, which must be steel shot, with nothing larger than T-shot. License and Duck Stamps are available at the lodge. Chest waders are highly recommended for hunters. The rate is $275 per day per gun. For goose season only, it's $230 per day per gun.

Trivia

Hernando de Soto crossed the Mississippi near Sunflower Landing, June 29, 1541. His search for food and gold took the Spaniards through the central part of the state, across the Arkansas River to Hot Springs, and down the Ouachita River to a site near Camden.

For more information call Cecil (Shorty) Owens at (800) 343–5944 or (870) 238–7856. During hunting season only, the lodge telephone number is (870) 697–2139. You can consult the Web site (www.pluck-a-duck.com), their fax (870–238–4481), or e-mail (info@ pluck-a-duck.com) for more information.

The town of **Parkin** on Highway 64 is worth a side trip if you enjoy archaeology. The **Parkin Archeological State Park** is excavating a site occupied from A.D. 1000 to 1500.

Evidence developed since the site was opened in the 1960s supports the theory that Hernando DeSoto visited here in 1541, making the Spaniards the first Europeans to cross the Mississippi River into what is now Arkansas. Tiny European-made glass beads, Spanish bells, and lead shot from a primitive sixteenth-century firearm have been found. The site dates from the Mississippian Period, an age when Native American villages were scattered across the Delta. The visitors center offers exhibits, a historical movie presentation, and a gift shop. A ½ mile trail provides a tour through the ancient village site. The park is situated just north of Parkin at the junction of Highway 64 and Highway 184. Hours are 8:00 A.M. to 5:00 P.M. Tuesday through Saturday; noon to 5:00 P.M. on Sunday. Admission is $2.00 for adults and $1.00 for children 6–12. During certain times visitors can assist at the dig, so call (870) 755–2500 for more information.

Highway 1 leads to **Jonesboro,** home to **Nancy Blades Pottery,** 2705 North Culberhouse Street, Jonesboro 72401, a combination studio and shop where Nancy makes both functional and decorative pieces in her several kilns. Nancy has been a potter for more than ten years and makes both wheel-thrown and handmade stoneware and porcelain pottery and jewelry. She will do custom orders for that special something you can't find anywhere else. She suggests you call ahead—(870) 931–9051—because her hours "vary wildly."

Arkansas State University Museum, 110 Cooley Drive, Jonesboro 72401, will not remind you of the dusty museums of your grade school field trip days. This museum connects yesterday with today and ancient Native American cultures with that of the early settlers, all done in colorful links that adults and children can easily follow. It shows artifacts from the world's oldest known cemetery found near Jonesboro, burial

Trivia

During the Civil War about 58,000 men joined the Confederate Army and perhaps 6,000 served in the Union forces. After the Confederate surrender, the state was controlled by the U.S. Army.

place of the Paleo-Indian culture of the Pleistocene Age—a settled and domestic people once thought to be nomadic hunter-gatherers. Especially interesting are the bones of a paleolama, an ancient 1,000-pound species of llama, excavated near here. It is the farthest north that remains of the species have yet been found.

Visitors can compare prehistoric tools to the farm implements used by pioneers a century ago. They can see a reconstructed log cabin built by a family 125 years ago. The museum shows both Confederate and Union uniforms, weapons, and equipment.

The museum's newest permanent exhibit is Old Town Arkansas, which was seven years in the making and covers the turn-of-the-century period. Visitors enter the old Main Street through a replica of the courthouse tower, complete with the original bell. Everything here is original; there are no reproductions. The physician's office includes the city's first X-ray machine.

The museum is open from 9:00 A.M. to 4:00 P.M. weekdays and 1:00 to 4:00 P.M. on Saturday and Sunday and is free. Call (870) 972–2074.

MORE PLACES TO STAY IN NORTHEAST ARKANSAS

GATEWAY AREA
Batesville Best Western, 773 Batesville Boulevard, 72501 (junction of Highways 167 and 5); (800) 528–1234

Calico Rock Cabins, 508 Calico Street, 72519; (870) 297–4134

Mountain View Days Inn, Highways 5/9/14, 72560; (870) 269–3287

Newport Park Inn International, 901 Highway 367 North, 72112; (870) 523–5851 (800) 633–7275

GREER LAKE AREA
Botkinburg Mountain Market, Highway 65 at Highway 110, 72031; (501) 745–5249 (great burgers!)

Clinton Best Western, Highway 65/Bypass 65, 72031; (501) 745–4700

Heber Springs Holiday Inn, 3450 Highway 25B North, 72543; (501) 362–1000

SPRING RIVER AREA
Hardy Best Western, 3587 Highway 412/62W, 72542; (870) 856–2176

Frontier Motor Lodge, Highways 62/63/412 (5 miles east of Hardy); (870) 966–3377, 966–4911

CROWLEY'S RIDGE
Blythville Holiday Inn, 1121 East Main, 72315 (870) 763–5800

Forrest City Best Western, 2333 North Washington, 72335; (870) 633–0870, (800) 526–1234

Jonesboro Best Western,
2901 Phillips Drive, 72401;
(870) 932–6600

Paragould Ramada Inn,
2310 West Kings Highway,
72451;
(870) 239–2121

MORE PLACES TO EAT IN
NORTHEAST ARKANSAS

Mountain View Village
Dogwood Hollow Steak-
house, Highway 5–19
North, 72560; (870)
269–9200

SPRING RIVER AREA
Hardy Cutter's Grill;
Junction Highways 63 and
62/412, 72542
(870) 856–4212

CROWLEY'S RIDGE
Blytheville Holiday Inn,
1121 East Main, 72315;
(870) 763–5800

Paragould Ramada Inn
Restaurant,
2310 West Kings Highway,
72451;
(870) 239–2121,

Chambers of Commerce in Northeast Arkansas

Gateway Area

Batesville Chamber of Commerce;
409 Vine Street, 72501; (870) 793–2378

Spring River Area

Mammoth Spring Chamber of Commerce;
Box 185, 72554; (870) 625–3518

Crowley's Ridge

Jonesboro Chamber of Commerce;
Box 789, 72401; (870) 932–6691

Paragould Chamber of Commerce;
Box 124, 72451; (870) 236–7684

Greer Lake Area

Heber Springs Chamber of Commerce;
*1001 West Main Street, 72543; (800) 77–HEBER;
E-mail: chamber@heber-springs.com;
www.heber-springs.com*

Northwest Arkansas

The Buffalo River literally gets you off the beaten path and into a beautiful wilderness. It was the first National River Park, established by Congress in 1972. Now about 12,000 canoes are rented during June and July, along with roughly the same number of private boats. Add the number of motorized fishing craft, and you have something like 50,000 folks floating down the 125-mile river. That's a lot of sunscreen. But the Buffalo cuts a path through some of the most unspoiled beauty in the country—towering limestone bluffs, white-water rapids, and natural wilderness—drawing campers, fishermen, and other folks bent on getting away from city stress.

Buffalo Point, at Highways 14 and 268, was the only fully developed park on the river. In 1997 Tyler Bend, on Highway 65, was added. Both offer camping, hiking trails, and rustic cabins and are run by the National Park Service. Outfitters can be found at every access point, in almost every town along the way.

The Buffalo River is a tributary of the majestic White River, along which settlers built log cabins. These hardy settlers, isolated as they were from the rest of the world, developed a folk culture that still lives today in the backwoods and hollows along the creeks that feed the historic river.

It can reach 80 degrees or get plenty chilly by the middle of October, when dozens of arts and crafts fairs lure thousands of autumn tourists to the area. November and December have their own beauty; the winter has many mild days, with dramatic new scenes uncovered after foliage falls. Snow in these mountains can be from 2 inches to 2 feet, but it can also disappear quickly.

Crossing the Buffalo River

Like so many small towns across the country, *Leslie,* 20 miles southeast of Buffalo River on Highway 65, fell on hard times when the railroads moved on. This was the end of the "Dinky Line," the railroad that hooked up to the Missouri and North Arkansas Railroad. The rail line was used

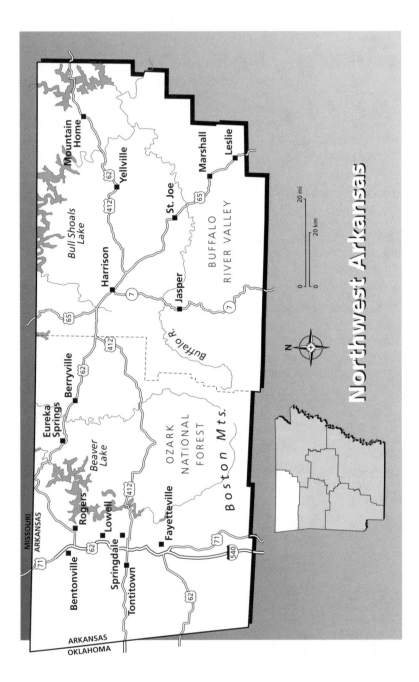

Northwest Arkansas

**BEST ATTRACTIONS IN
NORTHWEST ARKANSAS**

Champagne Flight,
Ponca; (870) 861–5514

Turpentine Creek Exotic
Wildlife Ranch, south of
Eureka Springs;
(501) 253–5841

War Eagle Mill, War Eagle;
(501) 789–5343

Ozark Scenic Railway,
Springdale; (800) 687–8600

James at the Mill,
Johnson; (501) 443–1400

Aunt Shirley's Sleeping
Loft B&B, Omaha;
(870) 426–5408

to "log out the hollers" around here, carrying lumber to the mills. When that industry faded, the town faded, too, in spite of the proud rock homes. The seven hotels mysteriously burned, one at a time, and Leslie went from being one of the biggest towns in northwest Arkansas to a shadow of its former self. Then longtime residents of Leslie donated money to help refurbish the town. Now the place is jumping again.

The *Ozark Heritage Arts Center and Museum,* 410 Oak Street, Leslie 72645, is a surprising treasure that any town would covet. This hill town of only about 500 people has a 400-seat theater, art gallery, and museum thanks to the philanthropy of Daphne Killebrew and her late husband, Rex. The museum covers the history of whiskey barrel manufacturing, which made Leslie a boomtown in the early 1900s. The Killebrew Theater was built over the high school gym and now offers the community repertory players made up of volunteers from the region. There is a large stage, comfortable high-rise seating, and twin balconies. The theater hosts musical performances, ranging from light opera to Ozark fiddlers. The Arts Center is open Tuesday through Saturday from 10:00 A.M. until 4:00 P.M. The gallery emphasizes the art of northern Arkansas, featuring primitive artists as well as abstract painters. Tours of the museum and gallery are free. For more information call (870) 447–2500 or visit www.ozarkheritage.org.

Leslie is also home to *Serenity Farm Bread,* at Main Street and Highway 66, where the aroma of healthy bread baking in old-world brick ovens greets visitors to Chris and David Lower's bakery. Each morning the ovens are fired up to 1,000 degrees Fahrenheit to heat the bricks. The floor of the oven is then scrubbed and allowed to cool to about 430 degrees for baking. The loaves are placed into the oven using a long-handled peel. Some starter is saved every day for the next day's batch, because the Lowers won't use yeast in the sourdough-type bread. (Actually it's Flemish *desem*—pronounced da-sum—bread.) Only organic grains, filtered water, and sea salt are in it. The culture that starts it is fed only whole wheat flour. There are other fruit-filled loaves, like the walnut raisin bread, which contains organically grown fruits and nuts. In all, the bakery carries more than fifty types of bread and pastries.

Lower wraps the loaves in bakers' linen—a tight wrap is part of the secret—which slows down the growth and makes the bacteria work harder. Each batch is different because of the effects of barometric

Christ of the Ozarks is off Highway 62, 1½ miles north of Eureka Springs on Statue Road. The statue towers seven stories above Magnetic Mountain and weighs more than a million pounds. The outspread arms measure 65 feet across, giving it the appearance of a gigantic cross when viewed from a distance.

pressure and temperature. With all this care, five kinds of gourmet bread are produced, and are they worth the effort! There is, of course, 100 percent whole wheat bread. But try the apple and fig almond-filled loaves, garlic herb and tomato olive focaccia, or the walnut raisin or European rye. You can sit and enjoy the gourmet coffee served here, including a local brew, Rozark Hills.

You can buy a loaf there in the bakery for $3.00 but don't cut it or eat it for several hours, because internal cooking is going on. The bread is best the third day after it is baked, therefore it is easily shipped to retail stores in the Midwest. It also freezes well. Call (870) 447–2211 for information. Serenity Farms has an informational Web site, www.serenityfarmbread.com, which includes their menu of available breads. But to order, you still have to call and talk to a real person. As it should be.

The town of **Marshall,** on Highway 65 between St. Joe and Leslie, has a great farmers' market on Saturdays starting at 6:00 A.M. until sold out, beginning in about mid-May and continuing through October. In addition to all sorts of fresh fruits and vegetables throughout the season, you'll find homemade crafts and fresh flowers from about thirty area farmers.

The Buffalo National River flows under Highway 65 north of the town of Marshall, and the Tyler Bend Recreation Area follows the river. **Gilbert,** on Highway 333, is a gathering place for canoers paddling the river. With its 1901 saloon-style front, the **Gilbert General Store** is the same now as then. Well, maybe not exactly the same—in 1906 the owner added onto it a bit. But the town post office is still in a front corner, and the potbellied stove, circled by rocking chairs, still makes a warm spot for the locals to gather. The store is the heart of this quaint town on the banks of the Buffalo River, where the population can swell from 43 to 543 on any summer day. Managers Ben and Cynthia Fruehauf have been here since the 1970s and can not only provide you with anything you need in the way of canoe gear but also tell you how to find all the secret waterfalls and cliffside swimming holes. Listed on the National Register of Historic Places, the store is open from 8:00 A.M. to 5:00 P.M. daily during the season, which runs from about March through October. Ben says they "shorten up the hours in the winter," which might mean it's closed entirely, but you never know unless you call (870) 439–2888 or

(870) 439–2386. Take Highway 65 to State Road 333; then go east on Highway 333 to the end of the road. If you want a preview, see their Web site: www.gilbertstore.com.

Tyler Bend Recreation Area has handsome camping facilities and a 6 ¹/₂-mile-long hiking trail at the put-in point just off Highway 65 at the Buffalo National River. The trail creates foot access to some of the best scenery along the river—high bluffs, long sandbars, and fast-water shoals. Most of the walk is along easy grades, but more difficult stretches occur along the ridgelines, where the vistas of Calf Creek are worth the effort. The trail is a series of loops adjoining one another and varying from just under 2 miles to nearly 4 miles. A 1,000-foot-long stone wall built during pioneer days and a 1930s log homestead are also found along the trail.

North of Tyler Bend on Highway 65, *Coursey's Smoked Meats* in *St. Joe* has been smoking bacon and hams for more than fifty years. The place has the original old smoker out front, but now it's all done inside in stainless steel smokers. Hours are from 8:00 A.M. to 6:00 P.M.— "only seven days a week." Jack Coursey is the owner, Mary Lu Coursey Neal is the manager, and they still make the best smoked bacon in the state. If you don't believe it, call (870) 439–2503 and order some or fax (820) 439–2300.

Also in St. Joe is *Ferguson's Country Store and Restaurant,* on Highway 65 just up from the scenic Buffalo River. The road to Gilbert, where canoeists drop into the river, turns off Highway 65 at Ferguson's. Down the road at St. Joe are other cutoffs to the river. The restaurant caters to busloads of tourists who come to eat the home-cooked fried chicken, pork chops, beans with cornbread, and cinnamon rolls and browse in the country store filled with handmade quilts, wood products, and doodads. The owner of this one-stop-for-everything store is Wayne Thompson. Call him at (870) 439–2234 for information. Behind the restaurant is year-round Ferguson Furniture Manufacturing. Folks who eat at the restaurant can wander through and look at the solid red oak tables, chairs, and hutches being made by the vanishing breed of craftspeople that once populated the Ozarks.

Fishing Country

The town of *Norfork* began as a changeover point for pioneers who followed the White River, then switched from boats to ox carts. Norfolk today is equally reliant on the river. Tourists come to the area for fishing,

OFF THE BEATEN PATH

and the many guide services and resorts are a major source of employment for Locals.

The **Wolf House,** built sometime between 1809 and 1825, is off Highway 5 in Norfork. It was the home of Major Jacob Wolf, sent as an Indian agent by President Thomas Jefferson. For more than a half century, it served as a courthouse, post office, and stage and steamboat stop. The historic house, said to be the oldest remaining log cabin in the state, is open for tours during the warm months and contains antiques and memo-rabilia dating from the 1700s—more than 400 pieces of interesting relics and furniture of the time, including items as unusual as a rare 1870 hanging mousetrap, a glass parlor fly trap, and an 1860 ruffle iron for ironing ruffles on ladies' dresses. Built by black and Native American craftsmen, the handmade bricks of clay—dug and fired on the property—compose the four fireplaces and two chimneys. Half-dove-tailed notched logs and original wrought-iron hinges, as well as the lock-raftered roof (no ridgepole is used), give fascinating insight into the labor and time required for the home to expand—the fam-ily grew to include the six children of two wives. Volunteers have the house open from 9:00 A.M. to 5:00 P.M. Monday through Saturday from April 15 to October 15. Call (870) 499–9653. There is a crafts shop next door designed to match the house. To find the house, take Highway 5 South ¼ mile past the North Fork River Bridge.

White River Pottery, on Highway 62, opens for the summer in April (and closes from January through March) and is where William Stephen-son creates many neat pieces you won't be able to resist taking home. Summer hours are from 10:00 A.M. to 5:00 P.M. Monday through Saturday. Colleen, William's wife, will be happy to show you around. Call (870) 425–2164 for infor-mation. **Earl's,** just west of Mountain Home on Highway 62 (across from White River Pottery), is a super place. His specialty is refinishing, and he has huge items, such as hotel bars, that are simply beautiful, as

Wolf House

well as interesting small stuff. It's a fun spot to stop and browse. Call (870) 425–8578 for information.

If trout dimpling around you in a cold stream is your idea of heaven, then Ken and Judy Epperson at the *Cotter-Trout Dock* in *Cotter,* the town just west of Gassville on Highway 345, can arrange float trips on the Buffalo, North Fork, or White Rivers. Both single-day floats, covering 15 to 20 miles of river, and overnight camp trips are available. All trips carry a guide and food. The overnight trips have a commissary boat operated by the cook and range from two to six days. You need bring only your fishing tackle and personal effects; everything else is supplied, and floats are tailored to your individual requirements. Guides with many years on the river ("We've been here as long as the trout have," says Judy) know where to fish. The cost is about $100 per person per day for day trips. Overnight trips on the White River are $160 each, with a minimum of four people and two days. The same kind of trip on the Buffalo River, where the smallmouth live, is $150 to $200, but fishing is good only April through June. Call (870) 435–6525, or (800) 447–7538 if you are outside the state, to arrange trips. Cotter-Trout Dock also has a Web site: www.whiteriver. net/cotterdock/; you can e-mail them at ctd@southshore.com.

The dock is under the historical *Rainbow Arch Bridge* on Highway 62B at Cotter. Built in 1930 at a cost of $500,000, the cement bridge, with its five rainbow stands, is very rare. It was the first bridge across the White River and is listed on the National Register of Historic Places.

Cotter has been an important spot on the White River since the Bluff Dwellers farmed the rich bottomland there. Steamboats brought people and goods from all over the country. Lake's Ferry was here first, and there was a steamboat landing at McBee's Place upriver about 1¹/₂ miles. Steamboats could make the trip from Batesville in about twelve hours when it took twenty-four to reach by land. Before the bridge was built, the citizens of Mountain Home and Yellville would meet at the ferry for picnics—stores would close in both towns, and everyone would trek to the Big Spring at the ferry in phaetons (light four-wheeled carriages), buggies, wagons, or oxcarts. A railroad bridge was built in 1904, and a tunnel was finished in 1905 for the White River branch of the Missouri-Pacific and Iron Mountain Railroad. Cotter was an exciting town. Mike Williams wants to see that excitement return and is doing his part to revitalize the Ozark river town. He now owns five buildings downtown and, with twenty years' experience in the high-quality antiques business, has begun to fill the 2,100-square-foot *Richmond Building,* at 122 McLean Avenue, Cotter 72626, with beautiful examples of carved-wood furnishings, fireplace mantels, and architectural items. Call (870) 435–2531 for information.

A walking trail starts in Cotter City's Big Spring Park and follows the river upstream for 2¹/₄ miles. It isn't unusual to spot an eagle or a fox as you follow the river. The best swimming hole in the Ozarks, according to the locals, is the Big Spring in the park. Rumor has it that there is a school in Cotter getting quite a reputation among fishermen—you can learn to make your own fly rod there. But you will have to ask a local for information if you are interested in this unique school. The best way to spend your time around here is to float the Buffalo River. Buffalo Point is located 14 miles south of Yellville on Highway 14. You can get equipment, canoes, or rafts from outfitters. Summer, when the river is tame and the bluffs are gorgeous, is a perfect time to visit this end of the river. In July or August, falling in feels good. It is a great river for first-time canoeists or families.

And speaking of historic places, **Whitewater**—now sometimes called "Whitewatergate" by the news media, due to President Clinton's involvement in this resort area—is located here in Marion County along the White River, southeast of **Flippin** on Highway 101.

Take Highway 101 South, (east of Flippin, and west of the Cotter Bridge.) Head for Ranchettes Access Area. The Whitewater Development is to the left, just before the Ranchettes subdivision. All you will see, though, is a gravel road and some third-growth timber. So take your fishing rod to fish at the access, because there was never much to see except a lot of reporters and now, even they are gone.

If you want fast food to take on a picnic or on the river, locals say **Sanders & Son** grocery store on Highway 62 (103 Main Street) has the best chicken and fixin's around. Their deli also has barbecue, cole slaw, and really big brownies. Hours are 5:30 A.M. to 6:00 P.M. every day but Sunday. Call (870) 453–2333 for information.

Many visitors to the Arkansas Ozarks come in search of beautiful handmade quilts, and rarely do they leave disappointed. Every little community here has active quilt guilds of hundreds of members. One place to match yourself up with their talents is at **The Curiosity Shop,** 9084 Highway 62 East, Flippin 72634. Paula Ross is the owner who started her business here in 1994 to sell quilting supplies and handmade crafts to travelers. She became interested in stained glass and soon her colorful creations began sparkling in the large open windows. She has combined her love of stained glass and quilting to offer matching patterns. Choose a pattern for a window in your bedroom or bath and she will design a quilt for the bed with the matching pattern. Paula has a large quilting machine inside the shop, and if you've never seen the process, she welcomes you to stop in and watch for she always has a quilt on the machine. (She admits, however, she prefers hand-quilted work). Paula says she's always in the shop, even summer holidays, but her posted hours are Monday through Saturday from 9:00 A.M. to 5:00 P.M. Her phone number is (870) 453–5300.

If you follow Highway 62 west toward Harrison, you will find a good B&B. The **Red Raven Inn,** at Highways 62 and 14 South near Yellville, near the lower Buffalo River, which is floatable all year long (unlike the upper Buffalo, which dries up after spring rains cease) is the perfect base for float trips. Don and Cam Semelsberger are hosts at the inn, which sits right on the banks of Crooked Creek (the creek is full of smallmouth bass). The stately Queen Anne–style early twentieth-century inn, with its wraparound porch, has five bedrooms, all with private baths and each decorated in a different theme. Cam particularly likes The Hummingbird Room, but male travelers are often at home in The Cowboy Room. The prices range from $65 to $95 and include breakfast—Don's *aebelskivers* (a Danish pancake with red raspberry jam) or Belgian waffles. You can invite local guests to join you for breakfast for $5.00. There is even a honeymoon suite. Call or fax (870) 449–5168 for information. A walking bridge across Crooked Creek behind the Red Raven leads to a very nice city park, which has a walking track, lit tennis courts, a volleyball pit, and lots of playground equipment for kids. Cam calls it "Six Flags over Yellville." Yellville has an annual Turkey Trot Festival in October.

The **Old Store,** in the Rush historic district at the end of Highway 26, off Scenic Highway 14, is in a deserted town that was once a thriving mining community. Silver and zinc were discovered here in 1882, and in 1883 a record-setting 13,000-pound piece of zinc was excavated and shipped to the Chicago World's Fair for exhibition. Today that piece is in Chicago's Field Museum of Natural History. The remaining structures in town now belong to the National Park Service, and hiking trails, boating access, and a camping area are nearby. There are also markers to help visitors relive the past in this historic old town.

In **Yellville,** the **Front Porch Restaurant** on Highway 62 East is in a delightful setting. It is an area destination as well as a place to eat. Owners Dave and Laveta Tablish have extensive plantings in the spring, summer, and autumn. There are rock work, waterfalls, and a bridge. All three meals are served in a country-style buffet that, on Friday nights, includes peel-and-eat shrimp. Call (870) 449–5500 for information. The restaurant has been mentioned in *Southern Living* magazine, as has the Red Raven Inn. Life on the Front Porch begins at 7:00 A.M. and rolls on until 9:00 P.M. every day. You can e-mail Dave and Laveta at burer@mtnhome.com.

Turkey Trot

Yellville has hosted the annual Turkey Trot since 1945, during which twenty-five live turkeys are tossed from a plane down into the crowd. The town does not sanction it. Their Miss Drumsticks Beauty Contest is judged by legs only (faces and bodies hidden). The festival is held in October.

Buffalo River Lodge, on Caney Road off Scenic Highway 14, sits on sixty-two acres of woods and meadows 14 miles south of Yellville. This three-level log lodge with a double deck and wraparound porch has five guest rooms, all with private baths. A luscious full breakfast is served in the dining room or on the deck in good weather. You can relax in the great room, with its stone fireplace and loft library, then enjoy the hot tub on the deck or retire to the Honeymoon Suite with an in-room Jacuzzi for two. You can also have gourmet dinners on Saturdays with advance notice. Innkeepers Stan and Glenda Erikson will happily fix you picnic lunches for canoeing trips on the river. Rooms are from $75 to $115. Call (800) 733–2311 or (870) 439–2373 for information and reservations. The lodge Web site is at www.buffaloriverlodge.com.

Harrison is called the "Crossroads of the Arkansas Ozarks" because scenic roadways to many mountain attractions meander through this small town. A visit should begin at the **Boone County Heritage Museum,** 110 South Cherry Street, Harrison 72601, at the corner of Central and Cherry Streets 1 block west of Highway 7 South. The museum houses a large collection of railroad memorabilia, Civil War artifacts, Native American items, and period costumes, as well as a fine collection of Ozark Mountain rocks. The museum is open from 10:00 A.M. to 4:00 P.M. Monday through Friday, March through November. From December through February, it is open only on Thursday. Admission is $2.00; kids are admitted free. Call (870) 741–3312 for information.

> ## Trivia
>
> *The Baker Prairie Natural Area near Harrison is a remnant of the prairie that was part of the Springfield Plateau of north-central Arkansas. With its limestone and chert substrata, it supports big and little bluestem grasses, switchgrass, and Indian grass. It is home to the ornate box turtle—its habitat is restricted to unplowed grasslands—which is endangered and protected.*

The Hotel Seville is located at 302 North Main Street, Harrison 72601, and was once the most luxurious lodging facility for hundreds of miles. Built in 1929, the hotel's interior remains like a step into fifteenth-century Spain and is a popular location for weddings and other social events in the area. You might want to spend the night; rooms range from $55 to $120. Or just stop in for lunch during a walking tour of the historic area of downtown Harrison. Maps for those tours are available in the lobby. Call (870) 741–2321 or visit www.hotelseville.com.

The **Lost Spur Guest Ranch** outside Harrison has four cabins and a cottage that accommodates up to twenty-four people. Crooked Creek runs through the ranch. You can fish, swim, or canoe in its shallow but clear waters. T. J. Hunter is the rancher who hosts this 116-acre ranch. His wife Lyn does most of the cooking and serving in the "dining barn," where a wood-burning stove and recliner chairs temp you to nap after a meal. T. J. takes visitors on trail rides across the meadows and through the woods along the creek. Guests can borrow any of six canoes to float

Couples travel thousands of miles to be married in the world-famous Little Bell Wedding Chapel on Highway 65 near Harrison. Services include elopements, proxy, off-site, reaffirmations, and baptisms, and you can even get a license on weekends or holidays. Complimentary flowers, photos, music, and candles are part of the service. Call (870) 743–2355 or log onto the Web at www.little-bell.com. Honeymoon information can be found at www.yournet.com.

the 6 miles downstream. Hayrides, chuckwagon cook-outs, and occasionally evening entertainment are part of the fun. The cooking pit with picnic tables alongside the creek is where the Hunters cook their "cowboy breakfast" (bacon and potatoes cooked together in a black cast-iron skillet and served with donuts and fruit). Stay for a week, Sunday through Saturday for $995, $590 for children through 17 years of age. A three-day stay, Wednesday through Saturday or Sunday through Wednesday, costs $495 for adults, $295 for children. Call (870) 743–7787 or (800) 774–2414 or e-mail at lostspur@aol.com.

Another interesting site is the **Baker Prairie,** seventy-one acres of America's vanishing tallgrass prairie filled with wildflowers, grasses, birds, and other creatures. It is 10 blocks west of the square on Goblin Drive.

It seems as though the mountains pop up as suddenly as spring mushrooms around here once you cross the border from Missouri—everywhere a view on Highway 65. There can be no doubt that this is Arkansas.

From Harrison go north 10 miles on Highway 65 to **Omaha. Aunt Shirley's Sleeping Loft Bed and Breakfast,** 7250 Shirley, Omaha 72662, is near Omaha—and yes, there is a real sleeping loft, one that will sleep five people. But even better, the loft is in a cabin next to the main house, so guests have complete privacy. The cabin can handle an entire family with three double beds, a daybed, and a quaint country bedroom on the main floor; the cabin also has such modern conveniences as a small refrigerator, a microwave, and a color television set to accompany the country motif. A complimentary bottle of champagne greets honeymooners. Shirley and Buddy LeBleu own the eighty lovely mountaintop acres. A couple of swings hang from the trees out front, and rockers on the porch catch the cool mountain breezes. There are quiet walkways and views everywhere. With plenty of space for kids to run free, Aunt Shirley's is far away from anywhere and anything. And though far from the madding crowd, the B&B is near enough to Branson, Missouri, and its fabulous collection of country music theaters to make it a good place to stay if Branson is too hectic and crowded (which it is).

Children are welcome at this open, country hideout. In fact, when they are along, "Aunt" Shirley fixes a favorite from her Arkansas childhood, chocolate gravy, to go on the homemade country biscuits she serves for breakfast. A big country breakfast with fresh biscuits and gravy, grits, and eggs is an everyday thing, but if you stay a week, Shirley fixes her specialty—Dutch pancakes (these look like cream puffs when they come out of the oven and are filled with wild blackberries picked on the property and topped with whipped cream).

The loft is available by chance or reservation but to only one family at a time. There's a room in the main house (with a waterbed) for extra people. Find Boone County Road 15 East off Highway 65—it winds about 3½ miles through the woods—or call (870) 426–5408. Rooms are $60 for two people and $5.00 for each additional person. Shirley's new Web site is www.auntshirleysloft.com.

While you are in Omaha, be sure to see the incredible stained glass made in a quaint old building at 11515 North Highway 65. *Burlington Store Stained Glass* is the place to visit for its extensive line of stained glass constructed on site. There are one-day free stained glass classes geared for visitors and glass and mosaic supplies for the hobbyist. You can buy Fenton collectibles and Yankee candles here, too. Suzy Aikman is the artist, who runs the store with the help of her sister, Debbie. They are the fourth generation of their family to operate a store at this location. Their potbellied stove warms the indoors in winter and an inviting front porch with swings welcomes guests in nicer weather. While visiting, be sure to ask Debbie and Suzy about the shoot-out with Jesse James on this site. Call (800) 654–3013 for class times.

Trout Heaven

*F*ishing on the White River is one of the most popular things to do in this area. Here's why: There are four main trout fisheries, all tailwater fisheries fed by cold water drawn from the bottom of reservoirs and run through hydroelectric dams to generate electricity. The water runs through limestone rich in nutrients that feed aquatic insects, fish, and crawdads. This flood of nutrients makes so much food available that the trout don't have to work hard to eat, which allows them to grow as much as an inch a month. No other location in the country can produce such a growth rate. The limestone is fertilizer, and state trout biologists say that in most streams the fish stop growing because they can't get enough food. Here, they just move up the food chain and keep on growing. The brown trout reproduce naturally, but the rest are from state and federal hatcheries.

To get to the **Bull Shoals Lake area,** take Highway 14 from Omaha back toward Yellville; then take Highway 178 North to the lake area. Fishing on the lakes and rivers below the Bull Shoals Dam near Mountain Home makes this region popular with fishing enthusiasts. The White and North Fork Rivers provide perfect trout waters for 100 miles downstream. The silver flash glimmering in the summer sunlight is often a record-threatening catch, and all the state trout records and a former world record (a thirty-eight-pound, nine-ounce German brown trout caught in 1988) reside here.

That record was broken recently when angler "Rip" Collins caught a forty-pound, four-ounce German brown trout in the Little Red River. The White River also produces National Fresh Water Hall of Fame line-class brown trout. Five of *those* fish are more than thirty pounds. So if you dream of piscatorial fame, these are the rivers to cast in.

The **Gaston White River Resort** in **Lakeview** is a good place to head-quarter for the adventure because the guides are among the best on the river. Much of the fishing is done with worms and salmon eggs, so be sure to specify a guide who appreciates fly-fishing. There's a landing strip here, and the resort is a popular fishing spot for celebrities like Phil Donahue, who flies in for an annual float trip. Call (870) 431–5202 for information. Their address is 1777 River Road, Lakeview 72642.

Gaston has a Web site at www.gaston.com and can be reached by E-mail at gaston@mtnhome.com. The restaurant is open every day from 6:30 A.M., so you can get an early start on the river, to 10:00 P.M. The restaurant's view overlooking the White River makes it a popular Sunday

Spelunking in the Ozarks

*A*rkansas is a spelunker's delight—there are more than 2,000 caves in the Ozark mountains. Scientists call caves "our last wilderness," and those dark, yawning openings still fascinate people. Our early ancestors took shelter there, in competition with bears looking for a warm place to hibernate. The Tom Sawyer or Becky Thatcher in all of us is drawn to the mysterious holes in the mountains filled with stalagmites, stalactites, and crystal waters. Many of these caves were thought to have been discovered in the past thirty years, but there is evidence that some of them were used to hide Spanish gold and Civil War supplies and munitions. Some have petroglyphs—cave drawings—in the ceilings dating back 1,000 years. A cave is considered young if it is less than ten million years old. So thousand-year-old petroglyphs are barely remnants of yesterday in earth time.

Trivia

You can cruise across Bull Shoals Lake at Peel Ferry, the only state-run ferry that still operates in the state.

brunch destination. Pilots from as far away as Chicago and Dallas will fly in just to eat fresh fish and homemade breads. There is a private club and bar where you can have a cocktail and talk about the fish you almost caught. (The restaurant is closed except for Sunday brunch from December 15 to February 15.)

The lake twists and turns for 80 miles through the Ozarks hills of north-central Arkansas and southwest Missouri. The woodsy hills and bluffs shelter the blue-green lake, leaving cool shadows. There are few boats on this lake, and you can cruise along in amazing quiet with seldom another craft in sight. Most of the shoreline is rough and undeveloped. There are no bridges and the only way across is the Route 125 Free Ferry to shuttle people from the north to the south side and back again. The spring-fed lake is refreshingly chilly for swimming on hot afternoons.

Now, for the nonfishing folks along for the ride, nature gave the trout a beautiful place to live, and you can enjoy it, too. Since you will be seeing the dew-kissed mornings along with the trout hunters, drive on over to **Mountain Village 1890** and tour an authentic Ozark village unmarked by time.

See ten historic structures moved to the village green from other towns in the state: The church stands on the highest spot in town for all to see; there's a nineteenth-century bank, a general store, a country school, a church, a dogtrot log cabin from Monkey Run, and the Lynch Flippin House, formerly the best house in Goatsville. Skilled craftspeople will be at work on pioneer arts and crafts.

Hear guides in old-style clothing pepper the tour with anecdotes that bring the old buildings to life. The "sinners' bench" in the church has some interesting stories to reveal.

Feel the hand-stitched quilts and rough wood of fence rails Native Americans split in 1828. April through October there are music and other special events. Admission also includes the magnificent **Bull Shoals Caverns,** 1011 C.S. Woods Boulevard, Bull Shoals 72619, with well-lit pathways to explore the underground wonders. The Bull Shoals Caverns are located just off Highway 178 in **Bull Shoals.** To tour the caverns and/or the Mountain Village, the entrance fee is $9.00/$13.50 for adults (that's for either/both) and $6.00/$9.00 for children six through eleven. Children under five are free. Hours are from 10:00 A.M. until 5:00 P.M. March 17 to May 15 (closed on Monday and Tuesday). From May 15 to Labor Day the caverns are open daily from 9:00 A.M.

until 6:00 P.M. The caverns are closed Tuesday and Wednesday from Labor Day until Halloween; in November they are only open on Friday, Saturday, and Sunday. If this totally confused you, Mountain Village can be reached by e-mail at mv1890@southshore.com or see the Web site at www.1890Village.com or call (800) 445–7177.

If you're ready for a bite to eat, stop by **Bush's Pizza and More** on the main drag through Bull Shoals. They've got really good pizzas, plus calzones and the biggest chocolate chip cookies you've ever seen and they deliver all over the lake area. It's just a tiny place, but while you're there, be sure to stick a pin in the big map of the world on the north wall. It shows where visitors have come from to eat this pizza. And as you leave, drop some crumbs to the wild cats on the front porch. These cats don't eat fish from the river, but prefer to eat leftover pizza scraps. Their favorite is pepperoni. If you don't believe it, call (870) 445–4100.

If you travel down Highway 62, you'll find about fifteen antiques, collectibles, and crafts shops, as well as several good eating places. Start shopping at **Country Reflections,** owned by Gary and Victoria Morgan and located at 1015 Highway 62 Southwest, Mountain Home 72653. They have four rooms of unusual things: old record albums in good shape, antiques, handmade baby clothes, pottery, used furniture—almost anything you could think of. The selection includes offerings from sixty-five of the best craftspeople in the area showing their wares. The Morgans are in the shop from 9:00 A.M. until 5:00 P.M. Monday through Saturday and enjoy directing people to interesting places in the area. Call (870) 425–7177 for information.

Bobbie Sue's Restaurant is located in a log cabin on Highway 62 East outside of Mountain Home. This eatery is a well-kept secret—even a lot of

Day Trip

*G**et up early for this day trip; a number of scenic highways are involved. Drive south from Mountain Home, taking a side trip on Highway 177 at Salesville for a look at Norfork Dam and the Norfork Federal Trout Hatchery. Then return to Highway 5 and continue south through Calico Rock on the banks of the White River* *and on to Mountain View for the Ozark Folk Center. Huge Blanchard Springs Caverns is nearby. The western edge of this tour via Highway 14 leads to popular access points for the Buffalo National River—St. Joe, Silver Hill, Gilbert, Yellville, and others. Just off Highway 14 the historic ghost town of Rush stands near the Buffalo River.*

Trivia

Diamond Cave, near Jasper, contains many passages. It has no diamonds, but the quartz crystals give a spectacular effect.

locals haven't discovered it—and the kind of place you might pass by without noticing. But people who do know about it head there on Wednesday at noon for the barbecued ribs. Usually boneless, these are cut from the end of the loin and are spicy and succulent. There is homemade bread for soaking up the sauce, as well as homemade beans and potato salad. Owners Bobbie McMillan and Sue Kasinger peel potatoes and make everything from scratch. There's a daily lunch special, and breakfast draws a crowd, too. Sue says, "We give everyone a hard time so they'll feel at home." It has a full bar and is open Monday through Saturday from 6:30 A.M. to 2:00 P.M. On Fridays, Bobbie and Sue stay open until 8:00 P.M. and serve a prime rib buffet. Call (870) 425–2923 for information.

Take the children someplace even better than the beach this year. Dress them in boots and jeans and visit **Scott Valley Guest Ranch** near Mountain Home. Then watch them do amazing things like jumping out of bed at 6:00 A.M. to help get their horses ready for the day's ride. You and the children will splash through small streams and over shady trails. Rancher Kathleen Cooper makes sure everyone knows how to ride. You can begin with practice in a meadow on starting, stopping, and steering your horse. You get to know your people-friendly steed before you leave. There are eighty-nine horses to choose from, most bred right there on the ranch. Along with the horses, there are 13 cats, 2 dogs, 2 opossums, 1 rabbit, 2 pigs, 2 geese, and 3 goats. But if riding is not your favorite thing, there are tours to Ozark Folk Center, fishing and canoeing on area rivers, and entertainment every night. There's a swimming pool and spa, tennis, and assorted other very active games. Summer rates are $145 per night for adults, $125 for children 6 to 12 years of age, $75 for children 2 to 5 years old. Guests must stay at least three nights. Call (888) 855–7747 for more information or visit the Web site at www.scottvalley.com.

The Beautiful Road

Scenic Highway 7 is just that, one of the loveliest drives in the state. It winds and curves and crests hills and skirts rivers. It is more than just a way to get somewhere in Arkansas, and there are some great little places along the way. **Brambly Hedge Cottage,** 4 miles south of **Jasper,** the hub of this area, on Scenic Highway 7, is a historic house constructed around a hundred-year-old cabin—built on Sloan Mountain before the Homestead Act in 1872. Hosts Billy and Jacquelyn Smyers have uncovered a portion of the original cabin and left it exposed on the screened porch. It was added onto in a sort of hodgepodge fashion in the 1940s and covered with stucco, giving the two-story house an English Cotswold look. (That's where the name came from: Jacquelyn loved British author-illustrator Jill Barklem's books about mice living in the brambly hedge.) The house was mentioned in an issue of the *National Geographic Traveler.* Now the cottage has three bedrooms, all with private baths, for guests (or you can use the quaint outhouse, if you prefer the feeling of the good old days).

Billy and Jacquelyn have also added a barn, which is popular as a guest cottage. It's a new structure, but looks old because of the old barn boards used in the construction. The rock fireplace and loft bedroom make the barn extremely popular for those looking for a romantic getaway.

The view from the cottage is "clear to Missouri" from the deck that overlooks the Buffalo River Valley. Sometimes the house is literally in the clouds; often it overlooks clouds or mist hanging over the valley. The rooms are from $65 to $100, and you can call the Smyerses at (870) 446–5849 or (800) BRAMBLY (800–272–6259).

Bordering the Ozark National Forest and the Buffalo River Park, *Ozark Mountain Cabins,* about ¹/₃ mile off Highway 7, 4 miles north of Jasper, offer a spectacular valley view, where elk and deer graze in the pastures. Each of the four log cabins sleeps six and has a gorgeous 20-mile view. The cabins are built of hand-peeled logs with pine tongue-and-groove walls and fireplaces of locally collected rock inside. Central heat makes the cabins a great place for winter vacations. The kitchens have everything you need; just bring food and drink. The cabins are about 150 feet apart, placed for the view, and with summer foliage they are hidden from one another. Summer rates for two people are $90 for one or two nights, $88 for three to six nights, $70 for seven nights or more; winter rates are quite a bit less, beginning at $60. Call for reservations at (870) 446–2229.

Ozark Ecotours are small group tours of no more than twenty-four people. You can create your own Ecotour to include a variety of activities. Choose from hiking, backpacking, camping, caving, canoeing, horseback riding, primitive skills, campfire cooking, map and compass reading—all put together with nature awareness. Explore the Ozarks with spring wildflowers coloring the limestone bluffs. Listen to storytellers weave tales while trekking along riverbanks. See elk graze in meadows and towering waterfalls. This is a responsible travel option that protects the environment. Activities begin on March 15 and go through June. They cover a wide variety of interests: Introduction to Caving, Photography in Nature, Outlaw Gangs in Legend and Fact,

Women in Nature—Three-Day Camping Skills. There are twenty-six tours to choose from, all customized to your interests and the number in your group. Write to Ozark Ecotours, P.O. Box 513, Jasper 72641, for a list of tours and rates. Call Kathy Downs (870–446–5898 or toll-free 877–622–5901). Their Web site is www.ozarkecotours.com; you can e-mail them at ecotours@yournet.com.

The **Point of View Restaurant,** 2 blocks off Highway 7 on Highway 74 West, is owned by Donna and Kyle McDaniels. The large wooden building is a noticeable red, with a tin roof and lots of windows across the front. It is on the river, but the name is "more of an attitude than a view," according to Donna, because the trees block the view of the river and "they won't let us cut them down." The specialty here is fried catfish, but people drive from miles around to have the steaks, too, which are charbroiled. The desserts are all homemade and unusual, including Reese's Peanut Butter Pie, which needs no description, and Millionaire's Pie, a creamy cheesecake with crushed pineapple and pecans. "One lady ate three pieces of it," Donna says, "which tells you something about it." (Also tells you something about the lady!) During the winter, hours are from 11:00 A.M. to 8:00 P.M. Tuesday through Sunday and closed on Monday. In season, hours are 11:00 A.M. to 9:00 P.M. Call (870) 446–2992 for information or e-mail at kfm@eritter.net.

After taking in the beauty of the Ozarks from above, try the view from underground. **Beckham Creek Cave House,** on a gravel road just west of Jasper near Parthenon, is perhaps the most unusual lodging you'll ever encounter. Built as a bomb shelter in the 1980s for a wealthy Colorado businessman and his family, the cave is now a popular destination for weddings, honeymoons, and people wanting something "different," according to manager Laura Magie. Deep in the crevices of a limestone cavern, luxurious accommodations are built right into the stone walls, including a hot tub in natural rock. But don't worry about bats or bugs. The bats exit the cave through another opening and eat all of the bugs and mosquitoes in the area. The cave is surrounded by 530 tree-covered acres where you can continue to enjoy the above-ground beauty of the Ozarks. Rates for the cave per night range from $200 to $300. Call Laura at (870) 446–6045 or toll-free at (888) 371–2283 or see the beauty of the cave rooms at their Web site, www.ozarkcave.com.

Arkansas House Bed and Breakfast, 217 East Main, Jasper 72641, downtown at the waterwheel, is an old building that should have been razed. Then Karen and Larry Visnosky discovered it and began restoration. Now it is an incredible place, called the "Jasper Ritz" by people around here. It is also home to Coco, a black bear who lives in a little air-conditioned house (with running water) in the backyard. But more about him in a minute.

The Visnoskys have a restaurant next door. What makes the building so fascinating, especially for people who like to study rocks, is that it is built from what Karen calls "recycled buildings." It is made of concrete and embedded with stone taken from places like Newton County's first jail. You may notice that lots of churches in Jasper are made of that same combination of concrete and stone. Look closely and you will see buried treasures: marbles, horseshoes, crystals, and all manner of things. The B&B is called Arkansas House because of a rock casting in the shape of the state in one wall. The restaurant has taken staring at the walls to new heights.

The five-room bed-and-breakfast is wonderful. There is a huge lounge of cedar and glass—called the plant room—two suites with whirlpool baths and chandeliers, televisions and VCRs. Each room is decorated in a lavish theme. The Garden Room is done in cranberry and hunter green in nineteenth-century style. The English Rose Room has a pink negligee in it. One of the most popular rooms is the Victorian Honeymoon Room, which is done in tapestry and has a private balcony. Karen's favorite room is Granny Nellie's Room, done in blue, white, and pink with a motherhood motif.

Now back to Coco, the real reason to visit Arkansas House. Coco was bought by Karen's brother, who had ideas about starting a petting zoo. He soon discovered that a bear cub is a lot like a baby, only worse. "They are a lot of work," she says. He asked Karen and Larry to "baby-sit" for a while. That was in 1994. ("I don't want anyone to think *I* was dumb enough to buy a bear.") Coco is very talented. He plays the guitar, which is most unbearlike. He is a member of the third generation of his family to be raised in captivity, "doesn't have a clue that he's a bear," according to Karen, and is a vegetarian. This cinnamon-colored sweetheart has a white collar of fur. He lets children play with him and kisses people. He has a playhouse in the front yard. Karen cautions that he is *very* strong (and doesn't realize it), so you have to be careful around him.

Breakfast is served in the B&B, of course, but if you have a hankering for a meal from the *Riverfront Dairy Diner* next door, anything on the menu will be delivered to you. The Visnoskys built a smokehouse on the property, which means excellent barbecue. Since they are from Texas, Mexican Monday means a great Tex-Mex menu is guaranteed. "We know *pico de gallo*," Karen says.

The courtyard—with rock garden, gazebo, and bridge by the river that

Coco the Bear

runs behind the property—gives you a beautiful and peaceful place to enjoy the area. Rooms are from $69 to $89. Call (870) 446–5179 or (888) AR–HOUSE for reservations.

The Buffalo National River rushes from Ponca to the White River. This most scenic stretch is floatable only in the spring, because once summer arrives it becomes a series of quiet pools. But when it runs, it runs, and it has plenty of roller-coaster rapids to enliven the scenery.

River Spirit is a quiet place near Parthenon where Ann Lasater offers guests more than just a cabin, she offers a spiritual retreat where you can escape the world for a few days and even have an hour massage for $50. The guest cottage rents for $85 and comes with VCR and stereo and overlooks a beautiful garden. There's a wood-burning fireplace to take the chill off the evening and a porch swing on which to enjoy the sweet air. It's a remote place, thirty minutes from Jasper, and 7 miles down a dirt road. Most people bring their own food, but Ann does some catering, too. The Mother Lodge, where Ann lives, is also for rent for larger groups. It can accommodate up to nine people. There is also a more primitive apartment in a barn on the property. It's cozy and comfortable with a kitchen and wood-burning fireplace, a splendid view, and an outhouse. It rents for $35. There's an outdoor hot tub near Mother Lodge that everyone can use. Ann hosts workshops throughout the year on a variety of subjects. Many guests over the years have participated in an ongoing group art project called The River Hermitage/Sanctuary. Using an old, English building technique, this structure is made of sand, clay, and straw using the hands, feet, and heart of the guests at River Spirit. Right now, it's being used for meditation, but when finished it will look like an adobe hut and will be available for rent as well. You can reach Ann at (870) 446–5642 or e-mail her at have@riverspirit.com. Her Web site is riverspirit.com.

Alum Cove Natural Arch is a 1 $^1/_{10}$-mile round-trip hike from the parking area. It's an easy hike, and the reward is an impressive natural arch. But you will also see some "cowcumber trees" and "goat houses," according to the natives here. (A stand of native cucumber magnolias grows along the north side of the arch, and wild goats may have sheltered under the namesake stone arch—as did Indians on hunting expeditions—according to archaeologists.) Each season has something wonderful to see along this trail. In the spring budding dogwood and redbud trees bloom, in fall vibrant colors abound, summer has wildflowers of many colors in the cooling shade of the hardwood forest, and even winter offers interesting ice formations. Drive 15 miles south from Jasper on Highway 7, turn west on Highway 16, and after $^1/_2$ mile, turn north and go 4 miles to the parking area.

A different kind of ride will let you float silently over the Ozark Mountains in the wicker gondola of a hot-air balloon. The ***Champagne Flight,*** leaving the Buffalo Outdoor Center in ***Ponca*** (population 20 in winter), has this thrill for only $225 per person (but your friends can ride in the chase vehicle with the crew if they want to). Leaving at sunrise, the flight is an hour, but with the time taken for inflation and for packing up after landing, it is about a three-hour adventure. Pilot and owner of the balloon Mike Mills will take you over the mountains from the valley where Ponca is nestled. Rising above the early-morning fog to see the peaks poking above the clouds makes for a lifelong memory.

And each flight is different; the wind is the navigator. Flights take place in summer and fall for the most part, with a few offered in winter (it's a bit too windy in spring). It's best to be flexible, because the weather plays such an important role in hot-air ballooning. For more information you can log on to their Web site at www.buffaloriver.com or e-mail Mike at boc@buffaloriver.com.

The **Buffalo Outdoor Center** also has rustic log cabins for $90 to $265 each that are equipped with a full kitchen, a fireplace, loft bedrooms, and a front porch swing. Of course, canoes and rafts are available, too. For further high jinks on the Buffalo River, call Steve McAdams at (870) 861–5514 or (800) 221–5514.

If you have never tried your hand at guiding a canoe down a river, it's never too late to begin. Doing so is not difficult, and first-time-outers often come back dry as a bone, having experienced no spills (but no guarantees, either). For those of you with more experience and perhaps a canoe lashed to the car, there are several put-in points in the area. If it's later in the season and the upper Buffalo is too shallow to canoe, you can put in at Woolum on the lower river, off Highway 65, and take a leisurely day trip to **Silver Hill** (16½ miles), where there's a U.S. Park Service station, or continue for a two-day trip (another 16 miles) to Maumee. The entire trip from Ponca takes about a week—from Woolum, about five or six days—and landings all along the river are about 4 to 20 miles apart. Canoe outfitters will pick you up where you plan to end. Hours are 8:00 A.M. to 5:00 P.M. every day.

The Buffalo Outdoor Center rents housekeeping cabins at Silver Hill, too. Call (800) 582–2244 or (870) 439–2244 at Silver Hill. Canoes rent for about $35 each, and transportation to and from put-in and takeout

Falling Waters

*T*here are some splendid water-falls along the Buffalo National River. A spectacular 225-foot waterfall on the Buffalo River lies between Steel Creek and Kyles Landing. You can reach Hemmed-In Hollow from the river or by a trail through the Ponca Wilderness Area. Park rangers or canoe outfitters can tell you how to get there. Twin Falls is a rugged 1-mile hike from Richland Creek Campground. If hiking or canoeing are not for you, you can view the Falling Water Falls nearby without a hike. Lost Valley waterfall is part of a 3-mile round-trip hiking trail that begins at the Lost Valley Campground near Ponca.

is about $20. The Buffalo River Tower at Silver Hill offers a spectacular view of five Ozark counties and the Buffalo River watershed. Horses are available for trail rides at Silver Hill.

Rimrock Cove is 180 acres of Ozark beauty near the upper Buffalo River. You'll enjoy a guided ride down quiet wooded trails and across meandering streams and see wildflowers in season. There is even a waterfall. If you don't ride, hayrides are excellent outings for families or groups. The thirty-minute trip takes you to an open meadow for a cookout. The horses are Suffolks, a breed of draft horse whose ancestors originated in England. The horses are raised and trained on this small farm. Rimrock Cove is on Highway 103 about 7 miles south of Osage or 5 miles from Highway 43. Rides are by reservation only. Toni and Dennis Albers are your guides. Prices are $15 for the first hour and $10 for each additional hour; or if you are ready for an all-day trail ride with lunch, it is $75. For more information call (870) 553–2556 or e-mail them at rimrockcove@ eritter.net.

There are so many places to stay around Japser that a lodging must offer something special to stand out from the competition. For example, the **Red Rock Retreat,** a beautiful and secluded spot 12 miles south of Jasper in the Arkansas Grand Canyon, has Lipizzan horses—the famous Dancing Stallions of Vienna—that Sandy Swayne raises here on the 130 acres surrounding two two-bedroom log cabins. The horses, which graze in a pasture in front of the cabins, are magnificent and worth the trip to see. There are riding trails, if you bring your own horse, and Sandy has facilities for horses for $10 a day.

The cabins are crafted of local rock and hand-peeled logs with a pine and cedar interior. The rock fireplace gives a rustic feel, while central heat and air-conditioning and modern plumbing make them comfortable for all seasons. Their many windows bring the Ozarks right inside, and a quiet creek whispers in front. Ceiling fans circulate air. The Cedar Creek cabin features a red cedar bathroom and antique claw-foot tub. Both cabins have kitchens that are fully equipped for cooking. From the front porch swing, there is a breathtaking view of Red Rock bluffs and Big Creek. The cabins are about $1/2$ mile from the Swaynes' house, ensuring privacy, and pets are welcome. The Cedar Creek cabin is $85 for two, plus $10 for each additional person. The Hickory Hill Cabin is $100. Call (870) 434–5316 for reservations. Check it out on their Web site: www.ozarkcabins.com/redrockretreat.

Eight miles outside of Jasper the **Horseshoe Canyon Ranch** looks like a dude ranch in Colorado—boulders jutting out of the ground and open meadows—where Barry Johnson and his father Jerry have ten yellow pine log cabins scattered on one side of the valley. They all have wood-burning stoves and a Western Native American theme. Often on Saturday nights, the Johnsons host horse games to liven up the evening. The price of $860 for a week ($460 for children under seven years old) includes a cottage, three meals a day, and "all the horseback riding your rear end can stand," as Jerry puts it. Family discounts and seasonal reductions apply. But if your kids demand television or a phone, this isn't the place to come. Rates change with the season, so call (800) 480–9635 or visit the ranch's Web site at www.horseshoecanyon.com.

"Off the beaten path" is a phrase meaning different things to different travelers. This next adventure will get you off the highways and into the forests, but the path is well-traveled by hikers. The **Lost Valley Trail** begins at the Lost Valley Campground just off Route 43 between Ponca and Boxley. It leads through the shady red cedar and sweet gum forest along Clark Creek, a tributary of the Buffalo River, to a pool below the gentle spray of Eden Falls. The creek begins about 1 3/4 miles up a narrow canyon of limestone bluffs and steep hills. The trail forks at a site known as Siamese Beeches, where the tree trunks have grown together high overhead. Take the right fork to Jig Saw Blocks (for the way they fit together) and on to a clear pool fed by water slowly carving a tunnel through the outcropping. Corn Cob Cave is at the base of the cliff, so named because Native Americans left corncobs here long ago. A spur leads on to Eden Falls. The terrain becomes slightly more difficult en route to Eden Falls Cave, 170 feet higher than the pool, but if you are adventuresome and have a flashlight, a bit of crawling will get you inside the cave where you will find another 35-foot waterfall hidden inside. But the falls below are a good spot for a shower among glistening rocks in the shallow pool, surrounded by fern and moss. It's almost paradise—that's why it's called Eden Falls. For information and a map, call (870) 741–5443; and for information about other trails, ask for the Arkansas Hikers' Kit from the State Trails Coordinator, Department of Parks and Tourism, One Capitol Mall, Little Rock 72201; (501) 682–7777.

Ozark National Forest

Due north of Kingston on Highway 21, you find **Berryville,** with lovely old homes that date back to the city's beginning. The town has a charming turn-of-the-century town square with a tree-shaded park, old-fashioned street lamps, and benches. There's a real five-and-ten, together with shops, restaurants, and museums, and a vintage drugstore that still has a soda fountain. The **Heritage Center** on the square contains a museum whose living history displays include a schoolroom, barbershop, and moonshine still. Moreover, a working village blacksmith shop shows you how tools were forged into the 1800s; Pioneer Park features vintage log cabins and an early jail; and a restored pump station houses the city's tourist information center.

The volunteers at the center will direct you to the **Saunders Memorial Museum** at 113–115 Madison Street. The museum has Pancho Villa's lavishly decorated .45 Colt—its right grip burned brown from the Mexican sun and its handle inset with gold, jewels, and a Mexican gold coin and nameplate. The guns of Jesse James, Billy the Kid, Annie Oakley, and Wild Bill Hickok are all part of the finest gun collection in the nation. But even if you're not a gun collector, there are many other novel items in the museum, which was a bequest to the town from the late Colonel C. Burton Saunders. Among the things to see are a tent, hand-embroidered with gold thread (made by a sheikh's 200 wives); a war bonnet and battle jacket owned by Sitting Bull (and his totem scalps); and displays of antique furniture and Native American artifacts. Mrs. Saunder's closet is there, too, with clothes and accessories, circa 1910, as well as vases, rugs, lacework, and silverware. The museum is open from May through October. Hours are 10:30 A.M. to 5:00 P.M. Monday through Saturday; you can call (870) 423–2563.

The long, redwood **Currey Studio-Gallery** is between Berryville and Eureka Springs on Highway 62, 5 miles west of Berryville. Displayed are the primitive watercolor and oil paintings of Grandma Fran (Frances Currey Brown), who works in the studio. She grew up on a farm in the time of coal-oil lamps. She cooked on a woodstove and milked cows, and these images stayed with her. She began her career quite by accident, sending small drawings to a granddaughter. Since that time her brightly colored, simple paintings of country life have been recognized in books and magazines and appeared in a large number of galleries, including the Royal Museum of Art in Brussels, the Smithsonian, and the Mykonos Folklore Museum in Greece. Grandma Fran is there year-round from 8:00 A.M. to 6:00 P.M. every day of the week except Sunday, when the gallery opens at 1:00 P.M. Call her at (870) 423–2073.

For a truly remote getaway, visit the **Little Portion Hermitage** near **Eureka Springs.** The hermitage is home to the Catholic-based monastic community wherein live both celibates and families, as well as cattle, chickens, rabbits, and the occasional pig. The large vegetable garden, apple orchard, and animal barns form an important part of the community. The garden is maintained according to organic or bio-intensive methods of natural growth. Bed gardens have soil sifted to a depth of 3 feet, the rock and clay replaced with compost and sand. Greenhouses prepare seeds and small plants during the colder months. The animals are organically fed in the barns and pasture.

The landscaped garden is centered around a statue of the Teaching Christ. Flowers and a running stream invite you in. The bell in the cedar bell tower, through which you enter, calls everyone to worship in the Charity Chapel, the heart of the community, three times a day at 6:45 A.M., noon, and 5:30 P.M. for monastic chanting of the psalms, communion, charismatic or spontaneous praise, and silent adoration.

The cloister/prayer garden, a freestanding cloister-arbor in local Ozark style patterned after European monasteries, is laid out in the form of a Celtic cross, with a gazebo in the middle. The garden includes rare flowers and grasses to provide solitude at various spots. The arbor is supported by wooden monastic arches that frame occasional stained-glass windows of Franciscan saints taken from the Franciscan community that helped birth the Little Portion.

The brothers and sisters also run the Little Portion Retreat Center a few miles away, where groups can meet or individuals may spend time in contemplation.

For more information call the hermitage at (501) 253–7710. To find the hermitage or retreat center, both of which are really off the beaten path, stop by the shop for a detailed map.

Highway 62 in this part of the state travels through numerous apple and fruit orchards. One of those belongs to Polly Newberry and her family, who also operate **Polly's Restaurant,** 5 miles east of **Green Forest.** They have about eighty acres of fruit orchards and, in the fall, sell produce from a garage adjacent to the restaurant. You can also buy homemade apple butter and cider, as well as jellies and fresh honey. A whole apple pie sells for $8.00. And while enjoying a slice of pie or any other dish on the menu, keep an eye on the herd of cattle across the road. In the springtime, guests often are treated to calves being born before their eyes. Call Polly and her staff at (870) 437–2233.

In the community of Green Forest is the **Cattlemen's Steak House,** one of the best places for a steak anywhere. On Thursdays, Fridays, and Saturdays, stop in to watch a cattle auction, but any time you're in a mood for a steak, this is the place to be. Call them at (870) 438–6021.

Highway 62 weaves from Berryville to **Eureka Springs,** which is not exactly off the beaten path. Yes, you have to look closely on the map to see it, but it is the state's premiere tourist town and a must-see for any Arkansas traveler. Shops and B&Bs come and go like cottonwood fluff in the breeze. Every year there are new and different places to see. There are some old standbys that would be a shame to miss and several small spots you might overlook. For example, the Bank of Eureka Springs on Main Street is an interesting place you might not think to visit. It is in a new building, but the interior is done in pure Victorian. The Carnegie Library has a rolling cart with photos of the town. There are sixty springs inside the city limits, and a walking-tour book will lead you along historical pathways to interesting places. There are old hotels, guest cottages, tons of antiques shops, myriad art galleries, and a batch of peculiar museums (featuring bells, frogs, bibles, musical instruments, or birds).

You'll also find a profusion of restaurants. The Victorian Sampler Tea Room (the most beautiful place in town) and Bubba's Barbecue ("It doesn't look famous, but it is") vie with a French restaurant (the Plaza) and a Czech-German restaurant (the Bavarian Inn) for your dinnertime dollar. You can find whatever you want at mealtime, from the most expensive (the Plaza, with a great wine list and dishes like duck with

Gaskins' Cabin

Gaskins Cabin Restaurant (501–253–5466), on Highway 23, is a simple red log cabin that will surprise you with a menu containing grilled walleye pike and escargot in garlic butter. It also has a great wine list. The cabin formerly belonged to John Gaskins, who was one of the first settlers in the county. Living along the creek 3 miles below Eureka Springs, he would watch crowds gather around Basin Spring to take the waters. He then

wrote about the many miracle cures he saw. When the Civil War broke out, he refused to serve in the Confederate Army and moved to Missouri, where the Union flag still flew. After the war he returned to Eureka Springs where he wrote his memoirs. He and his family rest in the nearby Gaskins Switch Cemetery, land he had set aside. In his memoirs he wrote: "I want to add that I believe we are raising boys here . . . who will have the brains for president."

Grand Marnier sauce) to the best bargains (Chelsea's—the most food for the least money—don't be put off by just looking in the door; go on in, order the Macho Nachos, covered with black beans, sausage, and alfalfa sprouts, and live a little) to places like the Oasis (mostly vegetarian food) and DeVitto's downtown (homemade pasta and bread and fresh trout worth the restaurant's long wait to get in) or Ermilio's (in an old house uphill on the Highway 62 loop; also Italian but very different from DeVitto's). The hours vary with the season, and many places are closed in winter, so check around.

Eureka Springs is also the place where you can find unusual things to do. For example, every day more than twenty people gather at The Old Town Pub on North Main to play *Jeopardy* along with the television show. The Mud Street Cafe is a couple of blocks away on North Main, downstairs in a comfortable little cellar. You can have curry or quiche and play games here, too. The cafe will deliver breakfast to cottages in the morning if you order the night before.

Just up the stairs from the Mud Street Cafe is a must-stop if you're traveling to Eureka Springs with children. At **Ted E. Bear's Toy Factory,** 1 Basin Spring Avenue, Eureka Springs 72632, you can make your own stuffed animal. Choose from a selection of about two dozen animal hides, then choose their eyes and ribbons. Kids will get a kick out of the pedal pump, which allows them to choose how fat or skinny their animal is. Paul and Sheryl Jones are the owners, who also repair music boxes and other gadgets. Call them at (501) 253–TOYS.

The many-tiered, sprawling Victorian village dates to 1879 on the rugged, hilly terrain of the Ozark Mountains. Today, because of the collective restoration of the town, Eureka Springs offers a microcosm of late-nineteenth-century life, making it a unique, historic tourist attraction. The streets are so steep that the entrance to St. Elizabeth's Catholic Church is through the top of the bell tower, and a motorized trolley roams the town's narrow streets, none of which intersect at right angles. The trolley follows the Highway 62 loop around town with a spiderweb of tiny culs-de-sac weaving off from it in all directions.

More than 600 artisans live and work in the Eureka Springs area, and their crafts are sold all over town. You can find quilts, knives, baskets, Quaker furniture, stained glass—almost anything—here. The shops are crammed with fine arts and oddities. The first thing to do is park your car and buy a trolley ticket. The streets are impossibly narrow, and there is never a parking meter vacant. You can get off and on the trolley as much as you want to and see a lot more that way. (The secret is to ride

As you walk through the streets of Eureka Springs, you'll note a flight of stairs that leads from Mud Street to Spring Street. This is Basin Spring Avenue, and even though it is a flight of stairs, the U.S. Post Office recognizes it as a legal street. Three businesses are located on Basin Spring Avenue, but you can't drive to them. Just climb the stairs.

it twice up hill and walk down, riding on the right side the first time and the left side the second time.)

The romantic setting of Eureka Springs draws hundreds of couples-in-love for weddings and honeymoons. No less than eight spots provide immediate, legal wedding services. One of the more popular locations for a prearranged service is **Angel at Rose Hall,** where more than 900 couples have married since 1993. Located at the west end of the historic district, Angel at Rose Hall, 56 Hillside Street, Eureka Springs 72633, is home to a 120-year-old Story & Clark pump organ and twenty-eight stained glass windows that are more than one hundred years old. Call Sandy Latimer to make arrangements for a truly memorable wedding or romantic getaway at (501) 253–5405 or (800) 828–4255. Their Web site is www.eurekaspringsangel.com. Sandy is also on the board of the state bed-and-breakfast association and will gladly put you in touch with other great inns throughout Arkansas.

Singleton House B&B is a pretty, two-story Victorian at 11 Singleton Street, Eureka Springs 72632. Innkeeper Barbara Gavron also has a service listing more than thirty B&Bs and cottages in the area. Barbara tries to match people up with the kind of place they want. She knows every street and path and is a gold mine of information. (She likes to send her guests out at night with a flashlight to see the beauty of the town after dark; go to the top of the old hotels and get romantic night views, she says.)

The Singleton House has five bedrooms, all of which have private baths. A breakfast balcony overlooks the garden and pond out behind the kitchen. A full breakfast is included in the $69 to $135 price. The phone number for Barbara's reservation service and the Singleton House is (800) 833–3394 or (501) 253–9111. Visit their Web site at www.singletonhouse.com.

Singleton Street is one of the web of streets winding off the main loop. A larger main street, Spring Street, is shaded by sycamores, colored with spring daffodils and irises, and lined with B&Bs and shops. The springs still flow from the bluffs that line the street, and a copper-topped gazebo was recently added near one of them.

When you have walked your legs off on the hilly streets of Eureka Springs, you will welcome the women waiting behind the picket fence at 31 Kings-highway. Unlike the psychologist who gives you a forty-five-minute hour, the massage at *Healing Benefits Massage Therapy Company* can last for more than an hour. Carol Brown's little pink-and-yellow Victorian house is open year-round, and she has a large following. Both she and Linda Parcher are reflexologists, too, so service is from your face to your feet. Soothing music and aromatic lotions relax you and silken your skin while you receive a first-class massage. Call ahead for an appointment at (501) 253–6750.

Smith Treur and Deborah Sederstrom have the *Rogue's Manor at Sweet Springs* at 124 Spring Street, Eureka Springs 72632, where seafood—especially from the northwest (they are from Oregon and Alaska)—and custom-cut steaks as well as vegetarian dishes are beautifully served. The Manor is open for lunch and dinner Wednesday through Sunday, with a Sunday brunch. The inn has two suites and a penthouse, all with room service at $85 to $135. Call (501) 253–4911 or (800) 250–5827, or click on www.roguesmanor.com.

As the name implies, Eureka Springs was once a spa. The *Palace Hotel and Bathhouse,* at 135 Spring Street, Eureka Springs 72632, is a restored Victorian hotel that has the only bathhouse in town and a staff of licensed therapists. Ask for "the works" and get a mineral bath, steam bath, clay mask, and thirty-minute massage for $56. The eight hotel suites contain king-size beds; a bar, sink, and refrigerator; and a whirlpool unit to modernize the comfort of the antique furniture. A continental breakfast of juice, coffee, and pastries and an evening snack tray are included in the price. Rates range from $110 off season from December through February to $165 in October. Call (501) 253–7474 for an appointment or a room.

> **Trivia**
>
> *The 18-inch-thick limestone-marble walls of the Crescent Hotel in Eureka Springs were fitted without mortar. In 1886 the "Castle in the Wilderness" opened with a gala ball attended by 400 prominent and wealthy social elite from several states. The hotel had its own orchestra for nightly dances, along with a bowling alley, swimming pool, riding stable, and fresh spring water on every floor for drinking and bathing.*

Like every historic town with lots of old buildings, some of them are considered haunted. If seeking out the supernatural is your thing, or if you just like the idea of haunted houses, check in with the folks at *Eureka Springs Ghost Tours,* located in the Crescent Hotel, 75 Prospect Avenue, Eureka Springs 72632. The Crescent Hotel is the perfect place for their ghostly office, since the hotel itself is said to be haunted with the spirits of several school girls and their teachers from the days this building was a girls' school. The tour takes you through several old mansions on Spring Street and the Eureka Springs Cemetery. Having the daylights scared out of you costs $12.50 if you are over 16; otherwise it only costs

$7.00. Tours fill up fast around Halloween when the spirits are their liveliest, so you may want to call in advance at (501) 253–6800.

Stone fences, old farmhouses, and creeks make for a lovely drive along Highway 187 north of Eureka Springs. If you want to take a nostalgic drive across one of the last single-lane swinging bridges left, take Highway 187 Northwest toward Holiday Island to the town of **Beaver.** You can also reach the bridge by driving 4¹/₂ miles back from the Highway 62/187 junction after you have visited these interesting places:

Outside of Eureka Springs on Highway 62 West, down a wooded trail, stands **Thorncrown Chapel,** a tall and glittering glass chapel tucked into the Ozarks woods. In May, when the spring canopy of leaves hasn't yet eclipsed the light, wildflowers carpet the forest floor. It is a peaceful spot, dedicated to God by a dreamer named Jim Reed and his wife, Dell, who hired E. Fay Jones, a nationally honored and recognized architect, to design the chapel of glass and two-by-fours that sits on eight acres of woods. The chapel, surrounded by blue sky and filled with sunlight, is just 60 feet long, 24 feet wide, and 48 feet tall, with eleven rows of bench seats. It holds only about a hundred people.

The base was made from the roughly cut sandstone of the surrounding hills. To avoid using building materials too large to carry down the path, cross-braced, hand-rubbed timbers 2 by 4 feet and 2 by 6 feet and in-filled with glass were used. The more than 6,000 square feet of glass in the walls and central skylight reflect the sunlight in patterns that change with the time and the seasons and let the chapel blend into surrounding timber as though it had grown there. It is called "Ozark Gothic"—Gothic in reverse, in that darkness becomes light. The chapel has seasonal hours: daily 9:00 A.M. to 6:00 P.M. April through October, until 5:00 P.M. in November, and 11:00 A.M. to 4:00 P.M. December and March. It is closed in January and February. Sunday services are at 9:00 and 11:00 A.M., with a special 7:00 A.M. service from June through October. The church is nondenominational, and the Reverend Doug Reed, son of the founders, is minister. Call (501) 253–7401 for information.

The area around Eureka has been an artists' colony since the 1930s and is a fine arts center. Galleries are everywhere and hundreds of artists live and work in the area.

No one around here laughs when you refer to opera in the Ozarks. They are not talking about Opry or country music at **Inspiration Point Fine Arts Colony,** on Highway 62. This summer opera workshop celebrated its fiftieth season in 2001 and consistently gives exceptional performances of such operas as *La Boheme* and *Die Fledermaus* (performed at the Walton Arts Center) in the 300-seat theater on Rock Candy Mountain. "This," says Jim Swiggart, general director, "is all about young people." It has a long history of giving aspiring young artists the push needed to pursue a professional career (one young singer calls it "the boot camp of opera") and giving patrons and guests an outstanding musical experience. People from both coasts call and request seats, and many performances are sold out well in advance. The group works in repertory style, so there is a different opera every night. Now they are raising money to move to a state-of-the-art theater on 200 acres overlooking the valley of Beaver Dam. All seats are reserved, so be sure to call ahead. Performances are at 8:00 P.M. during the season from mid-June to mid-July. Call (501) 253–8595 for information and reservations. The Colony also sponsors a barbershop quartet weekend, as well as blues and jazz festivals. Their Web site is www.opera.org.

Eureka Springs Gardens spans thirty-three acres of hardwood trees, flowers, and plants. The main floral season of this privately owned botanical garden begins in spring with displays of bulbs followed by the dogwood, redbud, and azaleas. Summertime is alive with stunning perennials and annuals native to the area. The fall brings a blaze of foliage along with chrysanthemums by the thousands. The garden is fitted with ramps as well as stairs, making it accessible to the physically handicapped, but for the best of the garden, wear comfortable shoes and take your time walking the trails.

Begin, if you are able, on the soft mulch path that descends the bluffs of the gardens on the series of stairways, allowing about two hours for

Where Shoes Come From

Tarantulas and armadillos dot County Road 187, but an even more interesting thing will appear along the roadway as you swing by Inspiration Point. Be sure to watch for the Shoe Tree. You will see brake lights come on and cars backing up and turning around. This huge tree has somehow grown thousands of shoes, boots, sneakers, slippers, and roller skates. It gets heavier each year with the strange crop. There are no signs leading up to it and no gift shop under it. It is one of nature's mysteries. So when the kids ask, "Mom and Dad, where do shoes come from?" you can take them here and show them one of the wonders of nature. It is an ever-bearing, year-round crop—not at all seasonal. But you have to watch for it, or you will drive right on by.

the walk. The alternate route on raised wooden walkways is engineered for the handicapped and is good for the return trip up the bluffs for everyone.

At the foot of the stairs, you will see the Spring Lagoon, where the waters from Blue Spring mark the beginning of the White River. *Blue Spring* is the star of the show; it bubbles up thirty-eight million gallons of water a day and is the natural source of the White River. It is a deep cobalt blue, but at times it appears as different shades of green. After heavy rains the surface water is picked up in local recharge areas, making Blue Spring brown for a couple of weeks.

The spring is dedicated to the Cherokee people who camped here along the Trail of Tears, but in 1971, a University of Arkansas archaeological dig uncovered a great number of artifacts, some dating back to 8,000 B.C. The cliffs are marked with hieroglyphs (crude markings, not pictures) from 8,000 B.C. to A.D. 1500 etched into the overhanging bluffs and show that Native Americans lived near this water since prehistoric times.

During the Archaic Period (810 to 500 B.C.), mobile hunters and gatherers depended on native plants and animals. During the Woodland Era (500 B.C. to A.D. 900), the people here tended gardens and domesticated barley, sunflower, squash, and maize, and by the Mississippian Era (A.D. 900 to 1541), they were agriculturists growing crops. Translations of the hieroglyphs appear near the crude markings.

Following the softly mulched path, you will pass through the Wild Flower Gardens, Meadow Gardens, and along the crushed limestone path to the dam. After crossing the dam (here is the archeological dig), the Rock Garden appears—an area simply planted in a rock garden created by nature.

At the end of the trail, the *Petal Pusher Gift Shop* is surrounded by benches where you can relax and enjoy the butterflies and humming birds. Call (501) 253–9244 for more information.

On a nice day look for the *Horizon Restaurant* just off County Road 187 and try the Grassy Knob Vegetarian Delight. It is a wonderful sandwich of marinated artichoke hearts, roasted sweet red peppers, alfalfa sprouts, and sun-dried tomatoes. Or you might want to try the Greek Pizza with marinated artichoke hearts, rosemary, and feta and Parmesan cheeses. The open deck, where a cool breeze makes it comfortable, is the place to eat. The Horizon is open Tuesday through Friday from 11:00 A.M. to 2:00 P.M. and from 5:00 to 9:00 P.M.; Sunday brunch is served from 9:30 A.M. until 2:30 P.M. Saturday service is from 11:00 A.M. to 9:00 P.M. Call (501) 253–5525 for more information. To find the Horizon, follow Highway 62 West to Beaver Lake, then turn left again on Highway 187, then left on Mandell Road, and go ¼ mile.

What to do with a lion cub that keeps growing beyond the "kitty, kitty" stage and begins wreaking havoc around the house? Well, rambunctious felines—some weighing more than 300 pounds—have a home here at *Turpentine Creek Exotic Wildlife Ranch.* Owners Donald and Hilda Jackson, their daughter Tanya Smith, and their son Robert call it a labor of love: this nonprofit home for unwanted or abused big cats. The ranch is 7 miles south of Eureka Springs on Highway 23 and is a federally licensed refuge for large carnivores. With 101 big cats, this is possibly the largest collection of these magnificent creatures open to the public. Saying "101 big cats" doesn't even begin to prepare you for the experience of actually seeing them.

When asked how it began, Robert said simply, "We've always been pet owners," but this collection of felines is beyond that. Don traded a motorcycle for a lion cub named Bum, who was a house pet the first 300 pounds of his life. Bum liked to lie around and watch television. Then a woman showed up one day with a horse trailer full of big cats, and the Jacksons couldn't say no.

Other guests at the ranch are Vain and Vada. Vain is a tiger who was abandoned for a week in a backyard. His owner was a construction worker who hauled him around in a trailer from job to job. Vada is a beautiful black leopard, rescued from an abusive owner in Montana who broke off the cat's four canine teeth. Over the years, she has had $10,000 worth of dental work. Robert's favorite is a Bengal tiger named

Trail of Tears

*Y*ou will notice splashes of lavender paint on trees and fence posts along County Road 187. This marks the Trail of Tears, the path from Echota, Georgia, to Parkhill, Oklahoma (near Tahlequah), walked by 13,000 Cherokee who lived at Chota Valley for 500 years. They were a settled people who, in September 1838, were uprooted and forced to march to a new land to make way for the settlers. After a cruel winter march of privation and grievous loss, only 7,000 lived to see their new home. They camped at Blue Springs for several days, resting and waiting for stragglers to catch up. This portion of the trail is held as a memorial to a staunch and valiant people.

S.A. S.A. who was a guard cat for an illegal drug operation—and he is mean. He was starved (and kept mean) by the drug dealers to make federal agents think twice about entering the place. Apparently it didn't work because now he calls the ranch home and is the most active and aggressive of the cats and wonderful to watch—from a distance. The other cats—cougars, lions, bobcats, and leopards—are in cages on the 463-acre ranch, which is open to the public.

Tanya talks to people about dying breeds, such as the Siberian tiger and the Sumatran tiger, which is now extinct in the wild. Some of the cats are most unusual—a lion-tiger mix called a liger, for example. Many of the cats are from abusive backgrounds. They come in cowering, sometimes starving, often covered with sores. In time, they settle in and lie in the sunshine eating chicken and becoming gentle. The cats make a "chuffing" sound, a sort of greeting sound to big cats. Tanya can walk up to any of the fences and a giant kitty will stroll over to rub against her, just like a house cat. But she emphasizes to the 2,500 schoolchildren who visit the ranch each year that these are not playthings. She shows them the cute, young tiger cubs Sara Jo and Jonathon, then shows them Jasper, the mature Siberian who weighs more than 800 pounds and eats twenty to forty pounds of raw meat every night. Although the love she feels for these cats seems to be returned by them—many turn their faces to her to be kissed—she always remembers they are wild animals and their moods may change suddenly. She takes no chances. Bum lived to be more than twenty years old, and Tanya says her father would often sleep in Bum's cage toward the end, he was so devoted to the cat.

Taking care of the cats is expensive, and it could not be done without dedicated volunteers, many of whom live on the property, and donors who provide chicken and vegetables whenever possible.

Lodgings are available on the site, too, at the *Call of the Wild Bed and Breakfast.* Two suites are available—decorated with the big cat theme—and are $75 per night with a continental breakfast. *The Tree House Cabin* is another option. Located high in one of the property's oak trees, the cabin sleeps four adults and one of the bedrooms looks right into a lion's den. The Tree House costs $100 per night. The Call of the Wild is at 239 Turpentine Creek Lane and has a Web site: www.turpentinecreek.org. Call (501) 253–5841 for information or e-mail tigers@turpentinecreek.org.

Because the meat bill around here is about $600 a week, donations are happily accepted. Visit between noon and dusk. The best time to get a good look is at feeding time, an hour before dusk. Tours are $10.00 for adults, $6.00 for anyone under thirteen or over sixty-four. There is a shop to browse in, too.

Off Highway 62 north of Rogers, the National Park Service has rebuilt the historic Elkhorn Tavern on the eastern overlook of **Pea Ridge Battlefield** (giving a good view of the western portion of the battlefield) and has fixed up the battle site with a visitors center for history buffs. A taped slide show and lecture every half hour and a walk-through museum or a drive-through tour (accompanied by recorded messages) of the battlefield make it possible for visitors to get both the Yankee and the Rebel perspectives on one of the only major battles fought in the state, but the battle that saved Missouri for the Union.

The second of architect E. Fay Jones's crystal chapels is in **Bella Vista.** It is a nondenominational chapel just off Highway 340, east of Highway 71. The **Mildred B. Cooper Memorial Chapel** has similar dimensions to those of the Thorncrown Chapel, 24 feet by 65 feet and 50 feet high, but this chapel uses steel, whereas Thorncrown is made of wood. The dominant pattern is curved, like a Gothic arch, rather than triangular, as is Thorncrown. It is open from 9:00 A.M. to 5:00 P.M. seven days a week; call (501) 855–6598 for more information.

West of Bella Vista on Highway 72 is the town of **Gravette,** where you will find the **Spavinaw Supper Club,** a hidden jewel set in a quiet tree-covered area with a view of Spavinaw Creek. Diners may sit on the deck and watch the hummingbirds and squirrels while enjoying a fine meal. Owners J. R. and Chris Martinez offer a different special each night as well as a full menu. Prime rib is a big favorite here, but then so is the rib eye steak with burgundy mushroom sauce. There is a wine list and a full bar (that's why it's a club in this mostly dry county). Desserts are all prepared by Granny, who has worked for the Martinez family for twenty years. Ask for her cheesecake. The old house, with its derelict barn and herb garden outside the kitchen, is about a mile from town on Highway 59 South and is open Tuesday through Saturday from 5:00 to 9:00 P.M. Call (501) 787–6363 for information.

If you are planning to spend the night in Gravette, find the **Gravette House Bed and Breakfast** at 401 Dallas Street S.W., Gravette 72736. Hosts Tom and Debi Boettcher have opened one of the town's original homesteads to guests who wish to enjoy the country setting, with a large porch for warm weather sitting and a sunroom for reading and relaxing. Rooms are from $55 to $75 with a full breakfast served in the dining room. Gravette is a quiet town near enough to Eureka Springs and Branson, Missouri, for a short drive to entertainment. Call (501) 787–6854 or (800) 419–3817 for reservations.

Bentonville is south of Bella Vista on Highway 71. Bentonville's town square has what looks like a 1950s five-and-dime—it even has a red and white awning—it is the *Wal-Mart Visitors Center,* 105 North Main Street, Bentonville 72712. Inside is a tiny office with a low ceiling, a room the size of an elevator, with an upturned apple crate for a chair. Here Sam and Helen Walton did accounting with wooden pegs stuck in the wall for hanging receipts and invoices. It is the American Dream: a five-and-dime called Walton's that changed business in the United States forever. It traces the phenomenal growth of the giant discount store chain—today's general store—from its beginning right through the year 2000. There are relics from such companies as Procter and Gamble, Johnson and Johnson, and Kimberly-Clark. This is a real "local boy makes good" story. At the time of his death in 1992, Sam Walton was the richest man in America. The center, at 105 North Main Street, is open from 9:00 A.M. to 5:00 P.M. Tuesday through Saturday; call (501) 273–1329.

The square is the hub of the town, of course, and every other weekend beginning in April there is a farmers' market where you can pick your favorite fresh produce and enjoy the camaraderie of the townsfolk at the *Filling Station,* a cafe on the square at 111 North Main where most everyone passes through at one time or another. This is a clean, lovely town, with many well-kept old houses. It is also the home of the annual Phillips Celebrity Golf Classic. Call (501) 273–0553 for information.

Let's do a little sightseeing around Bentonville. Begin with the Italianate three-story villa tower *Peel Mansion,* 400 South Walton Boulevard, Bentonwille 72712. It is made of brick, embellished with stucco, trimmed in white, and topped with rose-colored roof tiles. A covered front porch wraps around the side, runs the length of the house, and is surrounded by flowers and plants commonly found in this country during the 1800s. This home was built in 1875 by Samuel West Peel, a Confederate colonel, Indian agent, attorney, and the first native-born Arkansan to serve in the U.S. Congress. The 180-acre farm and apple orchard was known as The Oaks. A massive renovation program using local artisans and craftspeople has restored the home to its Victorian grandeur. The library has a rare Anglo-Japanese mantel. Gardening teams spent months of detailed research to replicate the historic plantings in the five gardens surrounding the Peel home. One garden is filled with wild-flowers; another has plants and flowers taken from the 1842 lists of a Fayetteville nurseryman. A pioneer garden has been added in recent years. Visitors enter the property through a log cabin that serves as a welcome center and gift shop. The cabin is a two-room structure that was dismantled log by log and moved from Brightwater to its present location. A map discovered in an attic in California, drawn by a Civil War army officer during the Battle of Pea Ridge, depicts the cabin as early as 1862. The Peel Mansion and Garden is open Tuesday through Saturday from 10:00 A.M. to 4:00 P.M. Admission is $3.00 for adults and $1.00 for children. In December the home is decorated for Victorian Christmas. For more information call (501) 273–9664 or look in at the Web site: www.biz.ipa.net/peel. You don't even need a ticket to take advantage of the archival library in the carriage house.

You might want to stop by **Morning Star Baskets,** 9186 Greenhouse Road, Bentonville 72712, where Martha Lue Featherston sells hand-woven baskets. Some of the more unusual items are the hen basket, designed to carry hens when it was common to share broody hens, and the egg basket, which is shaped to keep eggs from rolling around and breaking. Call (501) 273–5282 for information. Hours are Saturday 9:00 A.M. to 5:00 P.M. and weekdays by appointment.

When it's time to eat, **Fred's Hickory Inn** at 1502 North Walton Boulevard, Bentonville 72712, is the place to try if you like lots of noise and table-hopping. Fred and Lou Gaye feature Italian recipes handed down in Lou's family. Hickory-pit barbecue was Fred's passion, and so with fine seasoning and quality meat he went into the business. Silver-haired Fred has lots of regulars who call if they are *not* coming in. He loves to tell jokes, and his place is usually filled. Call (501) 273–3303 for information or reservations.

If you stay on Highway 71, you will be in the Rogers area. And, no, **Rogers** wasn't named for Will Rogers, although Will Rogers was married to a local woman (Betty Blake) here in 1906. The **Rogers Historical Museum,** at 322 South Second Street, Rogers 72756, was formerly the Victorian 1895 Hawkins House. Guides will give you a taste of the history of the area with old photos, handmade furnishings, and forgotten tools. A barbershop, bank, and dry goods store are assembled in great detail, right down to the clipped hair on the floor by the broom. The "Attic" is stocked with antique toys, clothes, and tools to explore. Rogers was a boomtown in the 1880s, when the railroad established a depot and apple orchards began to be planted; this was called the "Land of the

Big Red Apple." A red Frisco caboose is parked 4 blocks from the museum for children to climb aboard. Hours are from 10:00 A.M. to 4:00 P.M. Tuesday through Saturday; call (501) 621–1154.

A new museum opened in Rogers in 2000. The **Rogers Daisy Air Gun Museum,** 114 South First Street, Rogers 72756, has hundreds of interesting displays on the history of these popular toys beginning in the late 1800s. The company relocated to Rogers in 1958 and the corporate headquarters are still here, although the air guns are no longer manufactured here. The museum is open six days a week from 10:00 A.M. to 4:00 P.M. Call them at (501) 986–6873.

Downtown Rogers has been restored to what it was when the town was young. Go through the 9-foot-tall doors decorated with bas-relief sculptures of mortar and pestle and into **Poor Richard's** at 116 South First Street, Rogers 72756. It is as it was as a pharmacy both inside and out. Oak woodwork, glass shelves, and a marble soda fountain are accented with wrought-iron tables and chairs—a fine place for a cup of coffee on a chilly day. The building was constructed of marble from nearby Carthage, Missouri. The shop contains solid mahogany fixtures, and the marble soda fountain has a mahogany back bar and room divider that offers a fine example of the cabinetmaker's craft of the time. A large mahogany clock with brass movement hangs to your left as you enter the store; its enamel face has kept time since 1907. The tile floor and pressed-tin ceiling tiles are original. The porcelain drawer pulls are inscribed with the names of the various drugs—in Latin—and pharmaceutical supplies. The store is open Monday through Friday from 9:30 A.M. to 6:00 P.M., on Saturday until 5:00 P.M., and on Sunday from 1:00 to 5:00 P.M. and is especially delightful during the Christmas season, when carolers are on hand and the store is decorated in holiday sparkles and open later. Call (501) 631–7687 for information.

At First and Elm Streets, around the block from Poor Richard's, in a blue-and-white-trimmed building is the **Crumpet Tea Room** at 107 West Elm Street, Bentonville 72712. The cook, Sandy Boles, is now the owner. Lunch in this second-floor restaurant is from 11:00 A.M. to 2:00 P.M. Monday through Saturday. Good things like quiche join unusual things like the "crumpet potato," baked with vegetables and sauce, and the tearoom's famous orange rolls with orange frosting. Desserts? You betcha—chocolate pie and cheesecake. Call (501) 636–7498 for other daily specials.

If you want to try a hickory-smoked ham done in the Ozark tradition—slowly, over natural hickory smoke, using an old family recipe of Tom

Baumgartner's dating back to 1841—then stop by *Hillbilly Smokehouse* (501–636–1927) at 1801 South Eighth Street (Highway 71B South), Bentonville 72712, for sugar or salt dry-cured ham and bacon. The secret is slow curing and aging, which create the delightful taste and texture. Hours are Monday through Friday 7:30 A.M. until 4:00 P.M. and Saturday until 2:00 P.M. Call (800) 759–9439 for a catalog of other meats available— turkey, sausage, and chicken. Their Web site is www.hillbillysmokehouse.com.

War Eagle Cavern *east of Rogers and across Beaver Lake on Highway 12 is a bat-filled setting next to a finger of the lake. If you are a James gang fan, you will be interested to learn that Frank and Jesse hid out here. In more recent times, Randy Travis, Rob Lowe, and Bill Paxton filmed the movie* Frank and Jesse *on location.*

War Eagle, southeast of Rogers on Highway 12, is the site of the huge War Eagle Fair, a four-day event that brings thousands of visitors each May and October to see handmade, one-of-a-kind Ozarks crafts in tents covering acres of ground. The fair always begins on the first Friday in May and the third Thursday in October. Across a one-lane rusty steel bridge (with a two-ton-limit sign), the War Eagle Mill Arts and Crafts Fair competes on the mill side of the river, and what seems to be more than two tons of traffic and pedestrians flows back and forth. You can reach the fair from the south on Highway 303 for easier (and free) parking.

War Eagle Mill is a reproduction of an 1873 gristmill, powered by the War Eagle River, with three sets of buhr stones and an 18-foot redwood undershot waterwheel. First built in 1830, the mill washed away in 1848. The second mill was burned by order of a Confederate general to prevent the Union army's using it. This undershot waterwheel is the only one of its kind still operating. Inside is War Eagle Mercantile, an old-fashioned general store with all manner of jams, honey, herbs, mixes, rugs, toys, clothing, pottery, and dozens of other things. The working water-powered gristmill is still making buhr stone-ground cornmeal, whole wheat flour, rye, and yellow corn grits.

In the same building the *Bean Palace Lunchroom* serves War Eagle buckwheat waffles and biscuits and sausage gravy for breakfast; for lunch there are always beans and cornbread, smoked ham and turkey, and home-baked cakes, tarts, and cookies—all with apple cider and all made right there at the mill. The Bean Palace is open seven days a week from 8:30 A.M. to 5:00 P.M. but closes Thanksgiving and Christmas Day. The mill is open seven days a week from 8:30 A.M. to 5:00 P.M., except January and February, when it is open Saturday and Sunday only. Take County Road 98 from Highway 12, or call (501) 789–5343. The War Eagle Web site is at www.wareaglemill.com; the e-mail address is zoe@ipa.net.

Traveling south on Highway 71 makes it easy to detour over to **Tonti-town** on Highway 412 West. This is an Italian community separated from nearby Fayetteville by vineyards. Settled in 1898 by Father Bandini, Tontitown was named after the first Italian to explore the state, Henri de Tonti. The neat white **Tontitown Historical Museum,** on Highway 68 West, features an early grape press, wine bottling, and spaghetti machines. It is open June through August on Wednesday, Saturday, and Sunday from 1:00 to 4:00 P.M.; September through October it is open Saturday and Sunday from 1:00 to 4:00 P.M. The museum tells

War Eagle Tales

War Eagle Mill is well known around these parts. It's a bit out of the way, but the path is well beaten because of the annual crafts fairs held here. We went to War Eagle during the off-season, which is the best time to visit most of Arkansas's attractions.

I was fascinated with the products of the mill: cracked wheat and seven grains of flour to give a crunchy texture to breads; pastry flour, which is low in gluten to make a delicate, flaky crust; and, of course, bread flour, which is higher in gluten to allow bread to rise up high and proud. I love to bake, as you may have gathered. Since most of the products will keep in the freezer for a year or so, my poor husband found himself hauling twenty-pound bags of various grains to our car. There was one product with which I was not familiar: yellow corn grits. I am not a Yankee, being from Missouri's southern Ozarks, and grits are not commonly served in Kansas City, so I had never seen yellow grits. So I bought a five-pound bag.

Well, I loved those grits. They had texture—not all cream-of-wheaty

like white grits—flavor, and color. I made cheese-grits casseroles and fried patties for breakfast or just enjoyed a hot bowl with butter in the morning or late at night. They were gone as fast as a greyhound after a rabbit, and I yearned for more. I searched the War Eagle catalog for yellow corn grits, to no avail. I assumed they quit making them and sadly returned to white grits.

Two years later we returned to War Eagle Mill, and I once again searched for yellow corn grits. I read every package on the shelves and was now certain they had stopped making my favorite food. I approached a woman working behind the counter and asked her about it.

"Oh," she said, "They're right ova' there," pointing to a shelf I had just searched. I looked again. All I could find was a package of something called Yankee Grits. "That's it, honey," she said.

"Why," I asked, "do they call it Yankee Grits?"

"Well," she drawled, looking me dead in the eye, "'cause they're yellow."

the story of the settlement of the town, but to get the true feeling of the community, try to be there for the Tontitown Grape Festival, one of the state's oldest continual festivals, featuring homemade spaghetti and sauce, at the St. Joseph Church and school that Father Bandini founded. Call (501) 361–2498 for information.

There are three old Italian restaurants in town. *Mama Z's Cafe* has been around for years. Owners Edna Zubo (that's Mama) and her daughter Lisa Neil make homemade pastas just like in the old country. This relaxed family restaurant turns out great Italian food, freshly baked bread, and

Because of the large crowds drawn by the War Eagle Fair in the fall, other fairs are held at the same time, and in order to take advantage of the traffic, many handcrafted items are displayed on porches, antiques placed in yards, and quilts hung on clotheslines. The area becomes a shopper's dream.

tops it off with homemade pies and cobblers Tuesday through Sunday from 7:00 A.M. to 2:00 P.M. and from 5:00 to 9:00 P.M. It is about 2½miles west of Highway 71 Bypass on Highway 412 West. Call (501) 361–2750 for information.

The *Venesian Inn,* on Highway 412–Henri de Tonti, is owned by Johnny and Linda Mhoon and has been here since 1947, in the same brick building in which it began. It is always busy, but the service is immediate—the salad (just lettuce covered with a strong garlic and oil dressing that everyone seems to love) is brought right away; fresh warm bread served with honey, basic Italian fare (spaghetti or ravioli), and chicken or steak entrees follow. The restaurant is open for dinner Tuesday through Thursday from 5:00 to 9:00 P.M. and on Friday and Saturday from 4:00 to 9:00 P.M.; call (501) 361–2562 for information.

The third Italian restaurant is quite different. Tablecloths, soft lighting, and a good wine list make *Mary Maestri's,* 956 East Henri de Tonti Boulevard, Springdale 72770, (Highway 412 West and Maestri Road) more upscale. A more complete selection of homemade pastas and sauces, including excellent lasagna and tortellini, join Italian entrees like chicken piccata (a favorite—cooked on the grill with lemon butter), the best steaks in the region, and, of course, homemade spumoni, pies, and New York cheesecake for dessert. Owner Daniel Maestri is Mary's grandson, and the restaurant and its traditions have been here for about seventy years, since a poor grape harvest left Aldo and Mary Maestri looking for ways to increase their income. Mary, using her mother-in-law's spaghetti sauce, opened a restaurant in their home, and the place was such a hit that more and more tables were squeezed in. At one point even the beds were used as chairs, with small tables between them, and when that wasn't enough, customers often used their laps as tables. The fried chicken and spaghetti dinner was the favorite and still is. All the spaghetti you want with any entree is still traditional, so you will never leave hungry. Hours are 5:30 to 9:30 P.M. seven days a week; call (501) 361–2536 for information.

Yesteryears Antiques Mall at 548 Henri de Tonti Boulevard, Tontitown 72770, is considered the largest antiques mall in the state. The mall's 28,000 square feet includes Garden Gourmet Cafe, which is open 11:00 A.M. to 3:00 P.M. daily and from 6:00 to 9:00 P.M. Thursday through Saturday. But the antiques mall is open from 9:00 A.M. to 6:00 P.M. seven days a week. Call (501) 361–5747.

Stay on Highway 412 west of Tontitown to the Oklahoma border, where Sugar Creek flows through the town of *Siloam Springs.* The hundred-year-old town grew up around mountain springs. Restored Victorian homes and buildings dot the town, which is filled with art galleries, crafts shops, and picture-book parks. It is the home of John Brown University and the Sager Creek Arts Center for the performing arts.

Springdale is the home of Tyson Foods, and driving on Highway 71 behind trucks filled with chicken crates feels like riding in a ticker-tape parade of chicken feathers. If all those flying feathers put you in the mood for a good chicken dinner, stop in at *AQ's Chicken House,* about 2 miles north of town on Highway 71. AQ's is located in a lovely Victorian gingerbread house and has been serving up the best batter-dipped chicken since the 1940s. They are open seven days a week beginning at 11:00 A.M. and closing at 8:30 P.M. Call (501) 751–4633.

While you are here you might want to visit the *Shiloh Museum,* at 118 West Johnson Avenue, Springdale 72764 and see the history of families like the Tysons and Waltons. But most of the museum's space is dedicated to the people who turned the northwest wilderness into a state. The walls and furnishings from the 1843 cabin of Elizabeth McGarrah and the collected works of more than 130 area photographers, as well as more than 50,000 tintypes, prints, postcards, and stereo cards, are displayed here. The museum is open from 10:00 A.M. to 5:00 P.M. Monday through Saturday year-round. There is no admission charge. Call (501) 750–8165 for information.

There is an elegant bed-and-breakfast in town called *Magnolia Gardens Inn,* 500 North Main Street, Springdale 72764. This is one of Springdale's important historic estates. It is a lavish ten-bedroom inn built in the 1880s on ten shady, tree-covered acres. Owners Bill and Carol Kendrick have decorated the rooms with unusual antiques— one bedroom has a bed made from a huge 150-year-old weaving loom; another, called the "Swinger's Loft," has a swinging bed—and all have private baths. There's a garden tearoom, wine cellar, and the Rebel Pub, where beer, wine, and cocktails are served. A stroll on the estate will find many secluded areas for quiet conversations. An

evening snack and beverage and full plantation breakfast are served by the fireplace in the dining room. A "full plantation breakfast" means enough food to feed the Confederate Army, with fresh-baked breads and rolls, the usual southern feed of eggs, biscuits and gravy, and sausage. Rooms are $100 to $135 for two. Call (501) 756–5744 for information, fax (501) 756–2526.

The Arkansas and Missouri Railroad operates the ***Ozark Scenic Railway*** from the Springdale depot, which is based on the design of the city's original depot. The train leaves at 8:00 A.M. for an all-day adventure. Between two and five trains a week make the trip; and the bright-red locomotive pulls as many of the turn-of-the century mahogany-lined and perfectly restored passenger cars as required from April to the last weekend of October.

Passengers travel through the most rugged portion of the Ozarks—a 7-mile ride from Winslow, through the 1,700-foot Winslow tunnel, and across the three highest trestles on the line. After the 117-foot-tall trestle, the trains begin a series of steep grades and end in the town of Van Buren, where a three-hour layover gives you time to browse the historic town or take a ride on the *Frontier Belle* Riverboat. During the layover the train makes a three-hour, nonstop trip to Winslow. The cost of the Springdale/Van Buren trip is $34 on Wednesday and $38 on Saturday (in October the prices are $34 on Wednesday and $39 on Saturday); the Van Buren/Winslow trip is $20 on Wednesday and $22 on Saturday (in October the prices are $22 on Wednesday and $25 on Saturday). Call (501) 751–8600 or (800) 687–8600 for reservations. You can also find fare information at www.arkansasmissouri-rr.com.

Highway 23—from Highway 16 to I–40—leads into ***Fayetteville*** and is known as "The Pig Trail" to Razorback fans who travel north through a canopy of forest toward Fayetteville for home games. In Fayetteville you can wine and dine and shop till you drop and still be only minutes away from the unspoiled mountains, lakes, and streams of the surrounding countryside. It is home to the state's largest university, the University of Arkansas. Old Main, the most famous building on campus, rises on a hill with its massive redbrick walls and mansard roof. Its twin towers stand watch over the campus and the Razorbacks who call it home. You will probably see groups of people walking along looking at their feet near Old Main, because the names of every graduate since 1876 are etched into the sidewalks radiating out from the famous old building. You can choose an atmosphere to suit your whimsy: the laid-back, anything-goes attitude on Dickson Street; the beer-and-boots cowboy scene south of downtown; several college hot spots that mix hard rock with huge dance spaces; the disco crowd on the square; and a couple of fine listening clubs for the quieter set.

If you are a sports fan, while you are strolling the campus you might want to duck into the *Tommy Boyer Hall of Champions.* Glass cases hold glittering trophies and stories of athletes' performances. There are interactive stations in each section and touch-screen displays to help you relive great seasons. Exhibits show off star performers in many sports: Miller Barber in golf, Kevin McReynolds in baseball, Mike Conley in track (currently the assistant track coach here), as well as a basketball section devoted to Coach Nolan Richardson's 1994 NCAA championship team. Hours are 9:00 A.M. to 5:00 P.M. Monday through Friday and on Saturdays of home football games. The admission is free. Be sure to head over to the *Hog Heaven Gift Shop* to the left of the exhibit where you can purchase all sorts of Razorback souvenirs. If football is your sport, go to the Broyles Athletic Center, and you will be treated to the same interactive displays on football. Call (501) 575–8618 for more information.

If eating's your thing, Fayetteville is your town. Colorful taverns and restaurants surround the campus, and there's even an old-fashioned farmers' market every Tuesday, Thursday, and Saturday morning May through October, from 7:00 A.M. to 1:00 P.M., on the vibrant town square that's alive with flowers and trees, produce and crafts. A leisurely walk through the Washington-Willow historic district is a fine way to spend some time, get some exercise, and see sensational old homes. The opportunity to browse through the farmers' market and the stores along the downtown square or catch the scenic view from Mount Sequoyah makes the town a quiet oasis. You can attend a concert at the Walton Art Center or take home a treat from the Ozark Mountain smokehouse.

The first local brewery and pub in the northwest part of the state is the *Ozark Brewing Company* at 430 West Dickson Street, Fayetteville 72701. A half-dozen varieties of beer, brewed on the premises, are available to try. Brewmaster Michael Plott purchased the old buildings, which have held businesses since 1880, and has begun renovation. The pub serves traditional food, such as bratwurst, pizza, chili (made with

Trivia

Driving south from Fayet-teville along Scenic High-way 71, the signs read VERY CROOKED AND STEEP, an accurate description. The trip is almost worth ruin-ing your transmission. You will find old cemeteries, abandoned log cabins, and an ostrich farm.

their own beer), and sandwiches, as well as an eclectic mix of pastas, salads, and desserts.

The restaurant's heavy post-and-beam construc-tion is similar to the timber framing of eighteenth-century New England barns, using massive 12-inch beams and wooden dowels. Beer styles from all over the world—Czech Bud and German Koenig and Jeverpils—will be brewed in the stainless steel tanks visible from the glass-walled elevator carrying people to the second-floor restaurant. It is open Friday and Saturday 11:00 A.M. until 1:00 A.M. and on Sunday from 11:00 A.M. until 10:00 P.M.; Mon-day through Thursday 11:00 A.M. to midnight. Call (501) 521–2739 for information. Or you can e-mail the brewery at hops@ozarkbrew.com or check the Web site: www.ozarkbrew.com.

Johnson House B&B is located at 5371 South Forty-eighth Street, off Highway 71 or Greathouse Springs Road in *Johnson.* This elegant 1882 country home of handmade brick, which is on the National Register of Historic Places, has three guest rooms, all with private baths. The front parlor has a wood-burning fireplace and intricately painted ceiling. The window-filled dining room (or the upstairs veranda, when the weather is perfect) is where innkeeper Mary Carothers serves a gourmet breakfast. A smokehouse on the property is now used as an antiques and gift shop. Miss Texas, a friendly black Labrador who lives there, greets guests at the gate. Some of the rooms have tin ceilings, and there is a curving staircase leading to nowhere in the front hallway. The upstairs bedrooms (reached by another staircase) have queen-size beds (one has an extra daybed), and the downstairs bedroom has an antique double bed. Rooms are $105 for two people. Call Mary at (501) 756–1095 for reservations. See their Web site at www.touristguide.com/bandb/arkansas/johnson.

Trivia

The Washington-Willow Historic District in Fayette-ville is a neighborhood with Victorian houses and large shade trees. Guided walking tours through the historical society can be arranged at the old jail.

Inn at the Mill, between Fayetteville and Spring-dale at 3906 Greathouse Springs Road (the John-son exit off Highway 71/62), is only minutes from the city but a world away. You are greeted with cof-fee, tea, or wine (sometimes hot apple cider). A complimentary continental breakfast is served in your room, in the parlor of the historic mill, or on the deck overlooking the pond and waterwheel. The comfort of a country inn with the amenities of a first-class hotel—turndown service and a cookie by your bed—makes this place most pleasurable.

Rooms range from $77 to $105; suites are from $145 to $175. Call (800) CLARION or (501) 443–1800 for information. The cherry on this sundae, however, is the restaurant next door.

The "James" of *James at the Mill,* at 3906 Greathouse Springs Road, is chef Miles G. James, who serves Ozark plateau cuisine next to the beautiful spring-fed waterwheel in the glass-enclosed restaurant. The entrees are unusual and unbelievably good: roast Arkansas rabbit with crispy red-skin potatoes, rosemary, and asparagus ($18), or blue-corn-meal-crusted chicken with creamy grits, fried broccoli, and Roma tomato gazpacho ($13). An excellent wine list, cited by *Wine Spectator* (the only one in Arkansas to receive that distinction), accompanies the menu. The wine list contains some unusual liquors as well. The warm chocolate brownie with Jack Daniels chocolate chip ice cream and caramel sauce is the best thing on the dessert menu—even if you are a teetotaler. Call (501) 443-1400 for reservations. You can have lunch at the Mill Monday through Friday from 11:00 A.M. to 2:00 P.M. and dinner Monday through Saturday from 5:30 to 9:30 P.M. It is closed on Sunday.

Just down the highway a bit (and recommended by the staff at James at the Mill to its out-of-town guests) is *Miss Sarah's Country Kitchen,* at 2212 Main Street in Johnson, 72741. Owner Lynn Goodwin devises her menu on Saturday, and it is different every week. You can find really good down-home cooking here: meatloaf, fried chicken, Swiss steak, all served with salad and two vegetables. Fried okra is always one of them, and often there is hominy. Breakfast is served all day Saturday, and is it great! Homemade cinnamon rolls, blueberry pancakes (very popular), and omelettes ("bigggggg omelettes," says Lynn, who worked here ten years before buying the restaurant, "not those little flip-over tortilla-sized things") served with grits. Of course, there are *always* biscuits and gravy. Miss Sarah's opens every day but Sunday at 6:30 A.M.—so there is no excuse for missing this opportunity to enjoy home cooking as good as (or maybe even better than) your mom's—and closes at 2:30 P.M. Call (501) 442-9618 for information.

If you are driving along Highway 62, at a mile west of its intersection with Highway 71 in Fayetteville, you can probably follow your sniffer to the *Ozark Mountain Smokehouse* in a stone-and-wooden barn tucked into the base of Mt. Kessler. Free tours are offered from 9:00 A.M. until 4:00 P.M. Monday through Saturday. Apron-clad guides put a paper hat on your head and lead you into the smokehouse. Through picture windows you can watch the meats and cheeses being cured and flavored with mixtures of herbs and spices. The pungent, sweet aroma of smoke coming from four dark, smoking chambers where racks of hams and turkeys hang will stir the desire for a taste—and you *can* taste the smoked products (and fruit preserves) as well. Owner Frank Sharp has come a long way from the barn his father, Roy, burned down nearly fifty years ago while perfecting the art of smoking. It's not fancy—wooden tables and stone floor and walls—but it's comfortable, so stay for lunch. Call (800) 643–3437 for information or see their Web site at www.ozarkfamily.com.

The historic district at Washington and Willow Streets between Dickson and Davidson is filled with Victorian mansions and large shade trees. Tours of the district and of Headquarters House, an 1853 frame structure that served both sides during the Civil War, along with many of the town's historic homes, are included on a walking tour. A tour can be arranged through the *Historical Society at Old Jail,* 30 South College Street, Fayetteville 72701, (501) 521–2970.

The *Arkansas Air Museum,* located in the vast, all-wood White Hangar of Fayetteville's Drake Field on Highway 71 South (4290 South School), houses everything from famous racing planes of the 1920s and 1930s to an early airliner. Music of the 1940s plays in the hangar to help you drift back in time. But this is no ordinary museum; here the colorful displays take off and soar. The planes are maintained and licensed and can be seen in the air earning the name "The Museum That Flies." There are open-cockpit biplanes and closed-cabin monoplanes all up, up, and away at various times. The volunteers who run the museum from 11:00 A.M. to 4:30 P.M. daily are lifelong pilots and mechanics whose love of airplanes and sense of humor keep the hangar full of life. A free movie, *Aviation Oddities,* shows many of the bizarre contraptions people have built to try their wings. You can also watch antique airplanes being restored in the museum's restoration shop. Admission is $2.00 adults, $1.00 children over six for this nonprofit all-volunteer museum. A gift shop sells model airplanes and T-shirts. Call (501) 521–4947 for information. The Web site is at www.arkairmuseum.org.

The house at 930 California Street is where Bill and Hillary Clinton lived while they taught at the University of Arkansas Law School in Fayetteville. The couple was married in their home with just a few close friends.

Highway 16 between the "Pig Trail" and Fayetteville shows the beauty of the prairies and woodlands colored by the wildflowers that grow in the hollows and along the creeks. But digging these plants is not encouraged anymore, because of the delicate balance of the ecology.

The *Holland Wildflower Farm,* at 290 O'Neal Lane in *Elkins* 72727, on Highway 16, is where Bob and Julie Holland have another way to fill your yard—with the reds of cardinal flowers, the blue of flocks, the purple of coneflower, or the dramatic burst of color of the orange butterfly weed. The farm offers wildflower seeds and native plants. A visit to the farm is like a nature walk, abloom with native color. The gardens and flower beds, together with the fields of wildflowers and native plants, offer wild columbines, irises, and other native perennials—all nursery propagated. Bob has a degree in wildlife research and plant pathology, Julie is a biologist, and the two have plenty of helpful advice to offer on how to raise the plants you select. If you plan to visit, call ahead for an appointment (501–643–2622). They have no retail help on the property. The farm is ½ mile from Highway 16 off First Street. All sales are through their Web site, which is www.hwildflower.com.

Maguire House Bed & Breakfast, at 19154 Highway 74 East, Elkins 72727, stands where a pre–Civil War town once stood, complete with school, church, and cemetery just short of Elkins on Highway 74 East. The circa 1850 house is listed in Confederate chronicles and is an Ozark farm, complete with chickens. The four spacious rooms with two shared baths come with a hearty breakfast of homemade bread, sausage, and eggs. The antebellum home, with vernacular Greek Revival details, of Mike Musholt and his wife Maureen is situated near the main branch of the White River. Slaves once worked the large farm, which is built from bricks kilned by those slaves. Rates are $65 for two. Call (501) 442–2122 for information or find their Web site at members.aol.com/maguirebnb.

Hand Made Studios, 137 East First Avenue, Elkins 72727, is where Mim Wynne has the most eclectic shop you will ever find. This old roadhouse, built in 1864, has been completely restored. Two rooms are filled with very fine quality handmade European, Japanese, and American soaps. There is jewelry made by craftspeople across the country and other gift items as unique as cotton or canvas couch throws, handmade ceramics, Venetian blown-glass bottles, and even exotic bugs. Yes, bugs. You just have to come in and see it yourself. Gifts you won't find anywhere else and things you want for yourself are all here *and* Mim's own handwoven rugs, which are sold around the world and have been featured on the cover of the Neiman Marcus catalogue. Hours are Tuesday through Saturday from "about" 10:00 A.M. until 5:00 P.M. Mim has weaving class on Saturday, so call (501) 643–3025 or e-mail her at Manyrugs@aol.com. She is not hard to reach—her fax number is (501) 521–9094 and voice mail is (501) 443–0921.

You can find your Bluebird of Happiness at *Terra Studios,* 16 miles southeast of Fayetteville on Highway 16. The newest thing at Terra Studios is glassblowing. You can watch the famous little glass bluebirds being made by skilled glass craftspeople—or learn to blow glass yourself. There is a large stoneware pottery showroom, too. Rita Ward's clay-sculptured "Terrans," tiny elflike creatures who live at Terra, are popular with collectors of gnomes and such, and John Ward's unusual large urns are displayed out front. Classes in pottery are also available. The Ward family has produced elegance everywhere. This is one of the few working family studios in the nation. It has two complete pottery studios and a 5,000-square-foot hot-glass studio. The lovely grounds include a picnic area under the cedars, an arched bridge, and a garden; visitors picnic in the hand-built clay gazebo beyond the arched bridge. The facility is open seven days a week from 9:00 A.M. to 5:00 P.M.; call (501) 643–3185.

Otiz Zark restaurant is at Terra, too. This unique eating spot offers "peasant neuvo" cuisine, including vegetarian dishes as well as meat and fish selections. Lunch is served 11:00 A.M. until 2:30 P.M. every day but Sunday, when a brunch is served from 10:00 A.M. until 3:00 P.M. Dinner is offered Monday through Thursday from 5:00 to 9:30 P.M., until 11:00 P.M. on Friday and Saturday. Call (501) 643–4063.

An absolute *must* if you really want to get the feel of the Ozarks is the **Little O' Opry** in downtown **West Fork.** Dan Wiethop celebrates genuine Ozark homegrown music every Saturday night beginning at 7:00 P.M. It is the finest collection of real Ozark music anywhere, done by real Ozark folks—a nonprofit gathering of musicians offering "good, honest, natural music" grown on the banks of the West Fork of the White River. The staff band is made up of an acoustic flattop guitar, steel guitar, fiddle, bass, and drums, and it backs up singers from around the Ozarks. Call (501) 839–2992 for information.

Stop at the **Mount Gayler Tower and Gift Shop** in **Winslow** south of West Fork, at 22035 North Highway 71, 72959, and trot up the 100-foot tower to show you are in shape. It costs $1.00 to make the climb up the steel stairs, but the view is worth a million dollars. Jordane Bellis manages the shop, which has been in his family since 1931. Lake Shepherd Springs is to the south, and to the east are the bluffs of White Rock Mountain. Call (501) 634–2742 for information.

Trivia
The town of Winslow was made famous in 1971 when Smoke in the Wind, a Civil War movie starring Walter Brennan, was filmed here. Churches and stores built almost one-hundred years ago can still be found here.

ACES TO STAY IN NORTHWEST ARKANSAS

Jasper Mockingbird
Hill Hotel, 72641;
(501) 446–2634,
(800) 704–7970

Harrison Hotel Seville,
302 North Main Street,
Harrison;
(870) 743–1000;
www.hotelseville.com

Mountain Home
Holiday Inn,
1350 Highway 625 West
(downtown) 72653;
(870) 425–5101

Yellville Eagle's
Nest Lodge,
109 Highway 235, 72687;
(870) 449–5050,
fax: (870) 449–4456;
www.arkansasweb.com/
eaglesnest

OZARK NATIONAL FOREST
Bella Vista Inn
at Bella Vista,
1 Chelsea Road, 72714;
(501) 876–5645;
e-mail: iabv@arkansas.net;
www.iabv.com;
($110–$140)

Bentonville Best Western,
2307 SE Walton Boulevard,
72712;
(501) 273–9727

Eureka Springs
Best Western,
Highway 62 East/23 North
(501) 253–9551,
(800) 221–3344

Fayetteville Best Western,
Highway 62/71 Bypass,
72701;
(501) 587–1400

Ramada, 3901 North
College Avenue,
(Highway 71/71 Bypass),
72701;
(888) 443–4866,
fax: (501) 443–1927,
443–3431

Rogers Days Inn,
2102 South Eighth Street,
72756;
(501) 631–8952

Springdale Best Western,
1394 West Sunset, 72765;
(501) 751–3100

Chambers of Commerce in Northwest Arkansas

Ozark National Forest
Bentonville Advertising and Promotion;
(800) 410–2535;
www.nwanews.com/bbvchamber

Eureka Springs Chamber of Commerce;
P.O. Box 551, 72632;
(501) 253–8737

Fayetteville Chamber of Commerce;
P.O. Box 4216, 72701; (501) 521–1710,
(800) 766–4626;
www.FayettevilleAR.com

Harrison Chamber of Commerce;
621 East Rush Street, 72601;
(870) 741–2659, (800) 880–6265;
www.harrison-chamber.com

Calico Rock Chamber of Commerce;
102 Main Street, 72519;
(870) 297–4129

Yellville Area Chamber of Commerce;
Box 369, 72687;
(870) 449–4676; e-mail: chamber@yellville.com;
www.yellville.com

Springdale Chamber of Commerce;
Box 166, 72765;
(501) 872–2222; www.springdale.com

MORE PLACES TO EAT IN NORTHWEST ARKANSAS

GREER LAKE AREA

Jasper Dairy Diner (at the waterwheel), Highway 7, 72031; (501) 446-5343 (6:00 A.M. to 8:00 P.M. daily)

St. Joe Ferguson's Country Store & Restaurant, 72675; (870) 439-2234

GATEWAY AREA

Bull Shoals Village Wheel Restaurant, 1400 Central Boulevard, 72619; (870) 445-4414

Harrison DeVito's Restaurant, Highway 62/65 Junction (4 miles north of Harrison), 72601; (870) 741-8832

Harrison Neighbor's Mill Bakery and Cafe, 1012 Highway 62/65 South, 72601; (870) 741-MILL

OZARK NATIONAL FOREST

Elkins Laverne's Country Kitchen, Elkins, 72727; (501) 643-3696

Eureka Springs Sparky's Roadhouse Cafe, 41 Van Buren (across from McDonald's), 72632; (501) 253-6001

Fayetteville Joe's Mexican Restaurant, 324 West Dickson, 72701; (501) 521-0194

West Central Arkansas

I n Kansas the Arkansas River is called the Ar-KANSAS River, but when it crosses the state line it changes its name, because in 1881 the legislature appointed a committee to ascertain the right pronunciation of the word, and the result was a resolution declaring it to be ARK-an-saw.

The western Arkansas River Valley glides from Fort Smith to Little Rock and is quilted with pastures, vineyards, forests, and rice fields. Rocky, towering mountain ranges line both sides—the Ozarks to the north, with lakes and hardwood forests, and the Ouachitas to the south, with pine forests and waterfalls.

The river crackles with life. Locks and dams divide the river into long lakes (dotted with sails, skiers, boats, and barges). A bouquet of small towns cluster around Fort Smith and lie sprinkled along the 160-mile valley with old depots, stagecoach stops, a frontier fort, and a monastery.

Scenic highways connect the towns. Highway 22 rolls east from Fort Smith to Dardanelle through farmland nestled between the river and steep slopes of the mountains. Highway 7, of course, is one of the nation's most scenic drives, wandering through both the Ozark and the Ouachita mountains from Harrison to Hot Springs.

Arkansas River Valley

W hen **Fort Smith** was founded at the confluence of the Arkansas and Poteau Rivers, it was frontier America at its worst. Outlaws, bushwhackers, and gunrunners heading southwest joined whores and men seeking gold. This place had it all. It was a tough boomtown known as "Hell on the Border," where a federal judge and a band of U.S. marshals sent seventy-nine outlaws to the gallows. (Judge Isaac Parker, "The Hanging Judge," is famous for saying, "I never hung a man; it's the law.")

The fort was built at Belle Point on the Arkansas River in 1817, and the Butterfield stage line stopped here on its way to San Francisco. This was

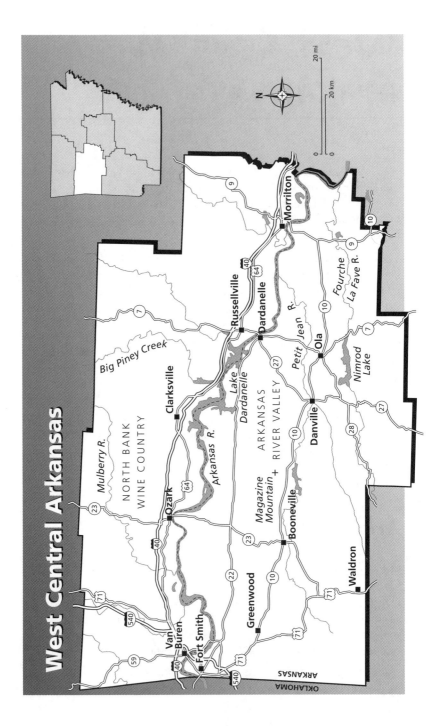

BEST ATTRACTIONS IN
WEST CENTRAL ARKANSAS

also the Arkansas terminus of the Trail of Tears, which sent the remnants of the five great civilized Native American tribes to the Oklahoma Territory.

The Victorian-era Belle Grove Historic District, on the banks of the Arkansas River off Rogers Avenue, dates back to the boomtown days. This charming time capsule has some of the best antiques shopping around. The **Fort Smith Museum of History,** at 320 Rogers Avenue, Fort Smith 72901, is 1 block away and has a nostalgic Trolley Museum, where a turn-of-the-century trolley has been restored. The museum depicts the growth of the town and contains a circa 1900 pharmacy, including a working soda fountain and a steam-powered fire pump. It's open daily June through August from 9:00 A.M. to 5:00 P.M. The rest of the year it is open Tuesday through Saturday from 10:00 A.M. to 5:00 P.M. (Sunday from 1:00 to 5:00 P.M.). Admission is $3.00 for adults and $1.00 for children. Call (501) 783–7841 for information.

Taliano's, Fort Smith;
(501) 785–2292

Grapevine Restaurant,
Paris; (501) 963–2413

Subiaco Abbey,
Subiaco; (501) 934–4411

Cedar Falls, Petit Jean
State Park, Dardanelle

Museum of Automobiles,
Petit Jean; (501) 727–5427

Tanyard Springs;
(888) TANYARD

Post Familie Winery,
Altus; (501) 468–2741

Wiederkehr Village,
Wiederkehr; (501) 468–2611

Ozark Scenic Railway,
Van Buren; (800) 687–8600

Old Van Buren Inn
Bed and Breakfast,
Van Buren; (501) 474–4202

Now pay a buck (50 cents for children) and climb aboard the restored electrified trolley, the last one to run downtown. The half-mile ride from the **Trolley Museum** at 100 South Fourth Street, Fort Smith 72901, to the national cemetery is accompanied by the clanging of the trolley bell as the worn brick buildings slide past. When the ride ends at the **Fort Smith National Historic Site,** at Third Street and Rogers Avenue, the driver walks down the aisle, flipping the seats over for the return trip—the car can't turn around, so the seats do. The museum includes three gasoline locomotives and other railroad memorabilia. The museum is open 10:00 A.M. to 5:00 P.M. Monday through Saturday and 1:00 to 5:00 P.M. on Sunday. From November through May the museum is only open on weekends—Saturday from 10:00 A.M. to 5:00 P.M. and Sunday 1:00 to 5:00 P.M. Call (501) 783–1237 for information.

Then you can experience something a little less modern than the old trolley; you can hitch a ride with Bud and Kate, two noble mules pulling a covered wagon down the street. The thirty-minute ride leaves the historic site from 10:00 A.M. to 5:00 P.M. Tuesday through Saturday. Call **Three "B" Carriage Tours,** (501) 667–3951 or 667–5857, for more information about excursions.

Trivia

Mount Magazine was named by French hunters. Magazin means "store-house."

Another option for touring the historic district is the **Fort Smith Trolley Bus,** which is air-conditioned in the summer and heated in the winter. Starting at 9:30 A.M. Monday through Saturday, the trolley bus departs the Fort Smith Visitor Center at North B Street and Clayton Expressway for a forty-five-minute tour of the historic sites that include Judge Parker's Court, the national cemetery and one of Belle Starr's past residences. The ride costs $1.00 and departs every hour until 4:30 P.M. March through December. The trolley bus is operated by the Fort Smith Transit Department and can be rented for large group events as well. Call (501) 783–8888 or 783–6464.

Admission to the historic site is $2.00 for adults (kids get in free), and it is open from 9:00 A.M. until 5:00 P.M. daily. Call (501) 783–3961 for information.

Looking for a B&B? Then go up the hill and into the driveway of **Beland Manor Inn,** at 1320 South Albert Pike, Fort Smith 72903, and fall in love with the Colonial manor wrapped in a porch. The winding open staircase leads to suites with such amenities as a Jacuzzi for two and four fireplaces. Innkeepers Mike and Suzy Smith almost always have something baking, so the scent of bread or chocolate will wake you in the morning. Down the hall from the suites, the refrigerator in the great room is stocked with beverages and ice, and the sofa invites you to stretch out. Big pine rockers give you a peaceful spot from which to enjoy the view from high up in the trees. Dinner is an experience in elegance: candlelight, soft music, fine china, and a table for two. Every-thing is made from scratch—pasta, continental cuisine complete with salad, French bread, and a very indulgent dessert. You can imagine what breakfast is like in the sunny blue dining room, or have it served in your room. In fact, Sunday breakfast features dessert! Suites are $75 and $165. One is on the first floor if stairs are a problem. Call (800) 334–5052 or (501) 782–3300 for information and reservations or check the Web site at www.fort-smith.net.

The **Fort Smith Art Center,** situated in the 1855 pink brick, Victorian Second Empire Vaughn-Schaap home at 423 North Sixth Street, Fort Smith 72901, was the first building restored in the Belle Grove Historic District. It displays the work of artists from around the world as well as area artists and hosts numerous art competitions throughout the year. But the home is worth a visit for itself alone. It contains a bathtub in which an entire Brownie troop, twenty-nine girls, once stood. Admission is free. Hours are from 9:30 A.M. to 4:30 P.M. Tuesday through Saturday and from 1:00 to 4:00 P.M. Sunday. Call (501) 784–ARTS.

The *Clayton House,* at 514 North Sixth Street, Fort Smith 72901, in the district, is an example of Classic Revival Victorian architecture from 1882. It has been restored and refurbished in period furnishings and contains original belongings. Hours are Wednesday through Saturday from noon until 4:00 P.M. and Sunday from 1:00 to 4:00 P.M. Admission is $2.00; call (501) 783–3000 for information.

Many of the volunteers at the Clayton House also volunteer at **The Darby House,** 311 General Darby Street, Fort Smith 72901. This was the boyhood home of William O. Darby who grew up to be a military general and leader of the U.S. Army Rangers in World War II. Darby was killed in action in northern Italy just two days before the armistice was signed. His home is decorated in that time period and is filled with great history of the Army Rangers and the European theater of World War II. The house is open Monday through Friday from 8:00 A.M. to 1:00 P.M. Call (501) 782–3388 for more information.

The National Register of Historic Places lists *Michael's Mansion,* located at 2900 Rogers Avenue, Fort Smith 72901. This Neo-Classical home was built in 1904 and was once a bed-and-breakfast inn. Owner Lynette Moore now opens her home for weddings and public tours. Call (501) 494–3700.

Ed Walker's Drive-In is certainly not fancy—you would probably drive right by. But it probably has the only curbside beer service in the state (maybe in the country) to go with its famous French dip or huge hamburger steak, which is smothered in onions and oozing brown gravy. Remember to flash your lights for curbside service, or go inside to enjoy the racecar memorabilia on the walls. You can drive in from 10:00 A.M. until 9:00 P.M. Monday through Wednesday and from 10:00 A.M. until 10:00 P.M. Thursday, Friday, and Saturday. You'll find the eatery at 1500 Towson, Fort Smith 72901 (501–783–3352).

Altus Grape Festival, Altus; last Friday night and Saturday in July; (501) 468–4684

Great Arkansas Pig Out, Morrilton; first weekend in August; (501) 354–2393

Old Timers Day, Van Buren; first weekend in May; (501) 474–2761, (800) 332–5889

Butterfly Festival, Mt. Magazine; last weekend in June; (801) 963–2244; www.butterflyfestival.com

Fall Festival, Van Buren; first weekend in October, 9:00 A.M.–6:00 P.M.; (501) 474–2761, (800) 332–5889

Annual Mount Magazine Frontier Day, Paris; first weekend in October; (501) 963–2244; Web site: www.paris-ar.com; admission free

Annual Native American Festival, Fort Smith; third weekend in September; (501) 784–2787; admission $1.00 (ages 12 and under free)

Trivia

Fort Chaffee Military Reservation, south of Fort Smith, is famous among rock and roll trivia fans. It was here on March 25, 1958, that Elvis Presley was inducted into the U.S. Army and received a G.I. haircut. The photo of that event is one of the most requested from military archives. Four days later, Elvis shipped out to Fort Hood, Texas, where he spent the majority of his military career.

Fort Chaffee continued to make international news in the 1970s when it became home to more than 25,000 Vietnamese refugees, many whom have now made their homes and businesses in the area. In the 1980s, Cuban refugees from the Mariel Boat Lift were housed temporarily at Fort Chaffee. The post has been deeply scaled back by the U.S. Army, but for more than seventy-five years, held a significant role in the history of western Arkansas and the United States.

Miss Laura's was once a bawdy Front Street "social club."

Well, it was a brothel, to be truthful.

Actually, Miss Laura Zeigler ran the best whorehouse in town, they say.

Now the historic building (you bet it's historic—if walls could talk!) is the Fort Smith Visitors Center, where volunteers will show you around the upstairs bedrooms furnished as they were in their heyday. You can buy a T-shirt in the gift shop telling the world that you visited a, um, social club in Fort Smith. It is the only (former) bordello on the National Register of Historic Places and is open Monday through Saturday from 9:00 A.M. to 4:00 P.M. and from 12:30 to 4:30 P.M. on Sunday. Just follow B Street clear down and across to the wrong side of the railroad tracks to the river park. You can hear the lonesome whistle as the trains pass the colorful house, which sits alone by the river at North B Street and the Clayton Expressway. Call (501) 783–8888 for information. A Web site will show you everything in town: www.fortsmith.org.

Taliano's, at 201 North Fourteenth Street, Fort Smith 72901, was born when Tom Caldarera and Jim Cadelli, childhood friends, wanted to start a restaurant. Across the street from Caldarera's home stood an old building, the Sparks Mansion, built in 1887, that Caldarera had made into apartments. The mansion, shaded by grand old magnolia trees, has been reborn. The chandeliers, the stained glass, the hand-carved wooden dividers, and the rest of its original Renaissance Revival beauty were restored, and it has since been placed on the National Register of Historic Places. Now the two men, whose families were from northern Italy (Jim's) and Sicily (Tom's), serve handmade pastas and sauces that reflect those heritages.

There are five dining rooms on the first floor. The original brass chandeliers have been converted to electricity, and the marble fireplaces were imported from Carrara, Italy. A white stone porch surrounding

Miss Laura's "Social Club"

one side has been glassed in, and there white wrought-iron tables and chairs also seat guests. For a quarter of a century Caldarera and Cadelli have done all the cooking, at first with the help of their Italian parents, and the recipes are still the same family favorites. The pastas are all homemade, as are the sauces, of course. Even the sausages are specially made. Prices range from $10.95 for the delicious Giardinara pasta, made with mushrooms and peppers, olive oil, and Parmesan cheese, to $22.50 for veal dishes, but everyone's favorite is Jim's lasagna. Taliano's is open for lunch Tuesday through Friday from 11:00 A.M. until 1:30 P.M. and for dinner Monday through Saturday from 5:30 to 9:45 P.M. They also have an all-you-can-eat brunch on Sundays from 10:30 A.M. to 1:30 P.M. Call (501) 785–2292 for reservations.

Drive along Highway 22 from Fort Smith. The highway parallels I–40 along the south banks of the Arkansas River. The river valley has mountains sloping up on both sides, creating rich bottomland for small farms along the roadway, where horses graze in the pastures.

Cowie Winery Cellars, at 101 Carbon City Road, is east of Fort Smith on Highway 22 in Paris 72855. The stone and cedar building is owned by Bob and Betty Cowie. A great-great-uncle of the Cowie family came from Switzerland to Altus, where he spent his life propagating new varieties of grapes—nine of them, to be exact. Today's bottles of Cowie wine have artist labels—pen-and-ink sketches of a ridge scene near the winery—and an annual series with limited edition prints is available.

Robert Cowie is the artist of the Arkansas wine industry, and the wines produced here reflect his art tempered with science. Old-world traditions and modern wine-making skills combine to produce some of the best wines in Arkansas. Tour the winery and enjoy a complimentary wine tasting. A good time to visit is during the Arkansas Wine Competition held the last Saturday in April. The winery is open Monday through Saturday 10:00 A.M. to 6:00 P.M. and Sunday noon to 6:00 P.M. For further information or to place an order, call (501) 963–3990 or visit the Web page at www.cowiewinecellars.com.

The *Arkansas Historic Wine Museum,* located adjacent to the winery, is the first museum in the nation devoted to the wine history of an entire state. It displays the area's finest collection of wine-making equipment, artifacts, and documents from the nineteenth century. A special collection highlights the life and works of Professor Joseph Bachman, an internationally known developer of grapes in the early years of the twentieth century. The museum exists to preserve the state's ethnic and wine-making traditions that led to the federal bonding of 147 wineries in Arkansas since the end of Prohibition. All but a few of these are no longer in operation. The museum is open Monday through Saturday 10:00 A.M. to 6:00 P.M. and Sunday noon to 6:00 P.M.

Trivia

*M*ount Magazine is home to 80 species of the 127 known species of butterflies in the world. One, the Diana Fritillary butterfly, is unique to Mount Magazine. It is simply beautiful and entomologists travel here to see the richly colored creatures. The male is a deep shade of rust and black, while the female is several shades of blue with black markings.

National Geographic *published an article about the butterflies of Mount Magazine in 1997, and the Logal County Chamber of Commerce had the first annual Butterfly Festival in August of that year. The festival is now held during the second week of June. For more information see the Web sites at www.Paris-AR.com and www.butterflyfestival.com.*

The newest addition to the Cowie winery is the **Winery Bed and Breakfast,** a romantic hideaway for two. It has a private entrance, a nice balcony view, and is quiet and secluded. A complimentary wine and snack basket awaits you when you arrive. The suite has a double Jacuzzi, and a continental breakfast is served in the morning. The suite is $75 a night. For reservations call (501) 963–3990.

Vineyards begin to appear along the roads outside of Paris. The scenery is *très bien,* as peaceful as a day in France, and there's even an old monastery looking down from a hill. This is wine country, and wine country is the same all over the world, *n'est-ce pas?* Rolling east on Highway 22 is like a drive in the Provence region of France, with low stone walls curving beside the road.

Paris is the gateway to Mount Magazine in the Ozark National Forest, the highest point between the Rockies and the Appalachian Mountains. Hang gliders and rock climbers practice their daring sports on these great sandstone bluffs watched over by an Ozark National Forest ranger station. Dramatically rising 2,750 feet above the view—which is, of course, spectacular—the mountain lures scientists, naturalists, and explorers. Like the rest of the Ozark Mountains, this was once the vast floor of an ancient sea and is home to several rare and endangered trees, including the Ozark chinquapin, the maple-leaved oak tree (not found anywhere else), and the yellowwood tree noted for the large, impressive clusters of flowers that hang from its branches in the springtime. Unlike the lush northern rim, the southern rim is dry and home to species of cacti and stunted and twisted oaks 200 years old and less than 50 feet tall.

Highway 309 leads to the top of Mount Magazine and connects with Scenic Highway 10. Blue Mountain Lake is hidden in the mountains between the Ozark and Ouachita National Forests, just off Highway 10 west of Danville and is a great spot for fishing and swimming.

The area along the Arkansas River was settled by German Catholics, who were reminded of their homeland and had brought along wine-making skills when they immigrated. Vineyards have prospered and produce some fine wines, using both imported and native grapes. A restored jail in Paris houses a small museum that depicts more of the region's history.

The first stop in Paris should be **The Grapevine Restaurant,** owned by Kenneth and Lisa Vines, a husband-and-wife team cooking great food there on Highway 22. Smoked meats, fresh-baked bread and cinnamon rolls, and sinfully delicious desserts join healthy fresh vegetables. Handwritten menus announce the daily specials. Lisa seems to know everyone in town and can direct you to the wineries and other interesting places to visit. The restaurant is open from 6:00 A.M. to 8:00 P.M. Monday through Thursday and until 9:00 P.M. on Friday and Saturday. The Grapevine is at 105 East Walnut, Paris 72855; call (501) 963–2413 for information.

Three clothing shops and a shoe store make it easy to buy Paris fashions in the shopping area downtown on the square. You can also send postcards from Paris to impress your friends. Tell them you are about to enter wine country—they'll be green with envy.

Then seek forgiveness for the little white lie at the graceful *Subiaco Abbey* in the tiny town of *Subiaco,* 3 miles east of Paris on Highway 22. The stone and red-tile-roof abbey is a Benedictine academy built in 1878 and is the only monastery in the state. It was built by the monks of locally quarried sandstone. Fifty-two tons of German, Italian, and Spanish marble and stunning stained glass imported from Europe accent the fine rockwork. The massive dome over the altar is supported by 20-foot white marble columns with a canopy made of balsam wood covered in gold leaf. From the canopy hangs a huge crucifix of carved wood with silver overlay. The abbey rises dramatically from the farmlands surrounding it, and the seventy monks welcome visitors to tour the church and courtyard and see the museum of local history. The abbey church has more than 175 stained-glass windows. The Coury House at the abbey offers guests a retreat wherein you can take time to meditate and relax without the distraction of even a telephone. The abbey's reputation isn't just built on its academic record, beautiful location, or spiritual life. It is also the perfect place to find peanut brittle. What began as a fund-raiser has become a best-selling regular industry. The delicious recipe was given to the abbey by a kitchen staff member's mother. Made by the monks and staff in the kitchen's big cast-iron skillets, the brittle costs $12.95 for a two-pound can. Rooms are $40 and up with private baths; meals in the guest dining hall are available for $6.00. The academy is a boys' prep school for grades nine through twelve. According to Brother Mel, a monk at the academy and director of Coury House, there are also organized retreats: marriage encounters and prayer retreats with monks or different denominational groups who use the facility throughout the year. The monks' Mass is at 6:30 every morning and open to the public; Mass on Saturday night is at 7:30, and Sunday Mass is at 10:45 A.M. Call Jean Rockenhaus, the Coury House secretary, at (501) 934–4411 for a schedule of retreats or for room reservations or visit www.subi.org.

Scenic Highway 22 runs along the river connecting Paris and Dard-anelle and is a beautiful side trip to get you off the freeway and into the countryside. It cuts across some of the coves of Lake Dardanelle and through the Ouachita National Forest.

Dardanelle is a historic old river town on the banks of the Arkansas River and Lake Dardanelle at the crossroads of Scenic Highways 7 and 22. Steamboat passengers landed at Dardanelle a century ago. The road climbing Mount Nebo's steep slopes was narrow, with hairpin turns, but the scenery and cool breezes made the trip worth the effort. Arkansas summers can be hot, and this was a great escape. It still is. The town sits at the hub of three state parks.

Mount Nebo State Park, on Highway 155 South, up gorgeous Mount Nebo, is a fine spot to get the feel of the Arkansas wilderness. This is the state's highest state park, with panoramic views of the valley. Ten rustic cabins dating from the Civilian Conservation Corps era, as well as five modern A-frames, are scattered around the top of the mountain above the Arkansas River Valley. Many of the cabins are very secluded and quiet, while others are very, very secluded and quiet. All are fully equipped and have fireplaces. The park is lovely, containing a large lake with the pine forest coming right down to the shoreline. The beautiful lake is spotted with islands and surrounded by softly wooded land. The park commands a terrific view from a plateau 1,800 feet above the river. Cabins rent for $75 to $125. Call (501) 229–3655 or (800) 264–2458 for information.

Lake Dardanelle State Park on Highway 326 allows campers to stake out shoreline sites at the campgrounds. Skiers and sailboats criss-cross the water, while fishermen anchor in coves, casting for bream, crappie, and bass. Record-making monster catfish weighing in excess of forty pounds are caught here under the dam. The oldest state fish-ing record was set in 1964, when someone caught a 215-pound alliga-tor gar on the Arkansas River near Dardanelle (he was using a minnow). The river here has sandy beaches and river access for boats on Highway 22 West. Rent an A-frame with fireplace for $75 to $95. Call (501) 967–5516 for information.

Beyond the city of Dardanelle lies flattopped Petit Jean Mountain near Morrilton. *Petit Jean State Park,* on top of the mountain, has eight rustic cabins and five modern duplexes. These are not as secluded as the ones at Mount Nebo. In fact a couple of them are near the highway, but there's little traffic at night. They rent for $65 for two people. A cabin with a kitchen rents for $85; the one with a hot tub for $150 with a two-night minimum. *Mather Lodge,* inside the park, has twenty-four rooms and a restaurant. This was Arkansas's first state park and still perhaps the best. Breakfast in the Mather Lodge is made even better by the Petit Jean ham and the panoramic view of the Arkansas River Valley. The cozy lodge, built in the 1930s by the Civilian Conservation Corps., is poised on the rim of Cedar Creek Canyon, and hiking paths weave more than 24 miles throughout the park. Call (800) 264–2462 or (501) 727–5441 for information. Rooms in the lodge are $50 with a queen- or king-size bed, or $55 with two double beds (slightly less in January and February).

Trails lead to the picture-perfect, 95-foot-high *Cedar Falls* within Cedar Creek Canyon, to delicate sandstone monoliths, and to Rock House Cave, containing ancient pictographs etched into stone by early inhabitants of the area. The falls are spectacular and worth the trip to see. The best time to photograph them is in late afternoon when the sun shines directly onto the falls and reflects sunlight in crystal sparkles. (During the morning hours the mighty falls are shaded and dark.) The falls are created by rainwater caught in the saucer-shaped mountaintop.

The park gets its name from the legend of Adrienne DuMont, a French girl who disguised herself as a boy (calling herself Jean) and accompanied her sailor sweetheart to America. She died before the return trip and was buried on the mountain. There is an unmarked grave on the mountain, and the legend begins there.

The *Museum of Automobiles,* on Highway 154 near the eastern edge of Petit Jean Mountain, displays privately owned antique and classic automobiles from collectors throughout the country and abroad. The museum was founded by Governor Winthrop Rockefeller and features some of his personal cars. The 1929 Rolls Royce Phantom I coupe is worth the price of admission, which is $5.00 for adults and $2.50 for children. The Museum of Automobiles is also home to the only car President Bill Clinton ever owned (since he was in public service his whole career, he was provided with transportation). The 1967 six-cylinder, light blue Mustang convertible waits there for him to return to Arkansas. The place is in a constant state of change, so you can visit it again and again if you are an auto buff. About twenty cars are in the permanent exhibit, but another forty or so change throughout the year. There are memories here in chrome and leather, as well as cars you've only heard about. Several Harley-Davidsons from 1913 to 1946 are in the motorcycle section. The facility is open year-round from 10:00 A.M. to 5:00 P.M. and

Cedar Falls

has a gift shop on the premises. The museum is situated 15 miles southwest of Morrilton via Highways 9 and 154. Call (501) 727–5427 for information.

Tanyard Springs, at 144 Tanyard Springs Road, Morrilton 72110, on Highway 154 on the west edge of Petit Jean Mountain, calls itself "The Un-Resort" and lives up to that billing with thirteen rustic-looking but handcrafted cottages, each different and each designed to fit the setting. None of the natural beauty of the area has been changed; the cottages are tucked into the woods near a stream or a pond. Big porches with swings and rocking chairs allow the sounds of the woods to penetrate even the most stressed-out soul. Each cottage is perfectly reproduced in incredible detail, with wood-carvings, handcrafted antique furnishings, and accessories to ensure historical accuracy. Each is also decorated around a theme. The most unusual, Stagecoach Cottage, has a full-size Butterfield stagecoach as a bed in the loft (the kids will love it). The kids will also get a kick out of the Woodsmen, where they climb a ladder to

Tanyard Springs Memory

The Arkansas River wound below. My husband and I sat on the edge of a cliff early in the morning enjoying the crisp air and warm sunshine. I know others have enjoyed this vantage point—perhaps Native Americans looking for campfire smoke in the distance or the French explorers who also wandered here.

Except for the electricity, the cabin we walked from on this particular morning was reminiscent of those built in the early 1800s. The thirteen cabins in the Tanyard Springs compound are scattered around the historic springs named for the tanning pits that used to be on the site. Forty acres of trees and the magnificent Cedar Falls are tucked into the nearby 8,500 acres of pine-oak woodlands of Petit Jean Mountain State Park. A 1½-mile trail loops among the cabins, and 20 miles of serious hiking trails interconnect in the park.

It was early winter, off-season at the resort, but for us it was the best possible time. We flew into the area in our Navion airplane, a huge beast of a plane—single engine, slide-back canopy—and landed at the airstrip here, which even though it is a daylight-only strip is more than a mile long. We stepped out of the cockpit and onto the wing of the plane and felt the cool breeze on our faces. We had come in just ahead of a rain shower.

Winter was always our favorite time in the Ozarks. We lived on the Missouri side. The quiet is intense, and the occasional call of a hawk or crow is clear and sharp. This was going to be a beautiful weekend.

Our cottage was the most romantic one in the compound, the Adrienne DuMont. When we arrived, a Crock Pot of beans and a chilled bottle of muscadine grape juice, locally bottled, waited for us. You can't call these cottages "cabins." Ours had a queen-size bed and a walnut headboard with a hand-carved lover's knot. Even with no telephone or television, we found enough to do to pass a very pleasant afternoon listening to the sound of the rain dripping among the dry oak leaves.

That night we had reservations at the splendid restaurant on the grounds, where we were offered a menu of continental specialties and a good wine list. It is sad that the restaurant is no longer there. The other option was to eat at Mather Lodge in the park, which is a mile-long, easy hike away. The next morning we awoke to find a breakfast of croissant, fruit, and orange juice waiting on the steps. Hidden inside the rustic kitchen were a microwave and coffeepot. The romantic feeling of stepping back in time was not at all lessened by not having to split wood—there was a neat stack by the front door. We poured a cup of hot coffee to warm our hands and built up the fire to take the chill from the room. My husband was from Michigan and firmly believed that sleeping with the windows open was the only healthy thing to do. That night we cooked steaks on a grill. The last day we had breakfast at Mather Lodge and enjoyed the spectacular view from the bluff over the canyon as much as the famous Petit Jean ham and eggs. This is, without a doubt, the most romantic and beautiful memory I have of Arkansas. It is not surprising that reservations are made a year in advance for summertime at Tanyard Springs.

their loft room. But these are more than just rustic cabins (that's why they're carefully referred to as "cottages," not cabins), as the price will tell you right away. Rates at Tanyard Springs are $150 Sunday through Thursday and $175 Friday and Saturday during the season. From December 1 through February 28, they are $125 and $150. Each cottage features an interior as comfortable as any fine city hotel's, with cleverly hidden appliances and large, comfortable beds. Food is brought to you, and each cottage has a complete kitchen and an outdoor grill. The food kits are already assembled for you to cook and eat in your cottage; you can order a breakfast kit, steak cookout kit, or hamburger cookout kit before you arrive or when you check in.

The resort is not a mom-and-pop operation, obviously; it is owned by Winthrop Paul Rockefeller, son of the late governor, and the cottages are all carefully tucked behind a security gate. A conference center is available for weddings or large family gatherings. Sometimes getting off the beaten path costs a little more—in this case it's worth it. It is about an hour northwest of Little Rock. From I–40 take exit 108. Go south about 10 miles on Highway 9 and turn right onto Highway 154 in Oppelo. At the top of Petit Jean Mountain, stay on Highway 154. The gated entrance is about 9 miles on the left. Call toll free (888) TANYARD or (501) 727–5200 for reservations.

South of Petit Jean Mountain on Highway 9 and about 40 miles west of Little Rock off Highway 10, the unique walking trail among the wildflowers at the *Heifer Project International Learning and Livestock Center* gives you a chance to learn how sunlight can be harnessed, bricks made of earth, and weeds thatched for roofing; how livestock can be raised in poor areas of the world; and how poor soil can be made to produce food. A longer hike along the wooded hillside will show sites where horses pull plows. The Guatemala Hillside, a farmhouse on two and a half steep, eroded acres, has blossomed into a farm with five species of livestock, ten tree crops, and more than fifteen annual crops and vegetables. Water harvesting and biogas fuel are a few of the innovative processes. The 1,225-acre ranch includes some Katahdin hair sheep. There are hands-on teaching units of swine to be slopped, goats to be milked, and poultry, rabbits, and bees to be tended. Informal visits can be made anytime, and a guided tour of the small-farm project can be arranged. A working visit, internship, or volunteer experience can also be arranged by calling the trail coordinator at (501) 889–5124. Signs will lead you to the center from Highway 10. The gift shop is open during the week from 8:00 A.M. to 5:00 P.M. and from 9:00 A.M. to 5:00 P.M. on Saturday.

North Bank Wine Country

ross to the north side of the Arkansas River at Morrilton and head back west on Highway 64, which parallels I–40. You will be following the same route the Butterfield Overland Stage followed. There's an old stagecoach at Ninth and College Streets in *Pottsville,* one of many that used to be headed for *Potts Tavern,* now a museum downtown. The beautifully restored antebellum house was a stagecoach stop and tavern on the Butterfield Overland Stage route. But there's more, if sombreros are your fetish: It is also one of the only two hat museums in the country. Five log cabins have been moved onto the property—one is the caretaker's home.

One of the cabins shows off a collection of about seventy-five dolls, all dressed in the inaugural gowns of all of Arkansas's First Ladies and the First Ladies of the United States. Hours at the Potts Inn museum complex are Wednesday through Saturday from 1:00 P.M. to 5:00 P.M. Admission is $3.00 for adults and $1.00 for children. Call (501) 968–8369.

Right across the street the *Pottsville Grocery Store,* at Second and Ash Streets, is more an old-fashioned general store, with groceries, hardware, plumbing supplies, and gifts. Aliene Morton owns it, and she says she "kinda takes care of people when no one's at the museum across the street." You can pick up all the supplies you need at Aliene's and garner any information about the area from her. You can usually find her and a few other folks watching television in the front of the store. Hours are from 7:00 A.M. to 6:00 P.M. (sometimes later) Monday through Saturday; 9:00 A.M. to 5:00 P.M. on Sunday. Call (501) 968–6703.

Russellville, on Highway 64, is small-town friendly, maybe because it's a college town, home of Arkansas Tech University.

River Valley Arts Center, at B and Knoxville Streets (1001 East B Street, Russellville 72801) in a natural stone building built by the Civilian Conservation Corps in the 1930s, is a former swimming pool and bathhouse that is now a gallery and more. There are two galleries, actually: the Artists' Gallery, which displays the work of ten or twelve local artists every month; and the Main Gallery, which features one-person shows of well-known artists, such as Ansel Adams or Leonard Baskin, Works Progress Administration artists of the 1930s whose work changed art in America. The gallery displays work from every medium—two- and three-dimensional art, weaving, sculpture, and photography. But there is more: Truly a center for the arts in the area, it has a community theater, a band, and a chamber chorus. There are educational arts programs, as well as the only pottery program in the state that is staffed year-round, for both children and adults. Associations like the River Valley Writers' Club, a songwriters' group, and an artists' support group meet here. The center is open Monday through Thursday from 10:00 A.M. to 5:00 P.M. and Friday until 4:00 P.M. Call (501) 968–2452 for information. Their Web site, which lists a calendar of events, is www.ohwy.com/ar/a/arrivavc.htm.

Ready for a sandwich? *Stoby's* is a one-of-a-kind place—a 1941 Rock Island dining car parked at a red brick and stucco depot, a replica of the real thing across the way. It's open for breakfast, lunch, and dinner with a menu that is both ordinary and extraordinary. They've received numerous awards for their meals from the statewide newspaper, the *Arkansas Times*. Take the Stoby's sandwich, for example. The number of meats, cheeses, breads, and toppings totals 3,000 possible combinations, according to the computer. Besides the full breakfast menu, there are homemade pies and cakes, since Stoby's opens at 6:00 A.M. and closes at 10:00 P.M. every day except Sunday. *Casual* is the key word here. The place offers an unusual combination of familiar things. It's just the right combination of quick food and full service, with prices in the very comfortable zone. You'll find Stoby's 2 miles south of I–40 on Highway 7, at 405 West D Street, Russellville 72801. Call (501) 968–3816 for information.

Would you like a taste of Arkansas, even if you can't make it to the Natural State for a while? The *Arkansas Pork Producers Association,* located in Russellville and representing about 600 farmers in the state, raises money for scholarships and environmental efforts by selling Arkansas hams and pork gift packages to people coast to coast. A factory in Pennsylvania orders more than 400 hams each year to give to employees for a holiday bonus. You just might get one under your tree this year. Call the association at (501) 967–3911 or order from their Web site at www.arpork.org.

Everybody's favorite restaurant seems to be the *Old South Restaurant* at 1330 East Main Street (East Highway 64). This mom-and-pop place has been here in this building forever, and although the building has been renovated, it is still the same wonderful building it was when it was built in 1946. Owners Mary and Jim Austin are proud of the diner, and their Old South cooking is in a league all its own: fried chicken and all the trimmin's and the famous Old South salad dressing. They even cut their own steaks and clean their own shrimp. You can eat there just about any time because it opens at 6:00 A.M. and doesn't close until 10:00 P.M. seven days a week. Call (501) 968–3789.

Jimmy Lile's Handmade Knives is 2 miles south of Russellville on Highway 7 South at 2721 South Arkansas Avenue. Before his recent death, Jimmy Lile was considered one of the top five custom knife makers in the world. Lile was the designer and maker of the knives used in the Rambo movies, and this shop and showroom are filled with examples of his craft. Four presidents, the king of Sweden, and many people in the entertainment industry own his knives. The knives are recognized worldwide and are still being handcrafted by skilled workers trained by Lile. Jackie Weir runs the business of making all manner of knives—folders, hunting knives of all kinds with 4- to 6-inch blades, and both drop-point and upswept blades. She personally oversees production. According to the people in the shop, she considers herself "inspector number twelve—it's not finished till she says so." Hours are from 9:00 A.M. to 4:30 P.M. Monday through Saturday. Call (501) 968–2011 for information and check out www.lileknives.com.

Big Piney Creek, near Russellville, is a small stream flowing from the wilderness of the Ozark National Forest to the Arkansas River. Canoes and white-water rafts float on gentle tributaries like Big Piney and the Illinois Bayou. You can take a trip down Big Piney, winding along spectacular granite bluffs from Fallsville through the mountains and into Lake Dardanelle. Short afternoon floats or several-day trips can also be arranged. Although the Big Piney's 67-mile route has Class II and Class III rapids—the first, Split Decision, to the grand finale, Haystacker Rapid—it can be enjoyed by both the beginner and the experienced white-water paddler (areas containing Class III rapids need white-water experience).

The Big Piney Creek outpost at ***Moore Outdoors*** is 10 miles north of Dover on Highway 164 West and Long Pool Road. Kerry and Debbie Moore have canoes, rafts, wet suits, helmets, throw lines, dry bags, and other white-water accessories (for experienced people), as well as camping equipment and kayak lessons; the Moores will also shuttle hikers to the Ozark Highland Trail by the Ozone or Richmond campground. The creek is at its finest from March through May and, in wet years, sometimes as late as Thanksgiving. Moore Outdoors is open from 8:30 A.M. to 6:00 P.M. seven days a week in season. Call (501) 331–3606 for information or check out their Web site, www.mooreoutdoors.com.

Looking for a great collection of handmade quilts? Head up Scenic Highway 7 to just south of the little town of **Pelsor.** There you will find **Nellie's Gift Shop** and more than one hundred quilts made by Nellie Dotson and her friends in area quilting guilds. She also carries handmade oak and cedar chests, to store your quilts or other valuables, and a myriad of ceramics and other collectibles. Nellie lives right behind the shop and says she's open just about seven days a week or any other day you stop by. Her phone number is (870) 294–5317.

Also along Highway 7 are two shops that specialize in handmade split oak baskets, and the owners are related to each other, so if you can't find what you want in one store, they'll be glad to call to the other one to see what's available there. The shops are **The Triple O** (870) 294–5290 and **The Treasure Chest** (870) 428–5282.

Back south along Highway 64 and Highway 103, you'll find **Whitetail World,** a deer hunter's paradise. Dayne Phillips and his wife, Kanna Lou, run the 10,000-square-foot show room that displays more than seventy-five of the world's most magnificent bucks, including the top ten bow-kills in the world. Dayne is a big hunter and will talk to you about some of the best places in Arkansas to hunt for big buck, but he also appreciates fine art that includes wildlife. Their gift shop includes ceramics, photography, weaving, and other art that incorporates the Phillips' passion for the outdoors. Whitetail World is open 9:00 A.M. to 5:00 P.M. Monday through Saturday. Call (501) 754–8620.

Looking for a remote spot in the mountains near the Mulberry River, one of the state's premiere white-water streams? Well, this may be the place for you. It was for James and Sandy Wright. A couple of years ago they bought fifty-three acres 8 miles from the nearest highway and 5 miles from their home. On that property stood an old house. They decided to renovate it, and as they began to peel off old wallpaper, they discovered layers of newspapers with dates showing the house to be at least one hundred years old. As they continued to gut the house, they found a layer of boards, and under the boards was the original log structure, a double-pin log cabin with a dogtrot. It turned out to be one of the first homesteads built in this valley in the late 1800s. Now the cabin has been completely renovated and has become **Lizard Springs**

Lodging on the Mulberry. The original hand-hewn timbers still show in one of the rooms, as they did a century ago. The dining room table, which sits over an old well in the west part of the cabin, has a glass top. With a flashlight you can see the bottom. There is an old root cellar on the property. The cabin is available to canoeists ready to float the Mulberry, which is just a stone's throw from the front porch—you can hear the rush of water as you fall asleep at night. It is surrounded by woods with trails for hiking and mountain bikes. Ask the Wrights about the trail behind the house. It will lead you to the graves of two Civil War deserters who hid out in these hills. They were killed by locals who accused them of raiding and looting the area. The Ozark Highland Trail is within hiking distance, about a quarter of a mile as the crow flies. Two bedrooms are available in the cabin. Located on either side of the dogtrot, each has two double beds and a fold-out bed. Sandy provides a continental breakfast your first morning. "We are not exactly a bed-and-breakfast," James says with a laugh, "just a bed, and bring your own breakfast." This BYOB arrangement is fine with hikers and canoeists looking for a wooded hideaway. There are certainly no restaurants around here, and the nearest store is at Turner Bend, 10 miles away. To get to Lizard Springs, take Highway 103 from Clarksville to Highway 215. After it crosses the Mulberry River, Highway 215 turns west. Go approximately 6 miles, and you will see a sign that says LIZARD SPRINGS. The office is James and Sandy's home, which is 7 miles farther up the road (west) on Highway 215. The price is $75 per two plus $10 for each additional person. Call (501) 667–4398 for reservations. Their Web site is www.lizardsprings.com.

The drive to the cabin is through the beautiful valley, past farms where cattle graze beside the roadway. There's even an old-fashioned country general store down the way a bit for odds and ends you might need. The twisting road curves up the Boston Mountains and tops out near Batson, then starts downhill again to the valley. It's about a forty-minute drive.

The Ozark Highlands Trail, running through the most remote and scenic wilderness in the Ozarks, has several access points nearby. It is a well-marked trail, and you can choose easy and short sections or longer hikes that could take several days.

The center of wine country on the north bank of the Arkansas River lies along Highway 64. *Altus* (which means "altitude") is the highest point between Little Rock and Fort Smith. Swiss and German settlers arrived during the 1880s and blanketed the valley with grapevines. Wineries dot the valley today and continue the tradition. Although not as well known, the 12,000-acre Altus region is a registered wine-producing region like Napa and Sonoma. There are tours and tastings year-round, together with festivals celebrating the harvest and barefoot grape-stomping contests among the families who own the wineries.

Post Familie Winery, 1 block north of Highway 64 on Highway 186, was founded in 1880. Wine-making tours take visitors through the process from grape to cork. The prolific Post family has twelve children, all grown now, and, for the most part, all in the wine business. Paul and Veronica Post manage this winery and Veronica also manages the city of Altus as its mayor. A variety of grapes, both those native to the state and those harder to grow here, are produced in the vineyards. The French cabernet grape is handpicked and lovingly cared for; it is at risk this far east, as a hard winter could destroy the root stock. But so far it is growing well, producing a wine that will surprise even connoisseurs. The Cynthiana grape, with its bright color and distinctive flavor, is, on the other hand, native to the valley. A must-try is muscadine wine, a traditional southern drink.

The winery has a gift shop that carries local crafts, as well as clever handmade gift items like wooden airplanes and trucks designed to be used as wine bottle holders. Quilts, grape leaves brushed with gold and made into earrings and pendants, and even smoked trout make the gift shop and tasting room worth a stop. Hours are from 8:00 A.M. until 6:00 P.M. Monday though Saturday, and from noon until 5:00 P.M. on Sunday. Call (501) 468–2741 for information or go to www.postfamilie.com.

Continuing up the mountain on Highway 186 will bring you to *Wiederkehr Village,* a Swiss Alpine-style village, home of the Wiederkehr Winery. The Weinkeller Restaurant is in the winery's original wine cellar, dug by Johann Andreas Wiederkehr in 1880 and listed on the National Register of Historic Places. A romantic little candlelit spot, it offers German food—the grandfather was from the German-speaking region of Switzerland—such as schnitzel, German fried potatoes, cheese fondues, and wines carefully aged in oak. Hours Monday through Saturday are from 11:00 A.M. to 3:00 P.M. for lunch and from 5:00 to 9:00 P.M. for dinner; Sunday hours are from 11:00 A.M. to 9:00 P.M. Call (501) 468–3551 for restaurant reservations.

Tours of the winery itself leave on the hour and half hour from 9:00 A.M. to 4:30 P.M. Monday through Saturday. The huge winery covers 350 acres and produces 50,000 cases of wine a year. The annual wine festival, held the last weekend in September, is worth a trip, with polka bands and a grape-stomping contest among the winery families of the valley. Call Linda Wiederkehr at (501) 468–2611 for more information.

At the crest of the hill is **St. Mary's Catholic Church,** built by the Germans who fled the Franco-Prussian war. The church is built of local sandstone and trimmed with gold leaf. It has a wonderful old pipe organ. Built in 1901, the church is on the National Register of Historic Places. It's open from 8:00 A.M. to 6:00 P.M. so that visitors can see the famous murals inside, done with local people as models (many folks here recognize great-uncles, -aunts, and grandparents). Call (501) 468–2585 for a tour or service times.

The trip up to Wiederkehr isn't the last of the wineries, though. *Mount Bethel Winery* is ¼ mile east of Altus on Highway 64. Eugene and Peggy Post and their eight grown children are the current owners. It was the original Post Winery but is now an entirely separate winery. The grown children come back to help at harvest time, when 15,000 gallons of wine are made here. Mostly sweet wines and fruit wines like blackberry and wild plum, these screwcap wines make no pretensions to greatness. But the Golden Muscat Port is similar to the Lagrima ports of Portugal, a very light and fruity wine, fortified with brandy to keep in a decanter for slow sipping. Hours are 9:00 A.M. to 7:00 P.M. Monday through Saturday and noon to 5:00 P.M. on Sunday. Call (501) 468–2444 for information. Their Web site is www.mountbethel.com.

Continue west on Highway 64 to the town of *Ozark.* The *1887 Inn Bed & Breakfast,* at 100 East Commercial Street, Ozark 72949, a block off the square, is where innkeepers Kay and DeWayne Jones have a 110-year-old Victorian inn nestled in the foothills of the Ozark Mountains. The inn has four guest rooms, three with private baths. It has been restored to its original beauty but with modern comforts. The Anniversary Room is downstairs and features a fireplace with a gas log. It would be perfect for celebrating any anniversary. Not only is there a four-poster bed, but guests may eat breakfast right in the room. It is also a romantic spot for a candlelight dinner, which the Joneses will provide for only $25 a couple. The room has a private bath with a shower and tub. The parlor and dining room are available for guests. There are three bedrooms upstairs. The Rose Room is done in dark greens and burgundies; the Magnolia Room and the Country Room are filled with beautiful things that give each room personality. Also, there are two bathrooms upstairs. A small television room upstairs has a refrigerator with complimentary cold drinks. The sitting area in the big hallway is always stocked with coffee, tea, and cocoa. The large front porch shares the shade with swaying ferns, and a walkway and ponds give you some-where to stroll. The side patio has a table and a comfortable swing. Breakfast is guaranteed delicious because the Joneses also run a cater-ing business and the cooking is excellent. Homemade muffins, omelettes, waffles, fresh fruit juice, and coffee are served. To find the inn from I–40, take exit 40 to the stoplight, then turn left, and go two blocks. The upstairs rooms are $50, and the Anniversary Room is $60. Call (501) 667–1121 for reservations.

The Ozark Bridge, which spans the Arkansas River on Highway 23, is listed as one of the sixteen most beautiful long-span bridges in the United States, according to the American Institute of Steel Construc-tion. If you can, be in this area at night. The lights on the bridge reflect-ing into the breadth of the river water at this point make a spectacular photograph or memory.

If you are in Ozark during business hours, stop by the **Bank of Ozark** at 600 Commercial Street, Ozark 72949. The 56-foot long wall behind the tellers' windows is a ten-panel mural telling the history of the area, begin-ning in the 1880s. The mural is made of redwood but was sandblasted with Arkansas river sand. It took thirty months to complete. The folks at the bank welcome tourists all the time and you don't even have to open an account. The bank lobby is open 9:00 A.M. to 4:00 P.M. Monday through Friday and until noon on Saturday. Call them at (501) 667–2181.

If you have time for a side trip, turn north on Highway 282 (it parallels Highway 71) near Van Buren and drive to **Mountainburg.** The route is steep and winding, with sharp turns, and provides glimpses of genuine log cabins—the kind with mud between the logs—hidden in the trees. The housing may not be modern, but folks living in these cabins have the kind of view out the back window that people in other parts of the country pay millions for. There is a spectacular view of Lake Fort Smith, Lake Shepherd Springs, and the river that makes them.

The White Mountain Wildlife Management Area is nearby, and 8 miles north of Mountainburg you will find *Artist Point,* on scenic Saddle Canyon off Highway 71, with an overlook that offers a view of the Boston Mountains that is a photographer's dream. The tiny gift shop there (501–369–2226) has a bit of everything, including homemade jams as well as a historical Indian museum.

On Highway 71 near Mountainburg (Highways 282 and 71 come together there) is the first *Ozark Mountain Smokehouse* to open in the state. This is where Frank Sharp began the enterprise that has expanded into a mail-order business and a string of rustic-appearing restaurants and shops that hide a very modern operation inside. Smoked turkey is the specialty. Frank Sharp and Vickie Teel offer sandwich buffet, where customers make their own sandwiches and pay by the ounce. The smokehouse makes bread, pastries, desserts, and even fruit preserves. Hours are from 9:00 A.M. until 5:30 P.M. Monday through Friday and until 5:00 P.M. on Saturday. The phone number is easy to remember: (800) HAM–SHOP.

The little town of **Alma,** population 2,900, is known as the Spinach Capital of the World. Area farmers produce tons of spinach that is packed by the Popeye Spinach Company. An 8-foot statue of the cartoon character keeps watch over the downtown square and the city's water tower is a huge can of Popeye Spinach. The Saturday morning farmers' market on the downtown square is a good place to purchase, you guessed it, fresh spinach. The market runs from about mid-April to mid-October.

The **Ozark Highlands Trail** begins in Lake Fort Smith State Park, which is deeply nestled in a wooded valley of the Boston Mountains. This trail offers hiking and backpacking through the Ozark National Forest, a 187-mile adventure as challenging as one anywhere else in the country. The scenery along the trail is outstanding, with hundreds of streams and more than 200 waterfalls and pools. Rambling through remote and rugged land, the trail is dotted by access points with parking and passes through eight campgrounds. There are several ways to go: A short day hike up White Rock Mountain will give you a pretty sunset, or begin at Shores Lake and take the 6-mile spur trail up to White Rock and spend the night. Hare Mountain lets you explore the remains of an 1800s homesite via a 6-mile hike from Highway 23 or a 2-mile walk from Hare Mountain Trailhead. One of the most beautiful spots, however, is the Marinoni Scenic Area, where the trail hugs a steep hillside and overlooks a creek. The Hurricane Creek Wilderness Area has deep green pools connected by white water and surrounded by towering bluffs. Swimming in the pools; lying on the large, smooth rocks; playing in waterfalls; going hunting, fishing, and camping—all are there. The *Ozark Highlands Trail Guide*—a 104-page handbook with maps, elevations, and mileage logs; information on scenic spots and campgrounds; a weather guide; and an animal and insect guide—is available through the National Forest Service at (501) 667–2191. The Evans Point Loop, a 6-mile trail circling the lake, is there for those who don't want to go overnight on the trail but still went to see waterfalls and caves. The park has six cabins with fireplaces near a large group lodge. From I–40 take exit 13 at Alma and go 12 miles north on Highway 71 to just north of Mountainburg. Prices are $60 to $75. For cabin reservations call (501) 369–2469 or (800) 264–2435.

Fort Smith and *Van Buren,* founded in 1818, are next-door neighbors. But there is so much to see in Van Buren's beautifully preserved Main Street Historic District that you can just plan to spend a day there. The town was called Steamboat Landing or Phillips Landing and was a stop on the Butterfield Stage Line from St. Louis to California. The name Van Buren was to honor Martin Van Buren, but, interestingly enough, the naming occurred before he was president—he was just a friend of Phillips then. Main Street in Van Buren is a restored delight, bustling with shops and restaurants and some of the best antiques shopping around. It retains its original nineteenth-century charm and has been used as the location for filming such movies as *The Blue and the Gray, Biloxi Blues,* and *Main Street Van Buren.* Stay on Main Street and sample what Van Buren has to offer.

The *Cottage Cafe,* at 810 Main Street, Van Buren 72956, has been a favorite hangout for a long time. It features biscuits and gravy, as well as homemade pies like chocolate peanut butter, pecan, and egg custard. The cozy atmosphere and friendly, down-home feeling make it the logical place to get a sense of the town. People there tend to be local folks and can give you directions to and information about the other places along Main Street. The cafe is right across the street from the Old Frisco Depot. Hours are 6:00 A.M. to 3:00 P.M. Monday through Saturday and 7:00 A.M. to 3:00 P.M. on Sunday. Call (501) 474–9895.

A vintage train excursion on the *Arkansas-Missouri Scenic Railway* takes visitors on day trips from the Old Frisco Depot (1901), at 813 Main Street, to the beauty of the Ozark Mountains. The 70-mile round-trip to Winslow takes three hours. You will pass over three high trestles and then go through a mountain tunnel surrounded by the lush Ozarks. The trip costs $20 during the week and $22 on weekends. An eight-hour trip to Springdale and back costs $33 and $38 respectively. Reservations can be made by calling (800) 687–8600 or (501) 474–2761.

The *King Opera House,* in the historic district at 427 Main Street, Van Buren 72956, is home to the King Opera House Players and, they say, the ghost of a traveling actor who was shot and killed by the father of a young lady about to run away with him sometime in the 1880s. You can pick up a performance schedule (for the opera, not the ghost!) by calling (501) 474–2426.

There's another ghost in town, too. Rumor has it that an "unseen presence" inhabits the second floor of the *Old Van Buren Inn Bed and Breakfast* owned by Jackie Henningsen, a native of California who came here and decided to stay when she saw the Old Crawford Bank Building at 633 Main Street, Van Buren 72956, in the historic district.

Jackie had found the ghost "friendly, so far" and decided to share the apparition with others. So she opened a California-style eatery and made the second story into a bed-and-breakfast. She's done quite a job on the old bank building, renovating it herself with hours of help from family and friends.

The restaurant is open and sunny. The meals are a delight. There's quiche, and great chili, and the homemade desserts—well, as they say

Ghostly!

*J*ackie was in the building alone. It was dusk, and the doors were locked because the restaurant was closed and she had no guests that evening. She decided to use the time to clean. She was bent over a table dusting in the dim light of evening when she looked up into the mirror above the table and saw him. "I screamed and whirled around, but there was no one there, just the empty room. I have never been so frightened," she said. "I turned on every light in the house and was whistling and singing and trying to convince myself that it was just a reflection of something that looked like a man.

"It took me a good fifteen minutes to get up the nerve to look into that mirror again, and when I did, of course, there was nothing there but the double doors of the wardrobe behind me."

But for Jackie it wasn't just a momentary apparition. "I can still see him. Our eyes were locked, and he was staring deep into my eyes. He was clean shaven, about thirty-six years old, blond."

"Jackie," I said, teasing her a bit, "he sounds like a very nice-looking man. Was he well dressed?" Her answer was fast: "He was wearing a white shirt with a high-button starched collar and a black jacket," she said without missing a beat. "I can close my eyes any time of the day or night and see him. He left an indelible impression on my mind."

Jackie can tell other stories that make this one all the more believable. She once had two guests who loved old buildings. She chatted with them in the restaurant one night about the bank. They asked if they could see other rooms, so she took them upstairs and showed them around. When they went into the Green Room, the woman kept talking but the man became silent and stared into a corner of the room. When his wife realized what was happening, she fell silent, too. "They are here, you know," he said to Jackie. "The man and his wife, are in the corner over there." He pointed to an empty corner. "He was the president of this bank. They are lost and confused. They can't move on because things keep changing here."

"The gentleman said he was a psychic or a channel or something," Jackie explained. "I don't know anything about that kind of thing, but he was sure impressed with the place. He said the room was alive—that they lived there and he could see them."

Old Van Buren Inn Bed and Breakfast

on the West Coast, the apple dumpling is "to die for." The desserts are the most incredible edibles you will ever be tempted by. Ask for grandma's bread pudding, made the old-fashioned way. While you are waiting for your lunch, browse *Jackie's Antique and Junk Shop,* which is there in the restaurant. A bit of everything to keep you occupied. The restaurant opens at 11:00 A.M. Wednesday through Saturday and just keeps serving until everyone is full.

There are two rooms available upstairs in the B&B, and each is filled with a soft bed, a rocking chair, and good books. The Victorian furnishings were hand-selected from antiques shops in the South. There are a half bath in the hall and a large sunlight- and plant-filled bathroom with a double tub.

The bed-and-breakfast now has a dayroom with television, games, and books for relaxing after exploring the town. Be sure to ask Jackie about the ghosts who share her home. The rooms are $69 each, or $100 if you want the whole top floor, but the ghost stories are free. Call (501) 474–4202 for reservations.

The *Silent Night Loft Bed & Breakfast* is part of *Christmas & Spice & Everything Nice,* across the street at 614 Main Street, Van Buren 72956. The shop offers a Christmas wonderland year-round. You can find elegant collectible ornaments in this beautiful shop and feel the excitement of the Christmas season in the heat of July. What makes it even more interesting is the bed-and-breakfast in the loft. Two bedrooms in Victorian style and a comfortable lounge welcome guests. The eating area, where a continental breakfast is served, is separated from the lounge by a skylight in the floor where guests can look into the shop below, enjoy the ambience of the Christmas lights, and watch people moving about. It is especially neat at night. Rooms are $63. Call (501) 474–1150 for reservations.

Big Jake's Cattle Company, at 1702 Fayetteville Road, Van Buren 72956, not only has really good steaks of any kind, (they own the meat-processing plant so you know the steaks are right) but pretty good pasta, too. Kids and adults love watching the elevated toy train circle the two-story dining room. Big Jake's is open seven days a week 11:00 A.M. to 9:00 P.M. Call (501) 474–5573.

Artist Ramonia Mitchell's shop, *Visual Enterprise,* at 610 Main Street, Van Buren 72956, is a quiet little gallery featuring Steve Payne's oils, along with much pottery, wood, and other artistic pieces. They've recently started carrying work of more Arkansas artists, such as Stone County Ironworks from Mountain View. It's open from 10:30 A.M. to 4:30 P.M. Monday through Saturday. Call (501) 474–3358 for information.

The *Antique Warehouse Mall,* at 402 Main Street, Van Buren 72956, is the kind of place you can wander around in for hours. Most of the things in the front of the shop are imported from England, Ireland, and Scotland. Two huge back rooms are filled with hundreds of stained-glass windows. The operation is the largest importer in the Ozarks. Hours are

Monday through Saturday from 9:00 A.M. to 5:00 P.M. and on Sunday from noon to 5:00 P.M. Call (501) 474–4808 for information or see some of their goodies on their Web site at www.antiquewarehouse.com.

After checking out all the shops on Main Street and the rest of the historic district, walk down toward the river, across the tracks, to the wall that protects the town from the Arkansas River. There, overlooking the river, is a park where you can relax and enjoy the soothing sounds of the river. But while you are contemplating the river, turn around and look at the back side of the wall, and you will see a mural depicting the history of Van Buren, painted by local high school students.

Park Place,
in the Civic Center, 72901;
(501) 783–1000

MORE PLACES TO STAY IN WEST CENTRAL ARKANSAS

MORE PLACES TO EAT WEST CENTRAL ARKANSAS

ARKANSAS RIVER VALLEY
Dardanelle Best Western, Frontier Junction of Highways 7/22/27, 72834; (501) 229–4118

Fort Smith Calico Country Restaurant, 2401 South Fifty-sixth Street, 72901; (501) 452–3299

Fort Smith Holiday Inn, 700 Rogers Avenue, 72901; (501) 783–1000

Thomas Quinn Guest House, 815 B Street North, Fort Smith 72901; (501) 782–0499

NORTH BANK WINE COUNTRY
Russellville Best Western, Highway 7, exit 81, 72801; (501) 967–1000

Van Buren Holiday Inn, 1903 North Sixth Street, 72956; (501) 474–8100

Chambers of Commerce in West Central Arkansas

Arkansas River Valley
Paris Area Chamber of Commerce; *301 West Walnut, 72855; (501) 963–2244, www.paris-ar.com*

Fort Smith Chamber of Commerce; *612 Garrison Avenue, 72901; (501) 783–6118 or (800) 637–1477; www.fortsmith.org*

North Bank Wine Country
Russellville Chamber of Commerce, *708 West Main Street, 72801; (501) 968–2530; www.russellville.dina.org*

Van Buren Chamber of Commerce, *813 Main Street, 72956; (501) 474–2761, (800) 332–5889; www.vanburen.org*

Southwest Arkansas

estern Arkansas's mountains, caves, and rolling hills provide the perfect terrain for those who enjoy rappelling, spelunking, serious hiking, biking, or just general messing around outdoors. The upper Ouachita River is a boulder-strewn stream with plenty of riffles and gravel bars. As the river turns south, it gets slower and deeper and forms three lakes: Ouachita, Hamilton, and Catherine.

The Diamond Lakes region covers five counties and contains five surprisingly uncrowded lakes, as well as the Caddo, Ouachita, and Saline Rivers. Water babies will revel in the lakes, streams, and rivers, loaded with bass and catfish and perfect for fishing, boating, waterskiing, canoeing, rafting, or just wading.

The Cossatot River crashes through here. It is called "Beauty and the Beast" because of its Class V rapids of crystal-clear white water. Definitely not for beginners.

Don't be tempted to take the easy way through the southwest corner of the state on I-30—try some back roads. This dense, piney woodland area is alive with natural attractions and some of the state's most exciting history. The old Southwest Trail passed through here, as did men as famous as Colonel James Bowie, Stephen F. Austin, Davy Crockett, and Sam Houston on their way to Texas.

Hot Springs Area

he mystical qualities of the clear quartz crystal gemstone has intrigued humanity for years—the New Age followers did not invent crystals. Millions of years ago silica-rich fluids and gas here in the southwest part of the state were subjected to high temperatures and fluid pressures. What was created is specimen-quality crystal, also used in electronics. There are only a couple of mines that allow visitors to dig for their own gems. *Coleman Crystal Mine* in *Jessieville* is one of them.

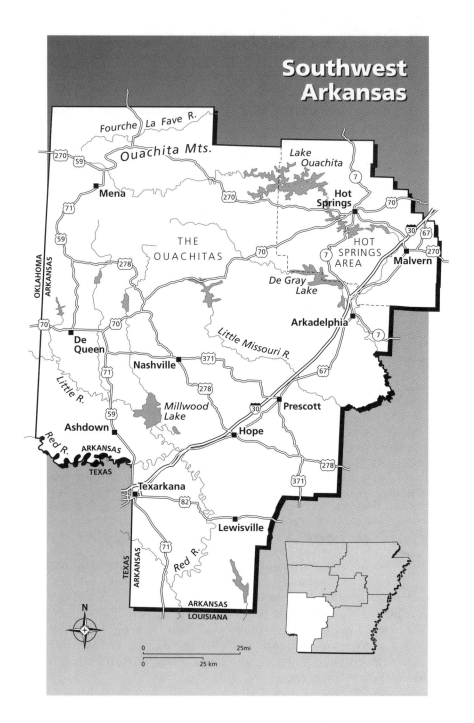

Southwest
Arkansas

SOUTHWEST ARKANSAS

BEST ATTRACTIONS IN
SOUTHWEST ARKANSAS

Herbs Plus, Jessieville;
(501) 984–5740

Mountain Thyme B&B,
Jessieville; (501) 984–5428;
Web site www.
mountainthyme.com

Fox Pass Pottery, near Hot
Springs; (501) 623–9906

*Maxine's International
Coffee House and Puzzle
Bar,* Hot Springs;
(501) 623–0653

Mountain Brook Stables,
near Hot Springs;
(501) 525–8393

The Owl Prowl, DeGray
Lake State Park, Bismark;
(501) 865–2801

Something Special,
Arkadelphia;
(870) 246–7544

*Crater of Diamonds
State Park,* Murfreesboro;
(870) 285–3113

*Beauty and the Beast
Cossatot River State Park,*
Langley; (870) 385–2201

Queen Wilhelmina Lodge,
Rich Mountain State Park;
(501) 394–2863

Ron Coleman, owner of the mine that bears his name, has found hefty chunks of good crystal, some of which he values at $80,000. Only two areas of the world—this one and one in Brazil—have this quality of quartz crystal, according to experts. Arkansas crystal is on display in a Zurich museum. Visitors leave with keepers every day. For a price per pound or set time limit (here it is $20.00 for all day, $5.00 for students, and free for children under six), visitors are handed digging tools and buckets and head off into the red dirt to find treasures—because crystals you find yourself are more powerful than those bought in gem shops, some say. The mines open at 8:00 A.M. seven days a week and close with seasonal hours. Call (501) 984–5396 for information.

At Jim Coleman's *Miller Mountain Crystal Mine,* also in Jessieville, the charge is $10 for all day; kids nine and under get in free. Jim is Ron's brother. Call (501) 984–5328 for information. The other mining area is near Mount Ida, 35 miles west of Hot Springs on Highway 270. The gift shop opens at 8:00 A.M. and closes at dusk, as does the mine.

Highway 7 squiggles through the mountains. Distances are deceiving on the map, so allow plenty of time if you want to get in before dark. Come into the Ouachita Mountains on Scenic Highway 7, and slow down about 3 miles north of Jessieville to watch for the signs leading to *Herbs Plus,* Kathy Seitz's hundred-acre herb farm; the barn-shaped building is not visible from the highway, so watch for signs leading to it or you might miss it. Sachets, herbal vinegar, and plants as well as fresh-cut herbs are for sale. From March through June the shop carries a large variety of live herb plants. This is not a medicinal herb shop; the sweet-smelling spices and herbs are meant for cooking. Herbs Plus also offers cooking classes lasting from about 10:00 A.M. to 2:00 P.M. These classes cost $15 and include enjoying the meal that is cooked. Classes are designed for about ten people and are especially popular now with the trend toward cooking with less salt and fat. Call (501) 984–5740 for a schedule of classes. Hours are Wednesday through Friday 10:00 A.M. to 3:30 P.M. and on Saturday from 10:00 A.M. to 2:00 P.M. Herbs Plus is closed from just before Christmas until February 1.

On the same site as the herb shop, Polly Felker and her daughter and son-in-law, Rhonda and Michael Hicks, built an eight-bedroom bed-and-breakfast, **Mountain Thyme Bed and Breakfast,** which fronts on Scenic Highway 7.

The Blue Goofus

*T*raveling on Arkansas's scenic highways can create the illusion that just over the next hill there will be a town. I call it an illusion because often there is nothing but more scenic highway, and more and more. I mention this as fair warning to carry a bag of trail mix or some cookies to quiet the growling of your stomach as the miles of evergreen forests pass by.

My husband was the real traveler in our family. He enjoyed cruising Arkansas's roadways and would choose curving scenic routes and spend hours pointing out little waterfalls and hand-mudded log cabins. I tried, in vain, to explain that I was a travel writer—that is, we were here not to enjoy the scenery but to find someplace to eat! I can only take so many notes about rolling hills and evergreen forests, no matter how beautiful they are.

But restaurants, ah, now there is something I can write about.

He would say, "Patti, I remember this road. When we [he and his golf buddies] drove to Hot Springs last year, there was this really great restaurant. It served the best fried chicken, had a fireplace, wonderful desserts, . . ." and on and on. "It had a funny name. The Blue something. It's right over this next hill, I think."

And I believed him. The next hill came and went. Several more slipped by. Still no Blue Something with great fried chicken.

"Bob," I pleaded, "are you sure this Blue Something place is on this highway? I am starving." I was eyeing the roadkill along the highway, and some of it was beginning to look appetizing—maybe deep-fried—and I was getting crabby. "I don't believe in this Blue Goofus," I grouched.

Then we crested a hill, and sure enough there it was: A smoky stone chimney surrounded by blackened grass and trees. Bits of broken glass caught the last light of day and winked in the fading sunlight. Charred boards leaned against the beautiful stone fireplace, and a broken sign announcing the Blue Goofus, or whatever it had been called, swung creaking on a chain over stone pillars. I could have wept.

But ever after that, when the going got tough and I got grouchy, Bob would say that there was sure to be a Blue Goofus over the next hill, and that would always make me laugh.

He was usually right. Arkansas is full of wonderful Blue Goofi, and I promise you, we found most of them and put them all in this book.

SOUTHWEST ARKANSAS

You can get a really good look at this B&B on the Web by logging onto www.mountainthyme.com, where you can tour each of the eight rooms of this pretty Cape Cod at your leisure. Rhonda and Michael wanted this to be the "perfect B&B" and looked to every detail to make it so. The sheets are soft, the towels thick, and the breakfast gourmet. Once you get settled in, you won't want to leave. Cozy up on the porch and listen to the woodland creatures—this B&B is on the edge of a national forest. It is no wonder that instead of just signing the guest book in each room, people write a page about how relaxed they are. Some rooms have a fireplace, or Jacuzzi, or VCR, and all rooms have books to read and perfect lighting to do it by. Prices range from $90 to $125 for the Honeymoon Suite. Call (501) 984–5428 or e-mail inn@mountainthyme.com. You can also reach the Web site by going to the Hot Springs Web site www.hotsprings.org and connecting through "lodgings."

The great burger search continues. President Clinton would be happy with the results. Latest find is **The Shack,** at 7901 North Highway 7, Jessieville 71949. The quarter-pound Shackburger—or the half-pound Super Shackburger—arrive wrapped snugly and fastened with toothpicks. Unwrap it carefully, because the wrapper also serves as a plate. When the weather is good, you can take in the sunshine at tables around the Shack while enjoying a thick milkshake. Shoestring potatoes come flavored in Cajun or ranch, and both are great. You can get a grilled chicken if you are weight conscious, but the fried catfish and shrimp are very popular with the rest of us. The Larry Special, named afer a family friend, is two beef patties topped with grilled onions and comes with fries and coleslaw. The owners of the Shack are Bill and Glenda Cockman. Hours are from 10:00 A.M. to 9:00 P.M. Monday through Saturday. Call (501) 984–5619 for information.

Best Annual Events in Southwest Arkansas

Annual Lake Catherine Tag Fishing Derby, Malvern; from May through December; (501) 332–2721; tagged fish are released into the lake and merchants sponsor prizes in value from $10 to $550

Annual Bull Stompin' Tour, Texarkana (at the Four States Fairground); (870) 773–2941; www.fourstatesfair.com; bull riding; admission $15.50/adults

Watermelon Festival, Hope; third weekend in August; (870) 777–7500

Annual Tea for Poets & Lovers, DeQueen; second weekend in February; (870) 642–6642.

Annual Boo Grass Picking Around the Campfire, Texarkana; Halloween weekend; contact Sam Strange at (903) 792–2481; picking, grinning, crafters, quilting, food, Halloween party; RV hookups available for $7.00 and $8.00.

Annual Christmas at the Ace of Clubs House, all of December; contact Ina McDowell at (903) 793–4831; e-mail: gcvanderpool@cableone.net; Victorian Christmas decorations throughout this historic home built in the shape of a playing card club; music and readings; admission $3.50

Fox Pass Pottery, off Highway 7 on Fox Pass Cutoff, is also the home of Jim and Barbara Larkin. They have lived in the stone house attached to the studio and surrounded by national forest for nearly thirty years. The Larkins use local quartz for glazing and silica sand from the White River in their creations. Barbara is the creator of Bud and Babe, a quirky twosome who show up frequently in her work in various guises. (Bud carries a cigar in his teeth and will show up on a Bud vase as well as in sculptures; Babe looks just as the name implies.) Jim creates more functional items. His colanders, mugs, and vases are fired in the kilns he built himself: The bisque kiln is the first step—it goes to 1,800 degrees, then cools. Then the "car kiln" reaches 2,400 degrees for the glaze; this kiln takes sixteen hours and two days to cool. To visit the studio take Highway 7 out of town two and a half miles and go ½ mile down Fox Pass Cutoff. Hours are Tuesday through Saturday from 10:00 A.M. to 5:00 P.M. Call (501) 623–9906 for information.

As it enters **Hot Springs,** Highway 7 is lined with big old homes set back on deep lots high on hills. The highway becomes Central Avenue and Bathhouse Row when it gets into town. Here's a city where you can have your palm read, enjoy a bath and massage, get married, go to the races at Oaklawn—or all of the above. And there are plenty of good restaurants for a city so small.

Even though former President Bill Clinton calls himself the man from Hope, his formative years were spent in Hot Springs, and it's hard to miss that information, with huge banners declaring HOT SPRINGS—BOYHOOD HOME OF BILL CLINTON flying across most main streets and signs in plenty of windows stating that BILL CLINTON ATE HERE.

Hot Springs was the hot spot in its day, no question. During Prohibition the Valley of the Vapors had bathtub gin, clanging electric trolley cars, speakeasies, and painted women. It was an odd combination of shady entertainment along Central Avenue: One side was shady as in illegal; the other side was shady as in a tree-filled national park managed by federal rangers.

People have been bathing at the spa since Hernando de Soto did in 1541. But he was just doing what the Native Americans had always done. According to legend the Indians soaked in steaming pools when they talked peace with warring tribes. Through the years traders, trappers, politicians, and gangsters have soaked in these waters. By the 1900s Bathhouse Row's most elegant establishment was the Spanish Renaissance Revival-style Fordyce Bathhouse, where water bubbled up from deep in the earth's center, reaching the surface at 143 degrees Fahrenheit, whereupon it was cooled for bathing. Fordyce Bathhouse visitors' center was restored by the National Park Service at a cost of $5 million; the elegant bathing facility is now open to the public—although you can't have a bath there today.

The water that flows from the springs in Hot Springs is naturally sterile. It is rainwater that is absorbed into the mountains and carried 8,000 feet underground, where the earth's heat raises the temperature to 143° F. The purified water makes its way back through pores and cracks in the rock in the form of hot springs.

The 4,800-acre **Hot Springs National Park** visitors center in the restored bathhouse has the decadent legacy of that bygone day. The only gambling done now takes place at Oaklawn Park during the spring thoroughbred racing season, although dinner in the circa 1875 Arlington Hotel's Venetian Room might help you replay some of that feeling under glimmering chandeliers, with jazz drifting in from the lobby bar.

This is the very place where Al Capone headquartered his gang during Prohibition days. Veined Italian marble, wrought iron, and hardwood railings are everywhere, as are classical sculptures and ornate ceramics. The third-floor sunroom is the true showstopper, with its stained glass, vaulted ceiling, grand piano, and wicker furniture. And the promenade behind Bathhouse Row is a nice place to stroll. The visitors center is open from 9:00 A.M. until 5:00 P.M. daily (until 6:00 P.M. in summer). Call (501) 623–1433 for information.

People came from miles around for the mineral water baths (health seekers, they claimed to be), so to fill the time between baths, gambling houses were run by the underworld of Chicago, New York, and Miami. The 1886 Majestic Hotel, 1 block away, is where "Bugs" Moran, Capone's rival, hung out. Today you can still "take the waters" in the warm steamy bathhouse. If you are lucky, you will meet Jim Lemons, who has been a bath attendant there for about sixty years, or Kathleen Crowe, across the hall in the beauty parlor, where she has been giving facials for almost forty-five years. The two of them delight customers with stories of the gangsters of the era while one is soaked, massaged, and pampered.

The new **Hot Springs Visitors Center** at 629 Central Avenue, Hot Springs 71902, is a good place to start a walking tour of the city. In addition to a computerized kiosk to help you find what you're looking for, the center has maps, discount coupons, and the latest information on shows and exhibits in the city. Hours are 9:00 A.M. to 5:00 P.M. seven days a week. Summer hours are extended until 8:00 P.M. Call (800) 922–6478.

Hot Springs is still a resort town, so there is more entertainment here than in other cities this size. There are many live-music places in town, and, as for eating, well, you've come to the right place.

Mollie's, at 538 West Grand, Hot Springs 71902, may be the only place in Arkansas to get tasty, deli cooking. The white brick house looks deceptively small, but the back overlooks the garden area, where patio dining is offered in good weather. There is more than just healing chicken soup, though. Owner Betty Forshberg (whose mother-in-law was the original Mollie) also serves a fine brisket of beef, potato pancakes, cheese blintzes, and, of course, chopped liver. Mollie's is open from 11:00 A.M. to 9:30 P.M. every day but Sunday. Call (501) 623–6582 for information.

A favorite place with the *cognoscenti* is **McClard's,** at 505 Albert Pike Street, Hot Springs 71902. This is an unassuming place with bright lights and, according to locals, the best barbecue in the state. The 1950s diner is always crowded, and with good reason: Not only is the barbecue great, but the tamale spread is fiery hot and, with a cold beer, hard to beat. It hasn't changed much since Bill Clinton and his buddies hung out here. It's open Tuesday through Saturday 11:00 A.M. to 8:00 P.M. Call (501) 624–9586 for information.

But "man does not live by bread alone." Hot Springs has recently become a fine arts center for the state. A Gallery Walk, held the first Friday of each month, is gallery open-house night to meet with artists whose works are being shown. About twenty fine arts galleries and arts-related businesses participate in the walk; refreshments are served, too. The **Hot Springs Arts Center,** located at 405 Park Avenue, is the heart of the city's art renaissance. Call Marla Crider at (501) 321–2835 for more information about the walk.

A significant contribution to the Hot Springs art scene is the new **Clinton Cultural Campus,** located in the old Hot Springs High School at 119 Oak Street, where the former president attended high school in the 1960s. The campus provides an interactive environment for artists and visitors to experience and participate in the creative process. The old school, built in 1914 and now on the National Register of Historic Places, is home to numerous artists in various mediums and their studios. Phone (501) 624–1964 for more information or visit the Web site, which is www.culturalcampus.org. A branch of the now infamous Clinton Presidential Library will eventually be built at this site.

Body and Bath Esscentials, at 124 Central Avenue, Hot Springs 71902, is filled with bath beads, bath oils, and skin creams, some very pricey. But the scent of vanilla, lilac, and lavender is so nice that one forgets the price. Call (501) 624–2025.

The *National Park Aquarium,* at 209 Central Avenue, Hot Springs 71902 (501–624–3474), is home to a ninety-pound snapping turtle that could take off your arm. While your children learn that it is part of the Chelydridae family and inspect the other reptile and fish inhabitants in residence any day of the week from 9:00 A.M. to 5:00 P.M., you can go to the *Arlington Hotel and Spa,* at 239 Central Avenue, Hot Springs 71902, enjoy the unique lobby with bright green leather sofas, and have a drink in the bar.

You might even decide to make a day of it in this grand old Southern hotel. Have a Day of Beauty in the full-service Beauty & Facial Salon, or try the spring-fed waters in the Bath House, where a staff of skilled attendants and massage therapists will pamper you with thermal whirlpool baths, hot packs, and massages. The outdoor mountainside hot tub and fifty of the sleeping rooms also have the thermal waters piped in. Rates run from $64 to $400. Call (501) 623–7771, (800) 643–1502; fax (501) 623–2243; or look at the Web site at www.arlingtonhotel.com for information about spa packages.

Or go to the *Faded Rose,* at 210 Central Avenue, Hot Springs 71902 a small cafe across the street from the Arlington Hotel. The high ceilings give this 1885 saloon an atmosphere reminiscent of the Cafe du Monde in New Orleans's Vieux Carre, with booths lining the walls all the way to the back and tables in the center by the long bar. Cajun-style food is the order of the day, with really good gumbo. (*They say* their specialty is steak.) Everything here is homemade, even the mayonnaise. Lunch is served from 11:00 A.M. until 4:00 P.M., and dinner is served until 10:00 P.M. seven days a week. Call (501) 624–3200 for information.

Send the kids into *The Fun Shop,* at 216B Central Avenue, Hot Springs 71902, where they can bypass the T-shirts and find magic tricks and an impressive assortment of hot gum, hand buzzers, and things designed to annoy their teachers. Call (501) 624–4002 for information.

On display at *Theartfoundation,* at 516 Central Avenue, Hot Springs 71902, is the three-dimensional aluminum-and-acrylic geometric

Trivia

Kellar Breland, a pioneering animal behaviorist, lived in Hot Springs during WWII and directed workers in top secret research. Dolphins were trained to attach mines to Axis warships, crows to carry listening devices behind enemy lines. Today, Educated Animals is an offshoot of that time. One-hundred-twenty performers wait in cages for their part in the ongoing show. A telepathic raccoon reads your mind and shoots baskets; a rabbit who plays the piano and a duck plucking a guitar provide music. But watch out, there's a rabbit ready to fire a cannon at the audience. It gets better. There is Andy, a pig who drives a Cadillac.

canvas painting of Italian-born artist Benini, who now lives in Hot Springs. Call (501) 623–9847 for information. Another gallery, this one with soothing music, is at 516A Central Avenue. *Taylor's Contemporanea Fine Arts* exhibits sculptures, paintings, and mixed-media art. Call (501) 624– 0516 for information.

Complementing the art scene in Hot Springs is great food. One restaurant that draws a crowd is *Belle Arti* at 719 Central Avenue, Hot Springs 71902. Owners Joseph and Penny Gargano were attracted to the city's reputation and moved here from New York in 1998. Belle Arti already had an established reputation for authentic Italian cuisine and the Garganos continue the tradition of homemade pastas, raviolis and tortellini, but their most requested menu item is the grilled portabella mushroom, which sells for $8.50. Hours for lunch are 11:30 A.M. to 4:00 P.M. seven days a week. Dinner, for which reservations are required, begins at 5:00 P.M. and continues until 11:00 P.M. To make reservations or ask for information, call (501) 624–7474.

A beautifully restored Queen Anne at 808 Park Avenue, Hot Springs 71902, is the home of *Wildwood 1884 Bed and Breakfast,* owned by Randy and Karen Duncan. It is a magnificent three-story home with five guest rooms, each with private bath. Three of the rooms have their own porches. There is original stained glass and many original furnishings and photographs. It is, of course, on the National Register of Historic Places. Breakfast is served in the dining room or morning room. You can preview the rooms at www.bbonline.com/ar/wildwood/ or call (501) 624–4267 or (888) 763–3707. Prices range from $85 to $95.

There are so many lovely old homes in Hot Springs and many of them are now B&Bs. Another is the elegant old *Williams House,* an 1891 Victorian brownstone and brick mansion with a carriage house at 420 Quapaw Avenue, Hot Springs 71902. Five guest rooms all have private baths. This one is also on the National Register and can be seen at www.bbonline.com/ar/williamshouse/, where innkeepers Karen and David Wiseman have shown the same attention to detail that will make your stay comfortable. Breakfast is served in the dining room between 7:30 and 9:00 A.M. Complimentary wine (or spring water) is served to

Downtown Hot Springs

· guests on arrival. Prices range from $95 to $145. Call (501) 624–4275 or (800) 756–4635.

The oldest building in Hot Springs is also one of the most luxurious. *The Stitt House Bed and Breakfast,* 824 Park Avenue, Hot Springs 71901, was built in 1875 and stayed in the Stitt family until the current owners, Linda and Horst Fischer, bought it in 1983. Situated atop two beautiful acres, the 6,000-square-foot home has four rooms named after the Fischer children and range in price from $100 to $125. Breakfast may be served in bed, in the formal dining room, or outdoors on the veranda. A large hot tub and heated outdoor pool add to the luxury. Call (501) 623–2704 or visit the Web site at www.bbonline/ar/stitthouse.com.

If you need some action, call Cyndy Anderson's *Outdoor Adventure Tours,* at 300 Long Island Drive, Hot Springs 71913 (501) 525–4457 or (800) 489–8687. However you want to tour, Cyndy can arrange it. Cyndy and her husband, Punch, lead hiking tours through Hot Springs National Park and can set up canoeing on the Ouachita and Caddo

Treatments at the bath-houses in hotels were interesting. Spa visitors were prescribed needle showers and sessions in steam-and-chill chambers, and syphilis sufferers had mercury rubbed on their genitals. Quack devices were also used (the Zanda machine). The treatment rooms contained not only showers and lockers, but also ornate stained glass and sculpture—locker rooms for the wealthy leisure class.

Rivers and biking in the Ouachita National Forest, which is only thirty minutes out of town. Most tours come in weekend or weeklong packages that include lodging and meals. They will even specialize a tour just for you. Tours leave from 350 Central. Rates are $15 for adults and $10 for children under 12 for a ninety-minute historic sightseeing tour. Mountain biking packages run from $310 to $650, including lodgings and meals. Hiking and canoeing packages are $250 to $350 per couple. They offer a lot more on their Web site, www.outdooradventuretours.com.

Maxine's International Coffee House and Puzzle Bar caters to the artistic set is at 700 Central Avenue, Hot Springs 71901. It's a great place to sit and enjoy any of one hundred different kinds of coffee while working a jigsaw puzzle or playing a game of checkers or chess. Maxine's also serves soups and sandwiches and alcoholic beverages.

Perhaps the place is not as lively as it used to be when the original Maxine had a bordello upstairs, but owners Hugh and Charlie Marshall are hoping to liven things up with contemporary bands performing now and then. Maxine's is open from 5:00 P.M. until midnight Monday through Thursday and until 2:00 A.M. on Friday and Saturday. Call (501) 623–0653.

To get an overview of the town, go up to the 216-foot ***Hot Springs Mountain Tower*** in the national park. Taking the glass-enclosed elevator to the open-air deck is a treat. The elevator operates from 9:00 A.M. to 5:00 P.M. Admission is $4.00 for adults and $2.00 for children. Call (501) 623–6035. But from the top of West Mountain, there's an equally good view; you can even see the tourists in the tower on the other mountain. The view is especially pretty at night. Pull your car off on the turnouts and enjoy the scene below—downtown Hot Springs glittering like the fabled spa it once was.

Going down from West Mountain onto Prospect Street, you will see a Russian villa at 634 Prospect. The fairy-tale house is vivid in red and yellow, with intricate decorations on the detailed shutters in the style of a northwestern Russian summer home, or dacha. It was designed and built by a former officer of the czar's army in 1930. Once abandoned, the house has been restored.

The Promenade, a paved path behind Bathhouse Row, is a pleasant stroll that offers a hint of the natural beauty of Hot Springs National Park. For the more adventurous, several paths lead to the top of Hot Springs Mountain. It's about a mile round-trip to the top.

A longtime feature at Hot Springs is **Dryden Pottery,** located at 341 Whittington Avenue, Hot Springs 71901, and offering pottery made of native clays and crystal quartz. For more than fifty years, members of the Dryden family have made their living at the potter's wheel. The showroom is filled with examples of the finished product. A mural painted on the building tells the story of the Indians and their pottery. Dryden is now listed in the *Antiques and Collectibles Price Guide* for its one-of-a-kind original pieces. Call (501) 623–4201 for hours and tour information.

Hot Springs Country Club Golf Course, 101 Country Club Drive, Hot Springs 71901, is open to the public. Its tree-lined fairways and hilly forty-five holes draw golfers from all over the five border states. Midwesterners vacation here in February and March, when the weather is usually golfable, but snow still covers the rest of middle America. (The fact that it's racing season doesn't disappoint anyone, either, if the weather is less than perfect.) For tee times, call (501) 623–4981.

Any tour of the president's hometown should include a drive past the two homes in which he lived—the two-story white house at 1011 Park Avenue and the brick house at 213 Scully Street. You can get a presidential self-guided-tour booklet at the visitors center and see places like the Malco Movie Theater (where Clinton liked to sit in the middle of the front row) and the Park Place Baptist Church.

If you are looking for a quiet spot, you will want to check out *Garvan Woodland Gardens,* near Carpenter Dam at the eastern end of Lake

Gators

*T**he Arkansas Alligator Farm, in business since 1902 at 847 Whittington Avenue, Hot Springs 71901, is stocked with more than 200 alligators of different sizes. Visitors may take a self-guided tour past the four ponds in which they live. You can watch the* alligators as they are fed Wednesday and Sunday at 11:00 A.M., noon, and 1:00 P.M. Open daily from May 1 to Labor Day 8:30 A.M. to 6:00 P.M.; the rest of the year from 9:30 A.M. to 5:00 P.M. Call (501) 623–6172 for information.*

Hamilton, accessible to the public only by boat. Visitors arrive on tours at the dock in a secluded shady cove.

The two large peninsulas with more than 4 miles of shoreline are all native forest and contain sweet gum, maple, redbud, and dogwood, as well as pine, oak, and hickory. The garden, which is more of an arboretum, has the best flowers in the spring and fall. It was donated a decade ago by Verna Garvan, who inherited the 232 acres from her father and wanted it preserved.

Trivia

Outdoor sculptures are hidden all over Arkansas. There is an Easter Island near DeQueen, a tribute to woodsmen in Gurdon, and a Statue of Liberty at Paragould. "Stone & Steel: A Sculptural Tour of Arkansas" shows you where to find nearly 400 outdoor sculptures. Call (501) 324–9880 or e-mail info@dah.state.ar.us for the brochure and map.

After climbing a steep 250-foot trail from the dock, you will stroll through the Top of the Walk Garden with dwarf azaleas, white cypress, ferns, mahonia, galax, and sarcococca. The white oak "walkout" turns brilliant red in the fall. You will see Japanese Maple Hill and Daffodil Hill, where several thousand daffodils bloom with blue French roman hyacinths and blue *Anemone blanda*. Walk the Camellia Trail surrounded by *Camellia japonica* and more than fifty sasanqua, interplanted with English laurel, *Euonymus sarcoxie*, *Osmanthus heterophyllus*, and hardy evergreens for winter protection. On Hawthorn Hill many kinds of parsley-leaved hawthorn grow; they established themselves when a tornado swept through the first-growth timber. Red yuccas have been added to the native cacti. Old Brick Hill is a road of solid red brick from the fuel house of a turn-of-the-century lumber company. The bricks were made at the historic Atchison Brick Company in Malvern.

One of the most striking features of the garden is the Verna Garvan Pavilion, designed by architect E. Fay Jones (designer of Thorncrown Chapel near Eureka Springs) in the Border of Old Roses near the end of the tour. The roof includes glass in the center shaped to resemble a flower opening. The garden has 110 varieties of old roses dating back to *Rosa gallica* from about A.D. 1300.

The season lasts from March to the second week of November, depending on the lake level. Almost 200 acres will be kept as a wildlife preserve for research by forestry and horticulture students. Because it is not a traditional tourist attraction with regular hours, make reservations by calling the Hot Springs/Garland County Beautification Commission at (501) 623–7871 or (800) 366–4664. Their Web site is www.garvan.org.

The fee is $6.00 for the tour and an additional $8.00 for the boat ride to and from the gardens. Wear good shoes for walking. Because the trails are quite steep in places, especially at the beginning from the dock, visitors should be in good health. A docent leads each group, relating historical and horticultural information. Tours are available Tuesday through Sunday from 9:00 A.M. to 6:00 P.M.

Five miles south of Hot Springs on scenic Highway 7 is **Mountain Brook Stables,** at 107 Stillmeadow Lane, Hot Springs 71913, where you can take guided trail rides in the Ouachita Mountains. Sunrise and sunset rides and day trips for both experienced and inexperienced riders are available. Gene and Deborah Sparling own the stable, which houses eight horses and two mules. The animals are gentle and well trained. A one-hour ride, which costs $18, crosses a stream and climbs a small mountain path through a hardwood forest to the summit, from which Lake Hamilton and downtown Hot Springs can be seen. The longer, two-hour ride, which costs $32, starts over the same trail but turns into a hardwood and pine forest to follow the stream to a gorge, where riders stop to rest by a waterfall before the ride back over a different route. The stable is open from March into December, or whenever the weather is good, with rides offered from about 9:00 A.M. to about 7:00 P.M. Call (501) 525–8393 for information.

The **Mid-America Museum** is in a heavily wooded, twenty-one-acre site about 6½ miles west of Hot Springs off Highway 270 West. The 50,000-square-foot building is divided into two wings, connected by a glass-enclosed catwalk over a stream. This is a hands-on museum, where the exhibits are designed to be touched. Here the arts and sciences come together with playful contraptions like the Featherstone Kite Open-Work Basketweave Mark II Gentleman's Flying Machine—the work of Rowland Emett, who designed the mechanical creations in the movies *Chitty-Chitty Bang-Bang* and *Those Magnificent Men in Their Flying Machines.* The lighthearted tone of the museum delights visitors.

The museum's Fine Arts/Science Program rotates original works by internationally renowned artists, such as the globular pop-art abstractions and brightly colored geometric images of Italian artist Benini, with the works of sculptors who are Arkansas natives. Cross the bridge to the west wing and explore exhibits in perception, energy, matter, and life, each display showing the connection between the arts and the sciences. The Balance Challenge alters your equilibrium with mirrors, the Walk-in Camera allows you to see how a camera lens views the world, and the Sun Scale-Earth Scale shows how much you'd weigh on the sun.

The Laser Theater uses laser beams and music to create a thirty-minute show. There's even a life-size mastodon like the ones that roamed the Ozarks 18,000 years ago. Hours are from 9:30 A.M. to 6:00 P.M. daily Memorial Day through Labor Day and from 10:00 A.M. to 5:00 P.M. Tuesday through Sunday the rest of the year. Tickets are $6.00 for adults and $5.00 for children and seniors. Call (501) 767–3461 or (800) 632–0583 for more information. Their Web site is www.ohwy.com/ar/m/mmcieeoa.htm.

The drive along Scenic Highway 7 is the most beautiful way to travel south in this part of the state. Birders especially seek out this area because **DeGray Lake Resort State Park** near **Bismarck** hosts many events for bird-watchers. Night owls will like **The Owl Prowl** on Friday and Saturday nights in summer (and in January); this event lets you see and hear barred owls, screech owls, and great horned owls by using taped calls to attract them. The annual **Eagles Et Cetera** in January is a weekend offering numerous opportunities to see bald eagles in the wild. You will learn how to identify birds or how to photograph them with some of the best birders in the state. The hour-and-a-half tour by barge—which can be chilly—offers more than a 95-percent chance of seeing bald eagles. The barge runs year-round on weekends and seven days a week from spring through fall. Tickets are $5.00 for adults and $3.00 for children ages six to twelve. Call (501) 865–2801 for information about the events.

The Eagle and Raptor Rehabilitation Program has these birds in temporary captivity, too. Other bird hikes continue throughout the day. Some other wildlife you might see include the common loon, great blue heron, raccoon, and gray and red foxes. All programs at the lodge and the bird hikes are free, but advance registration for hikes and barge tours is necessary because of limited space.

There are other special events here, too. March brings early-morning bird walks and the Easter Ecstasy spring wildflower walks (and annual Easter Egg Hunt). April's wildflower walks join the Tell a Tale Troupe Dinner Theatre, performing such classics as The Red Badge of Courage. And Full Moon Cruises are available from April through October.

Reservations at the ninety-six-room lodge should be made by calling (501) 865–2851 or (800) 737–8355. Lodge rates start at $65 for double occupancy; campers are charged $5.75 for water and electrical hookups and a dump station, with bathhouses containing hot showers also available. The park, which is located off Highway 7, 6 miles north of I–30 at Caddo Valley (21 miles south of Hot Springs), also has an eighteen-hole golf course, a pro shop, and a marina and offers guided trail rides on horseback. The Web site is www.degray.com.

Scenic Highway 7 ends at Bismarck, but if you take Highway 67 South through the Caddo Valley beginning at Malvern, the picturesque, 20-mile stretch will take you by a number of antiques shops (one in a town's restored train depot), a restored antebellum cabin, a petting zoo, and an old-time general store with woodcrafts and smoked meats. Highway 67 is the old route to Texas; if you want to get off of I-30, this is the way.

Bismarck is the home of *jo ann diffee studios.* Well, not exactly Bismarck. You have to travel down winding Highway 84 west of Bismarck about 3½ miles to a quiet spot where Jo Ann works. She is a self-taught artist who specializes in portraits but also does landscapes, wildlife, and still lifes. Her work reflects the colors of the mountains and desert and the feelings of the Southwest, where she grew up. The studio is open Tuesday through Saturday from 10:00 A.M. to 4:30 P.M. or by appointment if you would like to commission a portrait. Call (501) 865–2529 for information.

The area around here is a rock hound's dream. *Magnet Cove* on Highway 270 East near Malvern is said to have one of the country's most varied deposits of rocks and minerals. It is named for the magnetic iron deposits in the area.

The city of *Malvern* has such historical attractions as the Boyle House Museum and the Rockport Bridge. From Malvern take Highway 171 west past *Lake Catherine State Park.* This park has seventeen cabins. Some are rustic single units, where on chilly evenings you can enjoy a warm fire in the stone fireplace; others are modern duplexes. They are situated on a little peninsula on the lake, and most are on the lakeshore; the price is $70. But if you want to try your hand at roughing it, Rent-a-Camp provides tents, cots, a stove, and other camping equipment for $30 a night. The park has 10 miles of hiking trails and a nice swimming area. Call (800) 264–2422 or (501) 844– 4176 to make reservations.

The Ouachitas

B uilt along the bluffs of the Ouachita Valley, *Arkadelphia* was a river port during steamboat days. Now it calls itself the Wildflower Capital of Arkansas, and acres of them have been planted along the roadways and on public land. Take home a T-shirt saying GROW WILD IN ARKADELPHIA! The town has two universities literally across the street (and a ravine) from each other—Henderson State University and Ouachita Baptist University—and this arrangement has created one of the country's more interesting rivalries; their fierce athletic competition is legendary. Ouachita Baptist houses the personal library and memorabilia of Senator John McClellan, and Henderson State has a museum in a wonderful antebellum home featuring relics of the Caddo Indians. Both campuses are lovely, with huge oaks and interesting architecture.

Something Special, at 4 Pine Street Village, Arkadelphia 71923, is where Patricia Greenwood makes paper angels (similar to cornhusk dolls) that began as a hobby and became a business. The angels are shown at the War Eagle Fair and exported to shops in other states. The tree-topper, at 20 inches tall, costs $17.50; the doll-size angel, at 10 inches, costs $10.50; and the ornament-size angel costs $7.50. The shop also carries other handmade natural decorative accessories—grapevine wreaths, arrangements using all-natural dried flowers, herbs, and seasonal decorations. It's open Monday through Saturday. Hours are from 9:30 A.M. to 5:30 P.M.; call (870) 246–7544 for information.

The **Honeycomb Restaurant and Bakery,** at 706 Main Street, Arkadelphia 71923, took quite a bit of damage in the tornado but survived. The restaurant is owned by Group Living, an organization to help adults with developmental disabilities. Because the group offers training and jobs to people, a big effort was made to get the restaurant going again—

Peanut Brittle Capital

*A*rkadelphia is unofficially the peanut brittle capital of the state— there were three shops located all within 1 block of one another, all good. But in March 1997, a tornado swept through this city leveling most of downtown and killing twenty-six people. It was a most powerful and unusual tornado because it stayed on the ground for twenty-six minutes, according to news reports. This Class IV tornado was more devastating than Hurricane Andrew in the almost-mile-wide path it cut through the main part of the city. It left nothing but toothpick-size pieces of businesses and homes. (The only tornado worse is a Class V, which leaves nothing, *not even toothpicks, in its wake.*) Only one peanut brittle company remained in town—**Andrew's Candy Company,** at 2606 Pine Street (870–246–2796). Another company, **Juanita's,** was blown away, but it's been rebuilt, at 47 Stephenwood Drive. The new phone number is (870) 246–8542. In the wake of the tornado, President Clinton visited Arkadelphia and promised as much help as possible in its rebuilding.

they served carryout foods until the building was fixed—and now they are back in business. Everything here is homemade. Breakfast omelettes, biscuits and gravy, and pancakes are served from 7:00 to 10:00 A.M. Lunch, which begins at 11:00 A.M. and is served until 2:00 P.M., includes specials like chicken-fried steak, which come with a vegetable and salad, enough to feed a family of four. You can have one of their sandwiches—on homemade French bread—and dessert (with espresso!) until 4:00 P.M. Manager Barbara Eggar says absolutely nothing is ready-made, and the desserts are excellent. The restaurant is open Monday through Saturday. Call (870) 245–2333 for information.

At Seventh and Clinton Streets, appropriately enough, Martha Dixon, the designer of Hillary Rodham Clinton's inaugural gowns, has a shop. She was in the line of fire of the tornado herself but escaped unhurt. Her building sustained some damage, but **Martha's Designs** has reopened at 701 Clinton Street, Arkadelphia 71923. Martha is concentrating on scrub-style uniforms for food-processing and medical workers these days but still does some custom designs.

Highway 67 rolls into **Gurdon,** where the **International Order of Hoo-Hoos Museum** will answer the questions of the curious about the history of the Supreme Nine, who handle the business affairs of the International Order of Hoo-Hoos. Ever wonder about the history of the Snark of the Universe, called the Supreme Hoo-Hoo, leader of eight other directors—the Senior Hoo-Hoo, the Junior Hoo-Hoo, the Scrivenoter, Bojum, Jabberwock, Custocatian, Arcanoper, and the Gurdon? Want to know more about the State Deputy Snark and the Viceregent Snark? You can get all the details here. "What's a Hoo-Hoo?" you ask. People in this timberland know. It's a fraternity of lumbermen—its symbol an arching Egyptian black cat with its tail curled into the number 9—and it was formed to foster "elbow-rubbing" and the spirit of teamwork and is dedicated to health, happiness, and long life for its members. The museum is at 207 Main Street, Arkadelphia 71923. Hours are 9:00 A.M. to 4:00 P.M. Monday through Friday (it's closed at noon for lunch). Call (870) 353–4997 for information. And there is a Web site: www.hoohoo.org.

Between Gurdon and Texarkana on Highway 67 (which parallels I–30) lies **"A Place Called Hope,"** birthplace of William Jefferson Blythe IV, who would become the forty-second president of the United States. His grandmother's home, at 117 South Hervey Street, is where he and his mother lived after his father's death. The home is now open for tours at a cost of $5.00 for adults and $3.00 for children. In addition to the home there is a gift shop and replica of the Oval Office in an adjacent building. The tour takes about thirty minutes, but take time to enjoy the beautiful memorial garden planted in the backyard in honor of President Clinton's mother, Virginia Kelly. The phone number here is (870) 777–4455. When Bill was four, his mother married Roger Clinton and moved to a home at 321 East Thirteenth Street. Bill Clinton attended Brookwood Elementary School. But if you want to see it all, go to the **Hope Tourist Center and Museum,** the renovated Iron Mountain/Missouri Pacific Railroad depot in the heart of the downtown area at the intersection of South Main and Division Streets, now dedicated to Bill Clinton and the town's history. Just as President Clinton said he "still believes in a place called Hope," others here have faith that the town will come alive now that more than 20,000 visitors a year from all over the world see it. In 1992 the presidential candidate visited the Hope depot to have campaign photos taken. When he was elected, the citizens of Hope decided to restore the depot to its original luster. The Union Pacific Railroad donated the station to the city in 1994, and the renovators used a federal grant and local funds to restore the building in 1995. Photographs chronicle Clinton's family, and many are on loan from local residents. One shows his father, William Jefferson Blythe III, who died in an auto accident before Clinton was born. Other artifacts include a bell from the kindergarten Clinton attended, one of the president's report cards, and a toy train he played with as a child. In a state-of-the-art audiovisual room, visitors can see two videos on the history of Hope and southwest Arkansas. Call (870) 722–2580 for information.

Also downtown is **Cherry's Old Tyme Soda Fountain,** at 225 South Main, Hope 71801 (870–777–3424), where owner Cherry Stewart credits much of the revival to the efforts of the local businesspeople. Hope is a large watermelon-producing community, so in season, have Cherry fix you a Watermellon Fizz. Other new businesses downtown include the **Little Herb Shoppe** at 203 South Main (870–777–2535), and **The Melon Patch** restaurant, at 104 South Elm, where you can stop in for lunch and have some very southern cooking (chicken and dumplings!). Call (870) 777–8802 for hours.

If you plan to be at the southwest tip of the state to visit the **Conway Cemetery Historic State Park** near Walnut Hill, you might enjoy the ride across the river; then you can sing "Remember the Red River Valley" with more meaning. The park is dedicated to the memory of James S. Conway, the first governor of the state. The half-acre family cemetery where the governor is buried is on the eleven-and-a-half-acre site, which also contains the governor's plantation home, Walnut Hill. Take Highway 29 to Bradley and then Highway 160 West for 2 miles to Walnut Hill. Turn left on the county road, and proceed $1/2$ mile to the park entrance. No camping or visitors' services are available.

SOUTHWEST ARKANSAS

Trivia

One of Texarkana's attractions is the circa 1924 Perot Theater, a restored facility that features Broadway plays.

If you take Highway 355 about 10 miles to the east of here, you'll come to the little town of **Stamps,** population 2,200. It was here that acclaimed poet Maya Angelou lived with her grandmother and other relatives off and on from about age two to twelve. A neighbor woman became a mentor of sorts to Maya, encouraging her to read and to express herself in writing. Maya says her formative years in Stamps contributed to her award-winning novel *I Know Why the Caged Bird Sings.* City leaders are in the process of establishing a memorial to Maya, including a regular poetry contest at the town's library.

Texarkana: The name of the town is derived from TEXas, ARKansas, and LouisiANA, three states that border nearby. Photographer's Island, at the front entrance steps of the post office, is a spot where you can photograph yourself standing in Texas and Arkansas at one time. Scott Joplin, the "King of Ragtime Composers," grew up here; a colorful outdoor mural depicts his life, a must-see stop.

Before the coming of the settlers, the territory around Texarkana was the Great Southwest Trail, for hundreds of years the main line of travel between the Native American villages of the Mississippi Valley and those of the West and Southwest. The Great Caddos tilled rich fields, fished, and hunted along the Red River, where they raised maize, beans, pumpkins, and melons.

In the 1850s the builders of the Cairo and Fulton Railroad pushed through to meet the Texas and Pacific Railroad here. One of the first town lots sold here in 1873 now houses the Hotel McCartney. Quite a few really interesting things are on the Texas side of the line; there is a walking-tour map available that will lead you to many of them. So be sure and do the "trail of two cities" beginning on Stateline Avenue, where the only post office in the country that is in two states is situated, and then follow the 10-block walking tour to the other sites.

The 1920s have returned to Texarkana at the **Texarkana Historical Museum,** at 219 State Line, Texarkana 75504, actually in Texas, but a trip to the town wouldn't be complete without a visit to the museum. "This side of Paradise: the Jazz Age in Texarkana," at the museum, takes a close look at what the twenties were all about in this part of the country and in a border town. Prohibition, automobiles, and a change in women's attitudes are all documented here. Hours at the museum are 10:00 A.M. to 4:00 P.M. daily. Call (903) 793–4831 for information. Admission is $5.00 for adults, $3.50 for children.

Established in 1824, the town of **Washington** was, for more than fifty years, the jumping-off point for the unknown Indian Territory and Texas, a welcome sight for travelers on the Southwest Trail. The trail was an old Indian path and an important route for settlers, stretching diagonally across the territory from Missouri to Texas, forming part of the trail that 3,000 Choctaw Indians traveled when they were forcibly evicted from Mississippi and sent to Oklahoma on the well-known Trail of Tears.

The town of Washington is intertwined with **Old Washington Historic State Park,** a time warp back to those days. Like Williamsburg, Virginia, it's an authentic re-creation—as authentic as modern restoration and archaeology can make it—of a frontier boom-town of the 1850s. The entire town of Washington lies in a state park. Private homes are mixed with historic structures in the 1-square-mile area, along with the state's largest and most magnificent magnolia tree. The narrow dirt roads were laid out about 160 years ago when thousands of people were headed for Texas and stopped at the hotels in town to buy supplies. Davy Crockett, Sam Houston, and Stephen F. Austin passed through Washington headed west. During the Civil War Washington served as the Confederate capital after Little Rock was captured by the Union army in 1863.

> ## Trivia
>
> *The Grand Caddoes farmed this area and maintained six villages along the banks of the Red River. They were hospitable to the explorers and settlers. In 1840 a permanent settlement was established at Lost Prairie 15 miles east of Texarkana. Today all that remains are a number of mounds and other traces of the Indian civilization left behind as the native population moved westward.*

A blacksmith shop stands on the site of an earlier shop, and inside the glowing metal is still fashioned by leather-aproned men who hammer out knives like the first bowie knife, designed here by smithy James Black for Jim Bowie. Today people travel from great distances to learn the ancient art of knife making at one of the world's few schools of bladesmithing, classes sponsored by Texarkana College and the American Bladesmith Society. The shop is open year-round.

Spring brings splashes of yellow jonquils, scattered over the hillsides, along roadsides, and in flower boxes all over the city to celebrate the annual Jonquil Festival in the middle of March. The quiet town of 148 is inundated with visitors, more than 40,000 at last count, who come to see the bright display of flowers, some of which are descendants of bulbs planted by the pioneers—as are the aging, gnarled catalpa trees that shade the gravel streets. During the festival craftspersons carve walking sticks of sumac, make brooms of straw with antique tools, and weave rugs on looms. Bowie knives are displayed in the park's gun shop, which

Trivia

Half of the post office in Texarkana is in Arkansas, half is in Texas.

also contains a seventeenth-century Chinese matchlock gun, muzzle-loading rifles (demonstrated by costumed traders in town), and a German machine gun from World War II.

The Pioneer Cemetery is filled with pre–Civil War tombstones. Small markers dot the area where wagons bogged down in the bottoms of the Saline and Ouachita Rivers and where attacks by Rebel troops at Poison Springs, Marks Mill, and Jenkins Ferry killed 700. All these can be seen on the walking tours of the town—tours that take about two hours and begin at the 1874 Hempstead County Courthouse, which houses the park's visitors center. There are plenty of other sights visitors can explore on their own, too. A printing museum shows the evolution of printing during the nineteenth century; the B. W. Edwards Weapons Museum contains a collection of more than 600 weapons; and the Black History Museum, housed in a doctor's office built circa 1895, portrays the important role Black Arkansans played in the history of Washington.

Williams Tavern Restaurant, catty-cornered to the courthouse and now operated by the park, began as a "stand" on the road, an open house where, for pay, John W. Williams entertained travelers. It was one of the best-known spots between Memphis and the Red River. Today the menu is posted on the blackboard and features such homemade specialties as chicken and dumplings, potato cakes, and apple cider. Hours are from 11:00 A.M. to 3:00 P.M. The Pioneer Grocery also serves sandwiches. And the nearby Tavern Inn re-creates the feeling of the pioneer era: The bar has an antique brass rail, and pre–Civil War bottles line the shelves, just as in frontier days. Phone (870) 983–2890 for more information.

There are several Greek Revival homes, among them the Royston House and the Sanders-Garland Home. At both places women in period dress check their hoopskirts in the petticoat mirror before greeting visitors. The Royston home towers behind huge magnolia trees, and flowers line the dirt drive leading up the hill to the front door, which has stained-glass windows depicting the four seasons. (Looking through one blue-paned glass makes things appear as though a blanket of snow were on the ground.) The house is filled with Empire furniture. The L-shaped, 1845 Sanders-Garland house has a large back porch where the family spent warm evenings. A portrait of daughter Sara hangs over the fireplace. A third house, the Dr. James Alexander Purdom home, circa 1850, features exhibits on early medicine.

The Confederate capitol of Arkansas (from 1863 until the end of the Civil

War) is open to the public, as is the 1874 redbrick courthouse. For those interested in research, Washington is also the home of the Southwest Arkansas Regional Archives (SARA), dedicated to collecting and preserving source materials for the history of the area. SARA is in the Old Washington Courthouse and can be used by all serious researchers, including grade-school students. Although materials cannot leave the archives and must be used in the research room, copies can be made of most materials in good condition. The park is open year-round from 9:00 A.M. to 5:00 P.M. daily. Admission is $6.50 for adults and $3.25 for children. Call (870) 983–2684 for information.

A block west of the courthouse is the oldest active Methodist church in the

DeQueen for a Day

*O*riginally, DeQueen was to be called DeGoeijen, after the turn-of-the-century Dutchman who was to be the namesake of this town, but the word proved too much of a tongue twister—it's pronounced "de-gwen"—and it was decided that it would be a terrible handicap for a town to start life with such difficulties (plus the mail problems). Because his friends called him DeQueen anyway, that was the name that stuck when the town was incorporated in 1897. In the fall of that year, the first passenger train ran from Kansas City to Port Arthur. In a special car were Arthur E. Stilwell, Jan DeGoeijen, and his wife, Mena, after whom Mena, a town in northwest Arkansas, was named.

In 1828, when Sevier County took in several other counties, Paraclifta was selected as the county seat. The town took its name from a Choctaw chief at a nearby village who achieved a peaceful settlement when some pioneer men were accused of stealing horses. In the 1840s R. C. Gilliam built Paraclifta's most imposing house with two ground-floor rooms leading from a large entry hall and two more rooms upstairs. (On the fireplace mantel you can see where Gilliam carved the initials of his wife, Frances.) Gilliam was a cotton planter and was killed during the Civil War's Battle of Marks Mill. The town of Paraclifta is now almost totally gone except for the mansion. Tours of the mansion may be arranged by contacting the Sevier County Historical Society Museum in Dierks Park.

Outside the museum stands the last red caboose from the Kansas City Southern Railroad, which linked the fertile Midwest plains to the deepwater port on the Texas Gulf Coast. Arthur E. Stilwell built that line with the help of Jan DeGoeijen, who was a young banker in Holland with the foresight to embark on this project when others had refused. Hours at the museum are Tuesday through Saturday from 10:00 A.M. to 4:00 P.M. and Sunday from 2:00 to 4:00 P.M. To tour the Gilliam-Norwood House (also called Paraclifta House), call (870) 642–6642.

state. The congregation dates from 1818. The Old Washington Jail is behind the church and is now a privately owned B&B. *The Old Washington Jail* is the original 1872 Hempstead County Jail, which now has five guest rooms, each with a private bath. The building has been completely renovated and furnished with period antiques. A full breakfast is served in the dining room. Prices range from $99. The innkeepers are Larry and Margaret Stephens. You can visit their Web site at www.bbonline.com/ar/oldwashingtonjail.com or call (800) 747–JAIL or (870) 983–2461.

Another unique state park lies north of Washington on Highways 4 and 27. If diamonds are a girl's best friend, then women have a lot of pals around Murfreesboro—not in the quaint town square but in nearby *Crater of Diamonds State Park,* because there are not only diamonds forever but also practically free. These are not phony "diamonoids." They are the real thing, and this is the only—repeat, only—diamond mine on the North American continent. There is a $4.50 charge for adults and a $2.00 charge for children to enter the digging area, but after that anything you find is yours to keep. Yes, diamonds are free here; all you have to do is pick them up. It's finders, keepers, no matter how valuable they are, and almost 1,000 diamonds are found every year—the average is three a day. More than 60,000 diamonds have been found in the eighty-acre crater. It's tricky; all that glitters is not diamonds. But here's a secret that makes this book worth the cover price: Dirt won't stick to diamonds like it does to other rocks, according to Michael Hall park superintendent. And most diamonds are found in kimberlite breccia, which is a greenish rock. The gems are said to be from 95 million to more than 3 billion years old. Diamonds come in yellow, brown, pink, and black. And even if you don't find diamonds, you may find other semiprecious stones, such as jasper, opal, agate, quartz, amethyst, and garnet. There is even a geologist on the park staff to verify the gems; gems are identified and weighed for you. The 40.23-carat "Uncle Sam" diamond is the record, but the 34.5-carat "Star of Murfreesboro" and the 15.31-carat "Star of Arkansas" wouldn't make a bad piece of jewelry, either. They are among the biggest, and for most visitors, they whet the urge to dig.

The diamonds should be all gone by now, you say? Wrong. Geological forces push the diamonds upward slowly through the kimberlite soil, and the park plows the crater occasionally to increase the chance of bringing them to the surface of this thirty-five-acre field, which is the eroded crust of an ancient volcanic pipe. The park is on Highway 301 about 2 miles southeast of town and is open daily from 8:00 A.M. to 5:00 P.M. Call (870) 285–3113 for information.

Murfreesboro is a real gem (you should excuse the pun) of a town. It is just northwest of the park on Highway 301. Every Saturday night during the summer, there is free entertainment at 8:00 P.M. in front of the Conway Hotel, which also has a flea market and an outlet for the art and crafts of local artisans. The hotel is on the National Register of Historic Places. The *Jif-E Corner Bakery and Deli* is on the court-house square at 101 West Main, Murfreesboro 71958. Its long summer hours are from 6:00 A.M. to 10:00 P.M. Monday through Saturday and 11:00 A.M. to 10:00 P.M. on Sunday. Call (870) 285–3314 during other times of the year. They bake a great raisin bread.

The *Queen of Diamonds Inn* is located at 318 North Washington Street, Murfreesboro 71958, 1 block north of the square. Al and Jane Terrell bought the house and renovated it a few years ago, managing to combine Victorian charm and modern convenience. The office is in the 1902 home, which is filled with authentic furnishings. Motel rooms were built behind the home, and the forty-one guest rooms there are new and modern. A complimentary continental breakfast is served in the cheery breakfast room in the house. Rooms cost $66 for two people; call (870) 285–3105 for reservations.

The *Ka-Do-Ha Indian Village* is near town, about 1¹/₂ miles off High-way 27 on Caddo Drive. It is the site of a prehistoric Indian settle-ment—home of the Caddo Mound Builders—and many artifacts are on display. The village is a combination archaeological-dig-and-museum. You can tour the mounds and hunt for arrowheads on the sur-face, but state laws prohibit digging. The mounds are in fields surrounded by woods; they are open, although some greenery has grown up around them, and you can see the remains and artifacts. An article about the mounds appeared in *Archeology Today* magazine, but as yet the mounds are relatively undiscovered by tourists and there are no great crowds here. The gift shop and the Happy the Prospector gem-stone mine are here, too, selling bags of rough minerals you can take to the water sluice and wash for your own gemstone. Hours at the village are 9:00 A.M. to 5:00 P.M. in winter and to 6:00 P.M. from Memorial Day to Labor Day. Admission is $4.00 for adults and $2.00 for children. Cliften and Faye Crews are the managers; they offer a wealth of infor-mation about most places around town. Call (870) 285–3736.

Off Highway 27 (just off the Ka-Do-Ha Indian Village parking lot), sturdy Peruvian Paso horses are bred at *Arkansas Horse Park.* These handsome descendants of the Spanish animals brought to Peru have a natural gait that makes them the smoothest-riding horses in the world. Visitors are welcome to the farm by appointment. Call (870) 285–3718 for information. Admission is $4.00 for adults and $2.00 for children.

Diamond hunting isn't the only outdoor activity that glitters near here. The Little Missouri River flows clear and cold and is the home of possibly the best fly-fishing for rainbow trout in the state. It is also home to the scrappy smallmouth bass that provide some of the best action for sport fishermen. The tailwaters below the dam are icy, and you can fish from a canoe or flat-bottom boat or just wade in and do it the old-fashioned way. If that experience has made you happy, continue north about 9 miles on Highway 27/70 to Glenwood, where you will find the Caddo River—a beautiful, spring-fed stream full of those same smallmouths. It is floatable year-round, and canoes and guides are available in Glenwood for pack-in trips in the wilderness. Crawfish is the bait of choice.

You can see why fishermen favor this part of the state. *Daisy State Park,* in the foothills of the Ouachita Mountains near the northern end of crystal-clear Lake Greeson, is famous for its thirty-pound lunker-class striped bass, northern pike, and walleye. Above the lake on the Little Missouri lurk fighting rainbow trout, too. But this park has something more: It caters to motorcyclists with the 31-mile *Bear Creek Cycle Trail* on the west side of the lake. The trail goes to Laurel Creek and is open to motorcycles, all-terrain vehicles (ATVs), and nonmotorized bikes as well, although if you are pedaling, a mountain bike would be a good choice, for this is a 31-mile one-way trip and it's mountainous. ATVs are not allowed in the park except on the trail. There's a parking lot at the trailhead to offload your ATVs, and motorcycles can be driven to the parking lot by roadway. The trail and park are open year-round seven days a week. Call (870) 398–4487 for information.

In October the bike tour from Daisy to Crater of Diamonds Park 23 miles away is an annual event. There is an entry fee, but you get a free T-shirt for the tour. An interpretive program of guided hikes, games, crafts, and evening slide and movie shows in the park's outdoor amphitheater is free during the summer. Campsites have electric and water hookups, but half of the twenty-one tent sites are for hike-in camping only. The clear waters of the Caddo River begin their path to the sea in the Ouachita Mountains near Mena, and the Caddo Valley is ideal for camping in primitive campsites on the abundant sand and gravel bars. From the town of Daisy on Highway 70, go ¼ mile south. Call (870) 398–4487 for information.

Caddo Gap River's Edge Bed and Breakfast is the kind of B&B we all dream of finding when we are wandering around a new area. It sits high on a hill overlooking the Caddo River smack dab in the middle of nowhere. This spot on the river is where Hernando de Soto went as far west as he was destined to go; De Soto Gap allows passage between the mountains. It was the hunting grounds of the Caddo (Tula) Indians, and many artifacts can still be found here.

Bill and Rhonda Counts live in this country Tudor-style home on three wooded acres that slope gently toward the river. Hammocks hang in the trees, taking advantage of breezes off the water. You can get up early in the morning and go fishing on the river before breakfast, which is served in the Victorian dining room or on the deck overlooking the river. The house has a great room with 30-foot ceilings, wide windows, a huge fireplace, and the kind of furniture "people are not afraid to sit on," according to Rhonda.

There are three spacious bedrooms, a honeymoon suite (all with private baths), and an efficiency cabin with plenty of beds. Groups of up to seven couples can stay here for shared vacations. In fact, the place can, and often does, sleep as many as twenty people "slumber-party style" when big groups come for retreats or reunions. You can rent a canoe next door, and there is a golf course nearby (Willie Nelson stayed here and so did Randy Travis while filming the movie *White River Kid*). Not enough to do? The Counts can direct you to fishing, horseback riding, mountain biking, swimming, antiquing, and crystal digging. It is one mile from Caddo Gap, which is just a little ghost town, really.

Prices range from $95 to $125. To reach the property take Highway 240 West, cross the bridge over the river, and then turn left into the driveway. Call (800) 756–4864 or (870) 356–4864 for reservations or information. You can log on to the Web site at www.riversedgebandb.com.

Two beautiful sights in this region are the 4-mile Winding Stair portion of the **Little Missouri Trail** and the **Little Missouri Falls** near the Albert Pike Campgrounds north of Langley. From Caddo Gap turn on Highway 240 and go 10 miles to Albert Pike. Take the dirt road about 5 miles. You have to hike in to see them, but they are almost accessible by road via a short ($2/_{10}$-mile) hike from a picnic area with parking. The falls are a series of 10-foot stair-step falls in an area designated as "wild," meaning that all roads into the area are barricaded and closed year-round. This walk is a bit of a tester for older people because of about 25 yards of steps. But the trail winds along the river and through rocky, tree-shaded canyons, and the only sounds are the rocks kicking up riffles and the

Little Missouri Falls

birds and squirrels chittering in the trees. Or, if you are still feeling your oats, you can camp at Albert Pike and hike 6³/₁₀ miles along a trail of shortleaf pine, old-growth American beech trees, American holly shrubs, and plenty of white oak, hickory, and red cedars—a trail that parallels the Little Missouri River to the falls. The trailhead is at Forest Service Road 106, a good dirt road, 2 miles from the Albert Pike Recreation Area. Watch for the Forest Service emblem marking the trailhead.

The falls are only 6 miles from the headwaters, and the river is not wide at this point. The trail fords the river at the southern end and crosses a creek near the northern trailhead, so some wading is required. The falls are between Round Mountain and Hurricane Knob. To drive to the picnic area from the Albert Pike Campgrounds, go north on County Road 73 about 2 miles; then take a left turn on County Road 43 and go about 5¹/₂ miles, taking County Road 25 to the left for 1 mile and County Road 593 to the left about ¹/₄ mile. There are five picnic tables there, as well as parking. Be sure to take your camera or sketch pad.

If you prefer a canoe or kayak, the river is peaceful and shallow and lazes along in summer, looping around wide gravel bars, forming deep swimming holes and rock towers. After spring rains, though, the Winding Stairs portion of the river is crooked and steep and capable of producing Class III rapids after a big storm: not easy to navigate for beginners.

East of Langley on first Highway 84 and then Highway 4, you can meet "Beauty and the Beast" if you are in the mood for danger and adventure. *"Beauty and the Beast"* is what they call the Cossatot River, and 11 miles of the most rugged and spectacular river corridors pass through *Cossatot River State Park* near Wickes where Highway 4 meets Highway 71. The river begins in the Ouachita Mountains southeast of Mena and rushes south for about 26 miles into Gillham Lake. The waters are the home of two fish found only in the southern Ouachita: the leopard darter and the Ouachita Mountain shiner. The park covers more than 4,200 acres of wooded slopes and cascading clear water. There are Class III, IV, and V rapids on this wild-running river, thus making it a favorite with rafters, kayakers, and canoeists. They say that Cossatot means "skull crusher"; the river can be dangerous. It flows over and around upended layers of bedrock, sometimes dropping 60 feet per mile, and contains narrow valleys and lengthy rapids and falls. The river is not recommended for the inexperienced; it is called "probably the most challenging" white water in the state. How's that for understatement? Call (870) 385–2201 for information about the river.

Mena is where Highway 71 runs into Scenic Highway 88. The city is in the shadow of Rich Mountain. The newly restored, 1920 Kansas City *Southern Railroad Mena Depot Center,* at 514 Sherwood Street, Mena 71953, is a combination museum and visitors center. It houses the Mena Chamber of Commerce, a tourist information center, and railroad displays and memorabilia. Quality crafts from a 60-mile area are for sale inside. The center is run by community volunteers who know their way around the area quite well.

Highway 88 shows off the 54 miles of twists and turns along *Talimena Drive* as it winds along the crests of forested mountains between Mena and the Oklahoma border, within the boundaries of the 1.6-million-acre Ouachita National Forest, covering almost all of Montgomery County. The drive spans the highest mountain range between the Appalachians and the Rockies. Getting off the road is full of pleasures, too. Hiking trails wind through the forests along ridges, lakes, and streams. It's a heaven for nature lovers. The area is one of America's oldest landmasses, and the rock there tells the geologic history of the area. At the crest of Rich Mountain stands a historic fire tower 2,681 feet above the valley.

Rising high above the clouds on Rich Mountain, *Queen Wilhelmina Lodge,* in the state park of the same name, was destroyed by fire in 1973 and rebuilt in a style that reflects its past, with stone fireplaces, comfortable rooms, and a spectacular view; it is perched on the highest elevation in the park on steep and winding Highway 88. The first lodge was built

Trivia

in 1896 by the Kansas City, Pittsburgh and Gulf Railroad and was designed as a retreat for passengers on the line. The three-story lodge became known as the "Castle in the Sky" and was named for Holland's young queen (there was largely Dutch financing for the lodge). A royal suite was set aside for her in hope that she would decide to make an official visit someday, but she never did. Dining in the lodge's restaurant gives you a view above the clouds. Rooms are from $57 to $100 (for a room with sitting area and fireplace).

The Ouachita Mountains run east and west, rather than north and south like most American ranges. This makes the area difficult for pilots of small planes and backpackers who often become disoriented in the unusual terrain.

Other attractions in the park include a small railroad, miniature golf, camping, and an animal park with creatures to pet. Queen Wilhelmina State Park is 13 miles northwest of Mena on Highway 88, but in bad weather it is advisable to take Highway 270 to Highway 272 and then to go south for 2 miles; continuing west takes you to the Pioneer Cemetery historical marker before crossing the state line into Oklahoma. Call (501) 394–2863 or 394–2864 or e-mail QWSP@Arkansas.net for lodge reservations.

Talimena Drive crosses Highway 259 and begins to climb along the spine of the Winding Stair Mountains. There are several interesting spots along the drive: Billy Creek Recreation Area, Emerald Vista (which has not only camping but interpretive and equestrian trails), Lake Wister, Cedar Lake Recreation Area, Horsethief Springs, and Old Military Road historical sites all perch on the ridge of the mountains. You will have a sweeping view of the Poteau River Valley.

Highway 88 East from Mena leads to the only town in America named after a radio show—***Pine Ridge.*** If you are old enough to remember radio days and are at all nostalgic for them, first close your eyes and listen to your memories and then open your eyes and take a look at Dick Huddleston's ***Lum and Abner Museum,*** or the "Jot 'Em Down Store." Is it the way you thought it would be? You will never see Fibber McGee's closet. You will never see the Shadow ("Who knows what evil lurks in the hearts of men?"). But this museum is on the National Register of Historic Places, and you can walk right in and let your imagination take you back to those nights in front of the radio. Arkansas natives Chester Lauck and Norris Goff, better known as Lum and Abner, entertained listeners during the 1940s with a radio show filled with down-home humor, and today the store looks just as it did, or how we imagined it looked, back in the 1940s—an old potbellied stove near the post office window in the general store (with the museum situated in the next room). The museum is open Tuesday through Saturday from 9:00 A.M. to 5:00 P.M. and from noon to 5:00 P.M. on Sunday March 1 through October. You can call (870) 326–4442, and although neither Lum nor Abner will answer, postmistress Kathryn Stucker will.

If you have followed Highway 88 East, you will be entering an area called the "Quartz Crystal Capital of the World," and there are several commercial mines around here. *Wegner Quartz Crystal Mines,* 3 miles south of Mount Ida on Highway 27, are perhaps the only mines where you can find your own crystals. They are open year-round from 8:00 A.M. to 4:30 P.M. Monday through Friday and by appointment on weekends weather permitting. You don't have to dig very deep to find crystals in one of the three mines. The digging fee ranges from $6.00 for deposits nearby to $20.00 a day to travel to the mines—groups of ten or more only, and you can keep what you find. Tim, the manager, says that finding a crystal is almost guaranteed. One of the mines is a hike—1/4 mile up a mountain slope, a strenuous walk not recommended for older people—but you can be driven to the other location (in Tim's pickup truck), where you can dig in the red clay until you find all the crystals you want. Six-sided, single-point crystals are the most common and can be clear or cloudy quartz. The clusters are more difficult to find; they require more work and some luck, too. Crystals range in size from a quarter of a pound to ten pounds. Richard Wegner, owner of the mines, also has showers and campsites available near the retail area, which is 5 miles south of Mount Ida on Highway 27. Call (870) 867–2309 for information or visit their Web site www.wegnercrystalmines.com.

Several other mines operate in the easygoing town of Mount Ida: *The Ocus Stanley and Son Crystal Mine,* open from 9:00 A.M. to dusk, asks for a donation, usually $5.00 a day. Call (870) 867–3556 for information. At *Fiddler's Ridge Crystal Mine,* it's $16.00 a day, but if you bring your own hard hat, it's just $11 (870–867–2127). Hours are 9:00 A.M. to 5:00 P.M. seven days a week.

Some nice side trips to resorts and picnic areas can be found along Highway 270. This beautiful part of the state offers scenic drives worth exploring for an afternoon or a weekend. Premiere among them is the twisting drive to the summit of Hickory Nut Mountain that leads to a panoramic view of Lake Ouachita and its many islands. This region is remote and natural with small towns sprinkled throughout the hills. It is a fine place to escape the hustle of city life and enjoy the beauty of the Natural State.

MORE PLACES TO STAY IN SOUTHWEST ARKANSAS

HOT SPRINGS AREA

Hot Springs Best Western,
1525 Central, 71902;
(501) 624–1258

Park Hotel,
211 Fountain Street, 71902;
(501) 624–5323

THE OUACHITAS

Arkadelphia Best Western,
I–30/Highway 67, 71923;
(870) 246–5592

Holiday Inn,
150 Valley, 71923;
(800) HOLIDAY

DeQueen Palace Motel,
607 West Collin Raye Drive,
71932;
(870) 642–9627

Hope Best Western,
I–30/Highway 278,
exit 30, 71802;
(870) 777–9222,
(800) 528–1234
(Bill Clinton slept here.)

Mena Best Western,
Highways 71/8/88, 71953;
(870) 394–6350

MORE PLACES TO EAT IN SOUTHWEST ARKANSAS

HOT SPRINGS

Cock of the Walk
Restaurant,
4848 Central, 71902;
(501) 525–5050

Mrs. Miller's Dinners,
4723 Central, 71902;
(501) 525–8861

THE OUACHITAS

Arkadelphia
Continental Inn,
I–30/Highway 67;
(870) 246–5592

Hope Catfish King,
1012 North Hervey, 71802;
(870) 777–8526

Western Sizzlin' Steak
House,
I–30/Highway 4,
exit 30, 71802;
(870) 777–9222

Chambers of Commerce in Southwest Arkansas

Hot Springs
Hot Springs Chamber of Commerce;
P.O. Box 6090, Hot Springs 71902;
(501) 321–1700;
www.hotsprings.org

The Ouachitas
Arkadelphia Chamber of Commerce;
6th and Caddo Streets, Arkadelphia 71923;
(870) 246–5542;
arkadelphia.dina.org

Hope Chamber of Commerce;
P.O. Box 250, Hope 71802;
(870) 777–3640

Southeast Arkansas

$\int$ everal of the counties of southeastern Arkansas share the Ouachita
River, but high bluffs, unspoiled forests, and the river bottoms give
each area a distinct personality. If you enjoy gentle currents, a float on
the Ouachita, with your fishing gear, is perfect.

In the early 1700s, French trappers encountered the Ouachita Indians
living in small villages on the banks of the river. Ouachita is the French
way of spelling the Indian word, which sounds like "Washita," but the
meaning of the word has been lost—perhaps "good hunting," or "river
of many fish," some say.

This is where the timberlands begin, after the Ouachita Mountains, on
the way to the Mississippi Delta. The timberlands are where the Gulf
Coastal Plain and the Arkansas River Delta meet, too. This lush area,
covered with vast forests of southern pines and drained by sleepy bay-
ous and sloughs, is a favorite with sports enthusiasts because of the
exceptional fishing and hunting it provides.

The longest bayou in the world, Bayou Bartholemew, meanders through
the timberlands. The history of the country is seen from a southern
view in this part of the state, and plantations and antebellum homes dot
the Mississippi bottomland along the mighty river.

Oil and Timber Country

amden stands on a bluff at a horseshoe curve of the Ouachita
River. The Quapaw Indians, a branch of the Sioux, were friendly to
early Spanish explorer Hernando de Soto when he made his trip up that
river in 1541. The distance is 5 miles around the river's bend but less
than a quarter mile across the neck of the curve. In fact, a man named
Woodward once set more than a hundred slaves to digging a bayou,
which, had it been completed, would have become the main channel of
the river, leaving the town sitting high and dry on the loop.

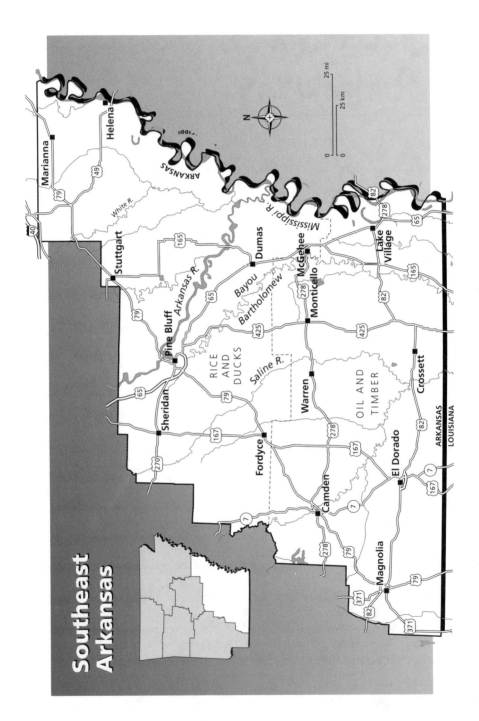

Southeast Arkansas

RICE AND DUCKS

OIL AND TIMBER

Marianna

Helena

Stuttgart

Pine Bluff

Sheridan

Fordyce

Camden

Magnolia

El Dorado

Crossett

Monticello

Warren

McGehee

Dumas

Lake Village

White R.

Arkansas R.

Bayou Bartholomew

Saline R.

ARKANSAS

Mississippi R.

ARKANSAS
LOUISIANA

25 mi

25 km

N

SOUTHEAST ARKANSAS

BEST ATTRACTIONS IN SOUTHEAST ARKANSAS

Big Boy Toys, Magnolia;
(870) 234–8899

Lois Gean's, Magnolia;
(870) 234–1250

Internet Cafe, El Dorado;
(870) 862–4335;
www.labella.net

Magnolia House,
McGehee; (870) 222–6425

Miller's Mud Mill,
Dumas; (870) 382–5277

Cajun Hideaway,
Pine Bluff; (870) 673–7460

Margland II,
Pine Bluff; (870) 536–6000

Klappenbach Bakery,
Fordyce; (870) 352–7771

Camden is an old Deep South city where cotton bales once lined the streets leading to the wharf. A varied collection of restored antebellum homes, including the circa 1847 **McCollum-Chidester House,** at 926 Washington Street NW, Camden 71701, attests to this heritage. The house, which is haunted (more about that in a moment), was used as headquarters by Sterling Price, a Confederate general, and Frederick Steele, a Union general, during the battle of Poison Springs in April 1864.

The house is filled with the original furniture and even has some bullet holes in the plastered walls of an upstairs room where stagecoach drivers slept: Union soldiers shot at stagecoach driver Colonel John T. Chidester—who had allowed Confederate soldiers to read Union mail he was carrying on his stagecoach—as he was hiding in a secret room near the stairwell. A pair of crystal hurricane globes, a mahogany and walnut secretary, and a sewing machine date back to 1850, along with Mrs. Chidester's needlework and clothing. The original dining table is set with Mrs. Chidester's silverware and china (which were buried under a tree in the yard to keep them safe from Union soldiers). The east bedroom is haunted by an apparition of a man dressed in a long coat, carrying a cane or sword. It appeared reflected in a mirror in a photo taken by a member of the historical society in 1985; copies of the photo can be purchased here.

The historical society has built a carriage house in the backyard. Because this was a stagecoach stop, a replica of one of Chidester's Concord stagecoaches and a turn-of-the-century surrey are parked there. The home is open March through October from 9:00 A.M. to 4:00 P.M. Wednesday through Saturday. Admission is $3.00 for adults and $1.00 for students. Call (870) 836–9243 for information.

The winters have been fairly harsh in southeast Arkansas for the last few years, which makes the annual **Daffodil Festival** in Camden each March that much more welcome. During the second weekend in March, the town literally blossoms with billions of daffodil bulbs planted by the city and private residents. The festival includes a tour of five historic homes and their gardens, street dances, gardening demonstrations, and arts and crafts. Call the chamber of commerce for more information at (870) 830–6426.

The Confederate Cemetery, at the junction of Adams Avenue and Maul Road, less than a mile from town, is the resting place of the more than 200 unknown young men killed here. It has many other interesting stories of the lives and times of the early setters. Beautiful examples of the almost-forgotten craft of wrought-iron work appear in fences around many plots. One unusual grave site contains only four weathered posts and a heavy iron anchor chain connecting them. It is said to be the grave of a child who died on a steamboat trip. The boat stopped only long enough to bury the little girl, and the crew used what it had on board to mark the spot.

From Camden take Highway 24 West to **White Oak Lake State Park,** which has 725 acres of timbered hillsides. Here in the hardwood forests, the Beech Ridge Trail offers a glimpse of the Gulf Coastal Plain. The gentle trail is 2 miles long and takes you from the thick underbrush of the edge of the woods into the shaded forest floor where life abounds. As the elevation drops, the pines of the uplands meet the lowland hardwoods, where the Caddo Indians lived some 200 to 300 years ago. Boardwalks cover the bottomland part of the trail to protect the unusual plants that live in this moist soil. Orchids grow here—in the early spring the twayblade orchid and later other orchids and arums (such as the jack-in-the-pulpit) are seen here. The park has recently added forty-five new campsites with electricity and water, which rent for $15 per night.

Trivia

During the Civil War near St. Charles on the White River, a cannonball was shot through a porthole of the Federal ironclad Mound City, *killing almost one hundred soldiers when it hit a steam pipe. Historians call it the single most destructive shot of the war.*

A bridge takes you across the stream, where the soil is mostly white sand, the remnant of an ancient shoreline that was formed as the Gulf of Mexico receded from the area more than a million years ago. The fine white sandhills lead around a slight curve and ascend into the sand barren, an isolated spot where the soil is infertile and few plants can survive—but the ones that do are unique to these zones. Riddel's spikemoss, for instance, looks like little sand castles and, like moss, dries up and waits for rain to revive it and release its spores. But unlike moss and more like fern, it has roots and, like pine trees, has a conelike megaspore. It is unique to the sandhills and is sort of a missing link between lower and higher plant levels. Call (870) 685–2748 or 685–2132 for information.

Logging trucks rumble down the highways, and trucks stacked high with chicken crates cruise in a confetti of feathers: Forestry and chicken ranching are the main businesses as you head south. But along Highway

79 between Camden and Magnolia, you'll see what is perhaps not the most beautiful of yard ornaments (but better than a birdbath)—oil wells—gracing lawns.

Six miles north of Magnolia on County Road 47, just off Highway 79 near the McNeil Highway junction, is **Logoly State Park.** This is not pronounced to rhyme with "by golly" but rather sounds more like "Low-ga-lie." The name has nothing to do with the loblolly pine, either. It is actually an acronym of the names of three families who gave the land to the state—the Longinos, the Goodes, and the Lyles. The park has medicinal waters bubbling up in eleven natural springs in the forest; people once traveled from far away to drink and bathe in the mineral waters. Logoly was also the state's first environmental education park, and observation stands and photo blinds dot the trails for nature observers and bird-watchers. The mineral springs and unique plant life make it worth exploring.

The visitors center houses exhibits of the park's history and natural environment. Summer hours are 8:00 A.M. to 5:00 P.M. daily; winter hours are 8:00 A.M. to 5:00 P.M. Monday through Friday and 1:00 to 5:00 P.M. Saturday and Sunday. Call (870) 695–3561 for information.

A lovely 1923 Mediterranean-style home with an Italian tile roof is just a few blocks from downtown Camden, which is on the Ouachita River near the Civil War battlefield at Poison Springs.

Umsted House Bed and Breakfast, at 404 Washington Street, Camden 71701, is where James Silliman offers hospitality to travelers. The buff-brick stone steps lead into this home, which is on the National Register of Historic Places. James has four bedrooms, all with private baths and decorated in period antiques. A graceful crystal chandelier lights the dining room, where James serves breakfast. You will find a menu in your room at night to help you select your morning treat. The specialty of the house

BEST ANNUAL EVENTS IN SOUTHEAST ARKANSAS

World's Championship Duck Calling Contest and Wings Over the Prairie Festival, Stuttgart; Thanksgiving weekend; (870) 673–1602, (800) 810–2241; Gumbo Cookoff and the Great 10k Duck Race

Grand Prairie Festival of Arts, Stuttgart; September; (870) 673–1781; juried show and sale, top exhibitors, miniature art show

King Biscuit Blues Festival, Helena, second weekend of October; (870) 338–8327

Magnolia Blossom Festival, Magnolia; third week in May; world championship steak cook-off (501) 836–6426

Crossett PRCA Rodeo, Crosett; second Wednesday in August; (870) 364–6591

Armadillo Festival, Hamburg; first weekend in May; (870) 853–8345; Armadillo derby and crawfish boil

Pioneer Crafts Festival, Rison; third weekend in March; (870) 325–7444; small admission fee

Frontier Days Festival, Hamburg; third weekend in October; (870) 853–5578; buggy rides, old time cooking

is a delicious creation named after the original owner, Sid Umsted. Eggs Sidney is a poached egg on an English muffin, much like eggs Benedict. But instead of just hollandaise sauce, this is topped with a crabmeat mixture and melted cheese. James also serves dinners or luncheons—with advance notice—for groups of up to twenty people. The landscaped yard is at its best in the early spring, when everything is in blossom. Rooms are $75. There's an antiques mall downtown, to which James can direct you. Call him at (870) 836–9609 or (800) 836–9609, or log on to www.umstedhouse.com.

James recommends the **White House Cafe,** at 323 Adams, Camden 71701, for lunch or dinner. This place has been open since the early 1900s, when it was built for railroad workers who were putting lines through for the lumber business, and has the oldest beer license in the state. It offers more than fifty kinds of beer, both domestic and imported, and is famous for cheeseburgers and steaks. One of its specialties is Mexican food. Teresa Lampkin is the new owner, who doubled the size of the restaurant seating when she bought it. She also brought in her family's personal collection of antique beer cans. Customers spend hours searching the walls for their favorite brand. Hours are from 11:00 A.M. to 10:00 P.M. for dinner Monday through Friday and noon to 10:00 P.M. on Saturday. Call (870) 836–2255 for information.

South of Camden on Highway 79 lies the city of **Magnolia.** As the name tells you, flowering trees grace this city's landscape. The courthouse is surrounded by them, and fragrant blossoms burst into bloom just in time for the Magnolia Blossom Festival, art show, and steak cook-off the third weekend in May.

The steak cook-off has become one of the biggest events around here. In 1996 they cooked 4,500 steaks and had 40,000 people attend the Magnolia Blossom Festival. This is the *official,* nationally sanctioned steak-cooking championship, attracting steak cookers from all over the country. It is sold out every year (you get a steak dinner with all the trimmings). Courthouse Square is a direct copy of the square in Oxford, Mississippi.

Big Boy Toys, at 2410 North Dudney at the Highway 79/82 Bypass, Magnolia 71753, is another must-see place. It is a combination art gallery, collectibles shop, and sort-of museum. Owner George Black says some items are not for sale, like the 1915 Model A car hanging on a wall. There are model trains, fountains, and a chandelier made of deer antlers (which *is* for sale). A good collection of emerging-images art is on display, too. In these paintings, nothing is quite as it seems at first glance. Something might appear to be clouds, but when you get closer you realize it is a herd of buffalo running across a prairie. By the front door stands a Christmas tree decorated in a western theme. The old tree done in bits and spurs is interesting, too. George recently added 4,000 square feet to the store, mostly to accommodate his hunting and fishing village, a separate room in the center of the store. In addition to antique hunting and fishing items, you'll find mounted animals, such as elk, deer, and bobcats. Some of them George shot himself right here in southeast Arkansas. George is an artist. He designs barbecue grills that look like a horse, a pig, or a rocket ship. The shop is open 10:00 A.M. to 5:00 P.M. Monday through Friday and 10:00 A.M. to 2:00 P.M. on Saturday. Call (870) 234–8899 for information.

If you are looking for a place to eat, search out the **Backyard Bar B Que,** at 1407 East Main, Magnolia 71753. It is well known around here for its baby back ribs and homemade pies. Glenda Jones is the "pie lady," and she has been here since the beginning. People line up outside for her special pies. You never know what kind of pie will be offered—it depends on her mood—but some of the favorites are chocolate chip cherry cheesecake, lemon icebox pie, any kind of chess pie you can imagine (chocolate and raisin are two favorites), and pecan cream cheese pie. Hours are Tuesday through Saturday from 11:00 A.M. to 8:30 P.M. Owners David and Susan Greer know that a lot of people are weight conscious, so they also have a low-fat menu. What, you might ask, could a barbecue and pie place have on a low-fat menu? Picture this: a rolled, steamed 10-inch tortilla with greens, chicken breast, steamed asparagus, carrots, fat-free cheese, and tomato slices.

Walk around the town square and feel the Magnolia-pride of this lovely town. Each shop represents the city's flowering trees in some small way, it seems. A gift shop sells marble eggs, music boxes, and items covered in magnolias. A framing gallery features prints with magnolias, and even the pharmacy has magnolia mementos. You can browse the antiques mall and give your feet a rest in the Let's Do Lunch loft while your eyes continue to shop, or be wild and find the **Magnolia Bake Shop,** which produces such mouthwatering treats as pecan sticky buns, rum cakes, and crullers. Located at 103 North Jefferson Street, Magnolia 71753, the bakeshop has been turning out fresh cinnamon rolls since 1928. Original owner Joe Stroope Sr. has passed the business on to his sons Joe Jr., Stephen, and Willie, who continue to turn out luscious baked goods daily. It has expanded beyond doughnuts and cookies, though, and now offers almost anything your sweet tooth can desire. Along with great bread, cakes (German chocolate), pies (apple, peach, and pecan), and Danish pastries, the men make fresh biscuits and sausage rolls for the breakfast crowd. (How does a German smoked sausage tucked inside a fresh roll sound? Or breakfast sausage inside a hot biscuit?) Everything is baked fresh daily, and the bakery opens at 6:00 A.M. and stays open all day until 5:30 P.M. Tuesday through Saturday, so you can go from early Danish to late-afternoon sausage roll. Call (870) 234–1304 for information.

Shopping for exclusive designer clothes, something in the $200 to $1,200 price range? Then stop by *Lois Gean's,* at 109 South Jackson Street, Magnolia 71753. The shop is listed right there with the high-dollar department stores in *Vogue* magazine as the place to buy designer clothes. The ad says, "Lois Gean's, Magnolia," with no state mentioned—because people "in the know" know where Lois Gean's is. People who want Donna Karan, Escada, and Anne Klein clothing and who like Valentino bags shop here and have come from miles around to do so since 1943. Lois Gean's started as a small gift shop and has bulged sideways to take in 4,400 square feet of the neighboring buildings. The rustic entrance, with its cast-iron stove and old brass mailboxes, belies the polish inside, and dynamic owner Lois Gean Kelly travels to New York on buying trips. The shop is open Monday through Saturday from 10:00 A.M. to 5:00 P.M. Call (870) 234–1250 for information. Check the Web site at www.loisgeans.com.

Open for tours is *Albemarle's Artificial Marsh,* 7 miles south of town on Highway 79. The National Aeronautics and Space Administration–inspired marsh is an environmentally safe wetland that serves as a natural water-purification system. There are more than 80,000 aquatic plants and feeding stations to encourage the habitat of beavers, otters, and raccoons as well as ducks, hawks, egrets, and other waterfowl. A teaching station explains the development of the marsh, and a freshwater aquarium is filled with Japanese koi, minnows, frogs, catfish, goldfish, and turtles. To schedule a tour call (870) 235–6000.

Southern Arkansas University's (SAU) Working Farm, at the north edge of Magnolia, also takes an environmentally conscious approach. The 670 acres of livestock, poultry, and plants are cared for by seventy-five students in the country's largest agricultural work-study program. The farm focuses on ways to reuse waste products, studies the benefits of tillage versus nontillage crop growth, and does applied research into breeding techniques and equipment. SAU is also home to the state's only official National Collegiate Athletic Association rodeo team, whose horse and practice stock are housed on the farm. The farm, which draws people from all over the country, can be toured by appointment by calling (870) 235–4340.

Georgia and Tommy Snider's restaurant, **Georgia's,** at 2630 Columbia Fifteen (at Burnt Bridge Road), Magnolia 71753, is in the house built in 1944 for Tommy's grandmother with lumber cut off the land itself; the original well and bucket are still on the back porch. The roomy house, with its L-shaped porch, is 6½ miles outside of town on four acres of crape myrtle and pines. Entering the house, you will be startled to see a huge carved bedroom suite with a bed so tall it almost touches the 9-foot ceiling. That's just the beginning, because all four dining rooms are filled with antiques. The Sniders serve catfish, shrimp, smoked pork ribs, and steaks—the couple won the annual steak cook-off with their secret recipe of herbs and spices one year. But the homemade rolls and fried pies are the specialties. Fruit pies, raisin pies, and coconut or chocolate cream pies are top sellers. Yes, you read that right: a fried chocolate cream pie.

There's a map on the wall in one room, and people from all over the country have marked it. At last count only Montana, Maine, and "a couple of those little states on the East Coast" were not marked. So if you are from one of those states, get over there and sign in. Hours are from 5:00 to 10:00 P.M. Monday through Saturday. Call (870) 696–3942 for reservations.

The **Weyerhaeuser Company Reforestation Center,** just outside Magnolia on Calhoun Road, is where fifty million seedlings a year are born from some 600 parent trees. The people at Weyerhaeuser know the ancestry of each tree ("It's sort of a stud farm for trees," says Lester Hutchins of the Magnolia Chamber of Commerce) and have chosen the area because the environment is perfect for reproducing pines. The birth and upkeep of these native trees are a full-time job in this timberland. In the spring, seeding operations can be seen; in summer the seedlings grow, covering the acreage with a soft green fuzz; in the fall, cone harvesting and processing go on; and in winter the seedlings are harvested to sell to forest products companies and individuals in a five-state area. Although southern pine predominates, other trees—different kinds of oak and some

Trivia
If you hear bells while walking around the town of Magnolia, don't think you've gone nuts. The campus of Southern Arkansas University is home to a 180-foot-tall bell tower that chimes every 15 minutes, 365 days a year. The sound carries for miles. During the Christmas holiday season, the tower is decorated and lit to look like a huge candle, and the music played reflects the season.

cypress—are grown in the forest. Respect and care for the environment are demonstrated in this area, despite the logging that sometimes strips hillsides bare before they are replanted. This is an environmental education stop worth a visit. Two videos are available: The first shows the birth and growth of the trees grown here; the second relates the life cycle of the forests. To find the forest, go south on Highway 79 to the first intersection (less than 1 mile), turn east onto Calhoun Road, and proceed about 6 miles to the center. Call ahead at (870) 234–3537; group tours can also be arranged.

Driving east on Highway 82 brings you to the city of **El Dorado.** In 1921 the town prospered when black gold began gushing and the sweet smell of crude oil pumping onto the land and into the once-pristine waters of the Ouachita River drew the get-rich-quick crowd of promoters, drillers, roughnecks, and thieves. The town filled with itinerant oil workers, and the population jumped to 30,000 persons who needed to be fed. A 3-block area called Hamburger Row sprang up. Now, more than seventy years later, more sophisticated restaurants line the street, and the city is not to be missed if good eating is high on your list of things to do while traveling.

El Dorado

*E**l Dorado stands among the proudest of the small towns. While others have lost retail business to outlying areas, El Dorado enjoys a 95 to 100 percent retail occupancy. It has the last grand movie palace in the state, the Rialto, still showing movies each night. When my husband and I went to El Dorado, I had just finished two terms on the city council and one term as mayor of our town. Our city had taken the same Downtown Redevelopment money used in El Dorado, but we accomplished very little compared with this sight. I was so amazed at El Dorado that I just couldn't leave without visiting every business on the square and talking to the owners. We stayed for dinner and saw the downtown blossom into a night center, too.*

The courthouse is magnificent, and many of the retail businesses are upscale specialty stores, located in a historic district that has been restored to reflect a 1920s ambience. Because of the four restaurants and the theater, however, there is a slight parking problem, something every small town in the country wishes it had.

In the 20-block downtown area, 750 trees were planted and the courthouse was relandscaped with more than 300 plants, including London plane trees, the street tree so common in Europe. There are old English phone booths, information kiosks, and street clocks dotting the square. Turn-of-the-twentieth-century light poles and sidewalk planters make the square a fine place to stroll.

Most of the buildings downtown were built in the boom days, when oil flowed freely from the wells around here. Now one of two "Main Street" cities in the county, El Dorado has been restored, and brightly colored awnings, pear trees, and park benches have been added to the old lampposts that line the streets. The place boasts handsome old homes and the South Arkansas Arts Center. The old Union County Courthouse on the town square, the heart of the community, is a massive, neoclassical building with more columns than any other structure in the state. The Rialto Theater, built in 1929 at 117 East Cedar Street on the square, has also been restored and is the state's only working art deco theater, with gilded, vaulted ceilings and waterfall curtains. To take a tour or to find out what's showing, call (870) 881–8771.

La Bella Gourmet Gifts and Delicatessen, at 101 East Main Street, El Dorado 71730, features delicious sandwiches, soups, meats, cheeses, and salads, as well as gift baskets. It is also well known for its cinnamon rolls and powdermilk biscuits. The building was an old department store built during the oil boom. It has a ballroom upstairs for parties and every day serves red beans and rice that is so good people from Louisiana take some home with them. The shop features the ***Internet Cafe,*** where you can surf the Net while drinking espresso. There is a $5.00 per hour charge to use the Internet or a $2.00 charge if you just want to check your e-mail. The one-hundred-seat deli sells such wonderful things as cream and butter fudge and uses Italian meats shipped in from "Yankee Land" (Massachusetts). You can order a jalapeño smoked turkey—injected with jalapeño spices and hickory smoked—and it will be sent to you for $54.95, plus about $10 in shipping. Jim Robinson is the owner of this place (you can't miss him, he's the big smiling man with the beard). It's open Monday through Saturday from 8:00 A.M. to 7:00 P.M. Call (870) 862–4335 for information or check out the Web site at www.labella.net.

The South Arkansas Arboretum is a seventeen-acre arboretum adjacent to the high school and city park. It has walking trails, pavilions, and picnic areas that are used for educational purposes and also for weddings. The arboretum is open from 8:00 A.M. to 5:00 P.M. daily. Call (870) 862–8131.

If you are going to spend a few days in town, Jim can direct you to other fascinating places like ***Creative Means,*** at 309 East Main, El Dorado 71730, where Caroline and Mike Means do quilt stretching and have work by local artists, prints, and posters. Hours are 10:00 A.M. to 5:00 P.M. Tuesday to Saturday (870–862–9881). At ***Mudslide Pottery,*** 207 East Main, El Dorado 71730, you can pay by the hour to make your own pottery and fire it right there. Or shop in a new gallery that features the work of potters from all over the state. Call (870) 862–9187 for information.

Tiger Harry's Restaurant, at 117 East Main Street, El Dorado 71730, is where water comes in quart mason jars with a wedge of lemon and a straw. You're going to need it, too, because a note on the menu says, "We put jalapeños on just about anything—just ask," and they do. A neon sign over the kitchen announces WE BE COOKIN'; a giant red neon Pegasus adorns the bar (where Rattlesnake beer and Rolling Rock beer are sold); and friendly waitresses let you sit back and relax. Trying to finish the half-pound Tiger Burger with jalapeños, cheese, tomato, and a huge load of spicy, unpeeled, steak fries is a real test of your eating capacity. But even more challenging is an order of the deluxe nachos—chips covered with sour cream, guacamole, beans, meat—enough to feed a family of five. "No one has ever finished them," the waitress said. Desserts include mug pie, a hot fudge pie in a mug topped with ice cream or Crispitos, and apple- or cherry-filled burritos, deep-fried and served with ice cream. Hours are 11:00 A.M. to 9:00 P.M. Monday through Thursday and 11:00 A.M. to 11:00 P.M. Friday and Saturday, Sunday 11:00 A.M. to 2:00 P.M. Call (870) 863–6611 for information.

The ***Old Towne Store,*** at 113 North Jefferson Street, El Dorado 71730, is a bakery and bulk-food shop offering foods prepared only with natural ingredients—homemade soups and sandwiches (with whole grain breads) and freshly baked pies and pastries. The aroma of baking bread and cookies fills the shop. Hours are Monday through Saturday from 7:30 A.M. to 6:30 P.M. Call (870) 862–1060 for information.

Even though it's tempting to spend the day on the square, the rest of the city has some surprises, too. There are plenty of antiques shops and restaurants tucked around town. If you get a hankerin' for alligator gumbo, head out of town about 3 miles south on the Haynesville Highway. The place is called ***Tina's Seafood,*** a family-run business that, among other things, serves alligator gumbo. Tina's family is from the Louisiana bayou country where alligator is a more common dish. They also serve frog legs and some of the best Arkansas catfish you'll find anywhere. Tina's is only open Thursday through Saturday from 5:00 to 10:00 P.M. Call (870) 875–2500.

Smackover, north of El Dorado on Highway 7, is worth a side trip because it is the other "Main Street" city in this county. The name comes from nearby Smackover Creek, which got its unusual name from the French explorers who found the banks of the creek to be covered with sumac and so named it Sumac Couvert. (Sumac Couvert soon became pronounced "smackover.") Boomtown murals are painted on the facades of the stores alongside Kennedy Park on Broadway Street; 1923 was a time when oil and money flowed freely and the town was prosperous.

The *Arkansas Museum of Natural Resources,* located 1 mile south of the oil-rich town on Highway 7 Bypass, is surrounded by twenty acres of woodlands. Six operational exhibits are on site, including a working oil well, pumping rig, and seven derricks. And surprise! Inside the 25,500-square-foot exhibition and research center, there's an art gallery, too, where local talent exhibits in the spacious auditorium. Each artist donates a piece of his or her work to the ever-growing collection in the fourteen galleries now being designed. This is the largest museum in south Arkansas and has a full-time staff to direct visitors through the permanent and changing exhibits made up of the archives and artifacts covering subjects that include geology, refining oil and brine, use of petroleum and bromine, and paleontology, as well as social subjects such as women's role in the boom era. Stop first at the information desk in the lobby for pamphlets describing the indoor and outdoor exhibit areas. Temporary and traveling exhibits are displayed in the Exhibition Center, with two video presentations depicting the discovery of oil and brine in the state. No admission fee is charged to see the machinery and equipment that made this area explode in the 1920s, when the Busey Number 1 oil well blew in. Notice the colorful murals by Phillip Grantham that depict the history of the oil boom. Videos, tapes, and transcripts of oral histories of the roustabouts and roughnecks who lived and worked in the boom era are available to the public. A gift shop in the museum offers a variety of unique gifts related to the petroleum industry and the 1920s, as well as locally produced treats of jellies, hams, and syrups.

The Smackover oil field was the largest in the country for a five-month period in 1925. Oil Field Park, the outdoor portion of the exhibit, has a 1920s standard rig and a 112-foot wooden derrick, the tallest known wooden derrick structure in the country. There's a spot to picnic, but if you want to see the real thing, you can get a tour through the forty-acre Smackover Field, just north of the museum, with acres of salt flats where the oil pioneers disposed of salt water that came from the ground along with the oil from when the oceans covered the southern part of the state. The museum, at 3853 Smackover Highway, Smackover 71762, is open Sunday from 1:00 to 5:00 P.M. and Monday through Friday from 8:00 A.M. to 5:00 P.M. There is no charge for this facility, but donations are accepted. Call (870) 725–2877 for information. The Web site is www.cei.net/~amnr.

Returning from Smackover, driving east from El Dorado north on Highway 15 is one of the more scenic drives in the southern part of the state. The 14-mile drive from Moro Bay to Hermitage is a tranquil journey on a good county road. Houses along Highway 15 are a mixture of Victorian and modern styles. There used to be a free ferry to whip you across the Ouachita River by Moro Bay State Park. It is now dry-docked, and you can walk through it. This is where Moro Bay and Raymond Lake join the Ouachita River.

The scarcity of B&Bs in the southern part of the state makes finding one a treat, so, after the restful ride on Highway 15, the town of **Warren,** famous for its pink tomatoes (the Pink Tomato Festival is the second week in June), has the **Bed and Breakfast of Warren,** The Burnett House, which you will want to check out. This Victorian home, at 111 N. Munn Street, Warren 71671, just 2 blocks from the historic Courthouse Square has three guest rooms, each with private bath. Innkeepers Greg and Jan Harton serve an extended continental breakfast in the breakfast area or formal dining room.

The Burnett House turned 105 years old with the new century. It was the first house in town to have indoor plumbing. It has high ceilings, and in the white country kitchen the original beaded-board ceiling was used to make the cabinets. The kitchen is filled with modern equipment, though, and people can do their own cooking if they have a mind to. The first thing you notice when you walk into this B&B is the 1850s square grand piano. There is also an 1874 pump organ in the dining room, and Jan plays both very well. A bowed psaltery was acquired in 1997 (an unusual, high-pitched string instrument that is mentioned in the Bible, it is one of the oldest known instruments). Jan plays it, too, and melodies, especially hymns, sound lovely. She also caters events in town. Her favorite affairs, though, are the tea parties she throws for area children. She serves heart-shaped peanut butter sandwiches, and the children dress up in feather boas and vintage clothing. She uses this time to teach them social graces. Within walking distance are quaint shops and restaurants. The price of a room runs from $50 to $65. Call (870) 226–5305 or (888) 999–6932 for information.

An interesting place to eat, or just to stop in and look around in Warren, is called **The Carousel.** It's a restaurant that features one of those great Arkansas catfish buffets and a dessert bar about a mile long. But it's also an antiques store that sells only memorabilia from carousels. Authentic carousel horses fill the windows, and the dining room has buggies and other items from old carousels. The price for dinner, at $5.95 a person, is a bit more palatable than the $10,000 price tag on some of the horses.

The Carousel, located at 104 E. Cedar Street, Warren 71671, is open only on Friday and Saturday from 5:00 to 8:30 P.M. Call (870) 226–5033.

Christmas is also quite a sight in town. A multimillionaire from Little Rock had a huge display of Christmas lights that annoyed his neighbors, who took him to court and won. The lights were donated to the town of Warren, and now Christmas on the Courthouse Square is lovely. At **Cathey's Country Store,** at 108 East Cedar, Warren 71671, owner Troy Cathey has the largest collection of antiques in southwest Arkansas. The store's hours are from 9:00 A.M. to 5:00 P.M. Monday through Saturday and from 1:00 to 5:00 P.M. on Sunday. Call (870) 226–3738 for information. In the same building is **The Sandwich Shop** owned by the Bradfords. They serve ice cream, sandwiches, beef stew, potato soup, and other good things at tables, the soda bar, or booths. Lunch, and dinner are offered seven days a week. There's even a pool hall in the back. Hours are Monday through Thursday from 11:00 A.M. to 3:00 P.M. and on Friday and Saturday until 8:00 P.M. Call (870) 226–3920 for information.

If you decide to go southeast from El Dorado on Highway 82 between El Dorado and Crossett, you will be passing through the **South Arkansas Wildlife Refuge,** which has a visitors center off Highway 82 at Grand Marais. Lifelike dioramas show the 65,000-acre Ouachita River bottoms with wildlife, native plants, hardwood trees, uplands, and permanent water. In the Native Inhabitants diorama, an archaeologist (an animated mannequin) unearths ancient artifacts and tells the story of Native Americans from the Felsenthal Basin. Pay attention during the tour. You can take a computerized test at the end to see how much you learned. The Saline River flows from the Ouachita foothills to the Ouachita River at the wildlife refuge, and here you'll find the world's largest green-tree reservoir—home to such rare species as the red-cockaded woodpecker, an endangered species that brings birders from far away (the loblolly pine is the *only* tree in which these birds will nest), the bald eagle, and alligators—as well as good bass fishing. Call (870) 364–3168 for information.

Crossett, on Highway 82 east of Lake Jack Lee, is a former sawmill town started by a lumber company in 1903. It has a multifaceted gem of a city park, with a 3-mile paved hiking trail circling Lucas Pond—a quiet little lake stocked with bass and crappie for fishing—cutting through thick woods filled with honeysuckle and grapevines, and ending near the zoo, which has alligators, wolves, and peacocks. East of the pond in a wooded setting is **Wiggins Cabin,** circa 1800—the oldest building in Ashley County. The cabin was restored by the Crossett Cultural and Historic

Society. Area senior citizens fired bricks and split cypress boards for the roof. The old house, a square-hewn cypress log dogtrot (with two living areas under one roof and a breezeway between), shows the labor of a man skilled with a whipsaw, broadax, and adze. Broadax marks scar the logs, and beveled horizontal lathes were used to fill spaces between the box-notched logs. The cabin dates from the settlement's earliest days in the "Great Wilderness" of towering cypress, canebrakes, and rattan vines of the Bayou Bartholomew. Today it looks as though someone lives there, right down to the strips of fabric trailing from a rocker onto the floor, as if Mother had just stopped her rug-braiding to fix dinner.

Next door is the *Old Company House,* built before 1910 by the Crossett Lumber Company for its employees. It, like all the other company houses, was painted "Crossett Gray," one of the cheapest paints sold at the time. It too looks lived in. A "four-eye" wood-burning stove stands in the kitchen with a pancake griddle and teakettle. Nearby is a washtub used for everything from scrubbing clothes and bathing to cleaning hogs. A bare bulb hung in each of the three rooms. Tours may be arranged by calling the Crossett Chamber of Commerce at (870) 364–6591.

Brown's Fish Market and Cafe, on Highway 52 North, started out as a fish market, but soon owners Buford Brown and his wife, Virginia, began cooking the catch and sending it out on plates. The next thing you knew, there were tables. Along with the Louisiana catfish, you can buy crayfish in the spring and buffalofish when it's available. Virginia makes hot yeast rolls, homemade pies, cakes, cookies, and hush puppies. The place is open from 11:00 A.M. to 8:00 P.M. Monday through Friday. Call (870) 364–2108 for information.

The Georgia Pacific Corporation has gained national recognition for its tree-farming methods. The *Levi Wilcoxon Demonstration Forest* at Hamburg, north of Crossett on Highway 82, has three distinct types of forest, interconnected by a nature trail winding around Lake Georgia Pacific. The forest contains 250-year-old virgin growth, as well as pine seedlings and pine sawlogs more than 70 years old. Near the forest stands the giant Morris Pine—a loblolly pine tree 130 feet tall that measures more than 197 inches in circumference at its base. It is estimated to be more than 150 years old.

Lake Village sits on the west bank of an old oxbow lake called *Lake Chicot,* the state's largest natural lake, an enormous oxbow of the great river forming the eastern border of the state. Lake Shore Drive follows 18 miles of waterfront through the city; it passes a marker designating the spot from which Charles Lindbergh made aviation history with his first nighttime flight. Highway 65 is only 6 miles north of the Louisiana border, and the rich alluvial soil reaches a depth of more than 1,000 feet (the world average is 7 inches); this is prime cotton-growing area, and the Mississippi River, just a few miles from town, creates some beautiful scenery.

Rice and Ducks Country

The city of *McGehee* is one of the old railroad towns in the southeastern part of the state. The proposed Rails-to-Trails Corridor, 74 miles of railroad tracks that are being converted to hiking trails, thread through the area.

The *Magnolia House,* at 310 North Third Street, McGehee 71654, is an English country cottage near downtown McGehee and in walking distance from the gift shop and drugstore (with a real old-fashioned soda fountain) downtown. Innkeepers Frank and Lu Alice Evans serve a continental breakfast to visitors in the five guest rooms, which all have private baths. The rooms are $60. Call (870) 222–6425 for information or check the Web site, www.magnolia-evans.com.

Now more about that soda fountain and gift shop. *Periwinkle Place,* at 310 North Second Street, McGehee 71654, is the kind of gift shop only a small town could have, and that is what makes it special. The ladies who run it have a "want list" on most of the folks in town, so that when a birthday comes up, someone can call for gift ideas. The personal shopper service is so good that they will wrap and mail the gift, too. The decor and merchandise change dramatically with each season, from floor to ceiling the place reflects the next holiday, whether it be graduation day or Christmas. Hours are 10:00 A.M. to 5:30 P.M. Monday through Friday. It closes at noon on Saturday. Call (870) 222–6218.

Kelley's Drug Store, at 300 North Second Street, McGehee 71654, has a genuine soda fountain and really great sandwiches as well. Hours are 8:30 A.M. to 5:30 P.M. Monday through Friday. It closes at noon on Saturday, too. Call (870) 222–5071.

Lu Alice and Frank also own the *Evans House* at 13 Wolfe Drive, McGehee 71654. It is a traditional house in a quiet residential neighborhood. The four guest rooms all have private baths and share inviting common rooms. A continental breakfast is served in the family-style kitchen. Reservations can be made at the same phone number as the Magnolia House. Rooms are $50 to $60.

Frank recommends places nearby to eat. One is the *Catfish Kitchen,* on Highway 65, not just because it is owned by his cousin, Craig Towles, but because the food is really good. The restaurant is open Tuesday through Saturday from 10:00 A.M. to 8:00 P.M. Call (870) 222–5471 for information.

In nearby **Rohwer,** on Highway 1 off Highway 65, is an interesting historic site—a Japanese-American relocation camp used during World War II to intern Americans of Japanese descent after the bombing of Pearl Harbor. (See sidebar.)

Miller's Mud Mill pottery shop, at 15 Lennox Street in Dumas 71639, north of Lake Chicot on Highway 65, is where Gail and Mitch Miller and their three grown sons, Mitch Jr., Matthew, and Carey, create hand-thrown stoneware pottery. Gail's trademark is a hand-painted cotton ball appearing on plates and mugs all over the shop. Her popular line has been exported to as far as Japan. Behind the shop five kilns are fired

Lest We Forget

A Japanese-American Relocation Center *site at Rohwer, on Highway 1 off Highway 65 and near McGehee, was established September 18, 1942, by the federal government in the aftermath of the bombing of Pearl Harbor. Unique monuments remain here, built by internees at this relocation center, where Japanese-Americans were detained during World War II. The center is on the National Register of Historic Places but until lately hasn't received much attention. The people of McGehee, under the leadership of Mayor Rosalie Gould, are working to establish a museum to document and interpret the site. Sam Yada, a former internee who lives in Sherwood, leads an effort to build a new monument to honor those Japanese-American soldiers who were killed in action during World War II while serving in the U.S. military.*

Today all that is left at the site is the cemetery, the monuments, and a brick smokestack. The monuments, exceptional works of sculpture built in 1944, show the fine artistic skills of the internees. One monument is dedicated to the Japanese-Americans from the camp who died while fighting for the U.S. Army in Europe; this monument is shaped like a tank, with a star-topped column rising in the center. Another monument is dedicated to those internees who died while in the camp; it features a column covered with elaborate Japanese script and topped by a globe with an eagle perched on it. The simple concrete grave markers were also made by the people living in the camp. The museum is being planned to show how relocation affected the lives of both the Japanese-Americans and the local people. The camp is about 12 miles north of McGehee on Highway 1 toward Rohwer. A sign on Highway 1 will direct you toward a gravel road leading to the site.

up, and on any given day you will usually find Gail working at the wheel. Out front, wind chimes, cookie jars, mugs, and all manner of neat things fill the shop, which is open from 8:00 A.M. to 5:00 P.M. Monday through Friday, "give or take," says Gail. Call (870) 382–5277 for information or log on to her Web site at www.millersmudmill.com.

On Highway 165 North you will find *Hopmann's Candle Factory and Store* (870) 382–4009, where you can pick up some wonderfully scented jar candles, pillars, and votive candles in twenty-eight different fragrances. Clay Hopmann makes the candles here, and hours of the shop are Monday through Friday from 8:30 A.M. until 5:30 P.M. and on Saturday from 10:00 A.M. until 5:00 P.M. Check out Clay's Web page: www.hopmanns.com.

In 1673 two Frenchmen, Father Jacques Marquette, a Catholic missionary, and explorer Louis Jolliet, set out to explore the Mississippi Valley, traveling down the river from a French outpost on the north end of Lake Michigan to where Helena stands today. In 1682 they were followed by French explorer Rene-Robert Cavelier de La Salle, who wanted to establish forts along the river. One of his officers, Henry de Tonti, stayed and established a trading post where the Arkansas and Mississippi Rivers converge. It marks the first permanent settlement in the lower Mississippi Valley. It was known as the Arkansas Post; homesteading began and, because the rich soil was perfect for cotton, was soon followed by slaveholding planters. Cotton became king. The main building is pioneer homestead-style, with an open fireplace in the kitchen, complete with cooking pots and offering a glimpse of how cooking and household chores were done. The Refeld-Hinman House, built about 1877 near Hinman Bayou, is an old log house that now serves as headquarters for the *Arkansas Post State Park.* The 1930s Child's Playhouse contains built-to-scale furniture and a wood-burning fireplace. The Peterson Building's lifestyle exhibits include one on pioneer wash day, as well as a country store, a farm workshop, and a vintage 1910 Stoddard-Dayton automobile. A gift shop is at the entrance to the Arkansas Post National Memorial. The museum is open year-round Monday through Saturday 8:00 A.M. to 5:00 P.M.; Sunday 1:00 to 5:00 P.M. Admission is $2.25. Call (870) 548–2634 for information.

The Arkansas Delta is land built by rivers and has its own special language for the lowlands—words like *levees, bottoms, backswamps, point bars,* and *oxbows.* When dueling was outlawed, the islands of the Mississippi were used as dueling grounds, because they were out of the jurisdiction of lawmakers. Hunters, of course, flock to this area just as the ducks do. The Mississippi flyway has a large number of hunting clubs and lodges, and when the season is right, they fill up fast.

The **Louisiana Purchase Historic Marker and State Park,** at the junction of three counties east of Holly Grove, preserves the 1815 benchmark used to survey the Arkansas area of the Louisiana Purchase Territory. It contains about thirty-six acres within a headwater swamp, a fast-disappearing ecological setting in eastern Arkansas. A boardwalk provides access to the monument in the swamp's interior that marks the "point of beginning" for the survey. To find it from I–40 at Brinkley, take Highway 49 and travel 21 miles south to Highway 362; then drive 2 miles east on Highway 362.

Rising above a bustling Mississippi port, **Helena** is an old river town on the slopes of Crowley's Ridge. It is steeped in history, with antebellum, Edwardian, and Victorian homes and buildings scattered among rolling hills. Because of its position on the river, Helena was of strategic importance during the Civil War, when control of the river meant cutting the Confederacy in half. The Battle of Helena was one of the bloodiest in the state. The Confederate Cemetery on Holly Street contains a monument to the war dead and a panoramic view of the Mississippi.

Helena, founded in 1833, is Arkansas's major Mississippi River port and one of the oldest and most beautiful communities in the state. Here wharf boats once tied up indefinitely to the landings on the river, with every kind of store and concession on board. Dozens of offices on Water Street and on Ohio Street made it a busy area. The street nearest the river began to drop off bit by bit as the river ate at its shores, and many buildings were moved from Water Street to save them. Most of the caving in of the riverbank occurred just after the Civil War. Soon Cherry became the main street.

Helena has built a park that embraces the river that gave the town its life. There's a boardwalk, fishing spots, picnic areas, campsites, and docks big enough to accommodate the *Mississippi Queen* and *Delta Queen* steamboats. Watch all of the activities on the riverfront by taking a 1.3-mile walk along the paved path atop the levee.

The **Delta Cultural Center,** at 95 Missouri Street in the downtown area, is an outgrowth of the city's blues heritage and rich cover of topsoil left by the winds and rivers of the area. The visitors center is in the Helena Train Depot, built in 1913 and now the home of the Cultural Center and Blues Museum. The building's arched windows and orange tile roof reflect the sunlight and sounds of the adjacent river. The museum contains exhibits of the changes in landscape and lifestyle of the Delta, with themes covering early inhabitants, the Civil War, and music of the region, using artifacts, film, and music. The gift shop offers handmade crafts, railroad memorabilia, and posters. A reconstructed houseboat porch lets you live the story of the "river rats" who inhabited the Black and White Rivers. A caboose, with its railroad sounds and elevated navigation seats, gives kids a hands-on sense of the railroad era. The most popular portion of the center is the darkened corner room, where music flows from hidden speakers. The rough wooden floor and counter stools evoke the hard life and gritty work of the early inhabitants of the Delta. Photos and artifacts from the clubs of the city recall the blues legacy of such musicians as B. B. King and Sonny Boy Williamson and of the roadhouse bands of "rockabilly" favorites Conway Twitty and Charlie Rich. The center has opened an educational complex with computers for children and free Internet access. Their Web site is www.heritage.ar.us.

The city has built a dock where riverboats from St. Louis to New Orleans will soon deliver passengers to the riverwalk. The center is at the corner of Natchez and Missouri Streets at the harbor, at the end of the city's business district. Hours are from 9:00 A.M. to 5:00 P.M. Tuesday through Saturday and Sunday from 1:00 P.M. The center is frequently open late on Fridays to accommodate special programs open to the public. Admission is free. Call (870) 338–4350 for information.

The area around the center is filled with shops and restaurants. Just across the way from the center is Kathy Sullivan's *This Little Pig Antiques,* at 105 Cherry Street. A nice shop for browsing, it has craft items, old silver, and antiques. The shop's biggest claim to fame is *Bubba's Blues Corner,* which houses one of the country's finest collections of blues recordings (LP, CD, tapes, videos) by the likes of Howlin' Wolf, Muddy Waters, and Memphis Slim. Kathy's husband, Bubba, was selected "Blues Retailer of the Year" not long ago, an honor usually taken by bigger shops in cities like Chicago. It's open Monday through Saturday from 9:00 A.M. to 6:00 P.M. Call (870) 338–3501 for information.

Good food, maybe the best, is at a variety of eating spots around Helena's waterfront. Come dinnertime, *Bell's Ducks by the Levee,* at 115 Cherry Street, Helena 72843 (870–338–6655), is the place to be. It opens for dinner only from 5:00 to 9:00 P.M. Monday through Saturday.

If it's too early for dinner or you are just craving barbecue, go north on Cherry Street, then west on Perry, which turns into Oakland, and stay on it to the first stoplight. If you turn left at the light, you will see *Armstrong's Barbecue* at 303 Valley Drive, Helena 72843. They start serving at 9:00 A.M. and continue until 9:00 P.M. Monday through Saturday. The phone number there is (870) 338–7746.

Cherry Street along the levee was once filled with many whites-only saloons. The black bars were on Elm Street, the neighborhoods segregated. Helena, like other Delta towns that relied on sharecropping and shipping cotton by river, had its rough side and its hard times. The great blues musicians like Roosevelt Sykes and Robert Lockwood let it all show in their music. In fact, this is the home of the Sonny Boy Williamson Blues Society.

Helena is the site of a Confederate cemetery built and landscaped by the women of the town. Soldiers were taken from the shallow graves near where they had died and reburied. A somber obelisk stands in the center of the graveyard.

Slowly, more of Helena's fine old buildings and private homes are being restored to their former elegance. *Magnolia Hill,* 608 Perry Street, Helena 72843, was built by a cotton merchant in 1895. In addition to being a private residence, the building has been home to a Presbyterian church and a USO Club during World War II. In 1993, Magnolia Hill was transformed to a bed-and-breakfast with eight guest rooms, private baths and cable television in each room. Rooms are $75 a night. Call (870) 338–6874.

Another private home turned bed-and-breakfast upon renovation is *Foxglove,* a 1900 Georgian-Revival mansion where blues artist W.C. Handy would play for after-hours parties arriving on the ferry. The home, located at 229 Beech Street, Helena 72843, has seven guest rooms that range in price from $79 to $149. Call (800) 863–1926 for information.

The circa-1896 *Pillow-Thompson House,* at 718 Perry Street, Helena 72843, is the grand dame of the Victorian homes. Turrets and gables of many shapes grace the roof line. Curved porches bedecked with gingerbread surround it, and a row of porthole windows gives it a unique look. It is every little girl's idea of a dollhouse and was built for fancy-dress balls. Five generations of Pillows lived in the house until it was donated to Phillips Community College by Josephine Pillow Shinault Thompson and her son, George de Man. Members of the Pillow family were among those serving on fund-raising and restoration planning committees. Much of the original furniture was given with the house. This wedding cake-style home is on the National Register of Historic Places. Because the house is now owned by the Phillips Community College, students in the hospitality program use the home and its kitchen as an educational laboratory and provide the community with a special reason to visit the home. Each Tuesday, the hospitality students serve lunch to the first twenty-five people to make reservations. The students prepare all sorts of dishes, depending on their unit of study. Some days, lunch may be a variety of soups, or appetizers, or salads, accompanied by a number of desserts. They make a great bread pudding and a spinach-stuffed filet. The menu is prepared by the students, so you have no selection, but for $8.00, it's a unique way to enjoy the home and its amenities.

The home is open for public tours Tuesday through Saturday from 10:00 A.M. to 4:00 p.m. and on Sunday from 1:00 to 4:00 p.m. It may also be rented for parties because of its commercial kitchen. Call (870) 338–8535 for more information, or visit the home's Web site at www.pcccua.cc.ar.us/pillowthompson.

There are three historic districts in Helena, each with its own interesting sites and a fine collection of antebellum and Victorian homes and festivals celebrating the town's Deep South heritage. Tours of the homes and a downtown walking tour of the city are available from the chamber of commerce.

In *Life on the Mississippi,* Mark Twain said, "Helena occupies one of the prettiest situations on the river," and so it does. Hernando de Soto crossed the river here, followed in 1673 by Father Jacques Marquette and explorer Louis Jolliet. The city is filled with large modern homes as well as dozens of sturdy Victorians. Rolling hills, trees, and deep Bermuda lawns line the wide streets. This is obviously a town of old money.

The blues have played an important role in America's musical heritage of jazz, rhythm and blues, and rock and roll. Such greats as Sonny Boy Williamson, Robert Junior Lockwood, and Robert Nighthawk have been broadcast on the *King Biscuit Time* radio show on KFFA in Helena since 1941, and the King Biscuit Blues Festival is celebrated in October to commemorate it. But Helena is also the hometown of lyric soprano Frances Greer and country singer Harold Jenkins, better known as Conway Twitty.

The deep yellow *Edwardian Inn Bed and Breakfast,* at 317 South Biscoe Street, Helena 72843, was built in 1904. It was the home of William Short, a cotton broker and speculator who spent more than $100,000 in 1904 to build his family's dream house. The home contains eight original fireplace mantels, detailed woodwork, wainscoting, and paneling. It has unusual wooden floors of "wood carpeting" parqueted in Germany from strips of 1-inch-wide wood mounted on canvas and shipped to town in rolls. The huge wraparound porch is a fine place to rock on a warm afternoon. The building is one of the most interesting structures in this historically significant town and is on the National Register of Historic Places. Owner John Craw watches over twelve comfortable rooms: The home has nine rooms and three suites, each with private bath, phone, and television. A full breakfast is served in the cheerful,

Cathy Johnson

Edwardian Inn Bed and Breakfast

latticed sunroom. The cost is $65 to $90. Call (870) 338–9155 for reservations. The Web site is www.edwardianinn.com.

The city of **Marianna** lies in the heart of the fertile delta and on the edge of the St. Francis National Forest, which has abundant wildlife, hunting, and fishing. The Marianna-Lee County Museum and the University of Arkansas Cotton Branch Experimentation Station are here.

The county museum, 67 W. Main Street, Marianna 72360, has a small collection of Civil War artifacts found in the area, as well as artifacts from the Quapaw Indians, who once called this region home. Other displays focus on agriculture in the region. The museum is open Monday through Friday and sometimes on weekends. Call (870) 295–2469.

A good place to eat after touring the town is **Cleo's,** at 381 West Chestnut, Marianna 72360. Cleo and Nancy Davis turn out good home cooking from 5:00 A.M. Monday through Saturday and keep on cooking until 7:00 P.M. (8:00 P.M. on Friday). Call (870) 295–6802.

More down-home country cooking can be found at **Sunshine's Cajun Kitchen,** about 5 miles west of town at the junction of Highways 78 and 79. Sunshine calls herself a true-blooded Cajun who puts her soul into the food she prepares, such as crawfish, étoufées, and red beans. But if you like, she'll whip up a great burger, steak, or just about anything else to suit your fancy. Sunshine's is closed on Monday, but open 11:00 A.M. to 8 P.M. Tuesday through Sunday. Call (870) 768–4499 for information.

The sign on Highway 79 says WELCOME TO STUTTGART. Take the "t"s out of the name and you have the word sugar, so it's called "Sugartown." Would you have figured that out? **Stuttgart** began in 1878 when a Lutheran minister born in Stuttgart, Germany, brought his congregation to the Grand Prairie region of Arkansas; nine years later the city was incorporated and named after the founder's birthplace.

Sugartown calls itself the "Rice and Duck Capital of the World." Farmers need oceans of water to produce rice, and this land is perfectly suited to this end. The waterproof layer of clay, known as "hardpan," stops water from seeping past the topsoil. Farmers use the "flush-and-flood" method: Fields are covered with water just after planting to germinate the new seeds; it stands for a day or two. When the shrubby plants are about 6 inches tall, the fields are flooded and left underwater for the duration of the summer. Although rice does not need standing water to grow, the water serves as a weed control device. That's why ducks have always been plentiful hereabouts; 1.3 million acres of rice is just too tempting to the migrating flocks, and ever since the Quapaw Indians tied decoys to their heads and submerged themselves up to the nose in the water among the cattails and weeds to wait for the ducks when they landed nearby (the Native Americans grabbed the birds by the legs, clipped their wings, and took them home to a pen), hunting has been as important as agriculture here. As agriculture increased, the duck changed from "an acquired taste" to a tasty delight, because the birds started out eating wheat in the Dakotas,

Trivia

The Smoke Hole Natural Area north of Stuttgart is a 455-acre tract of land that is a good example of a forested wetland. The name "smoke hole" refers to a small, chimneylike opening in the tupelo brake within the area, which makes the perfect environment for the river otters and wood ducks who live there. Part of the area is flooded from 60 to 90 days each year and most is flooded permanently. Marshes, swamps, and bogs covered in shallow water are home to plants and animals found in wetlands.

then dined on corn in Illinois, and finished up on Grand Prairie rice as they migrated south.

Life wasn't easy for farmers on the prairie. But when the chores were done and they put the hoe down, they knew how to have fun, too. The **Stuttgart Agricultural Museum,** at 921 East Fourth Street, Stuttgart 72160 (at Park Avenue), depicts the history of the pioneers who farmed the Grand Prairie of eastern Arkansas from the 1880s until 1921. You can see how they worked and how they played. The first families came to the area under the 1862 Homestead Act. An 1880 home is beautifully furnished from the era. A rustic prairie home and scaled-down reproductions of actual buildings once here on the prairie—a mercantile, a doctor's office, a photography shop, a millinery, a grocery store, a post office, and, of course, a jail—are all part of the intriguing outdoor displays. A beautiful new mural has been painted in the equipment room depicting the history of the prairie. The area was settled by German Lutherans, and the museum has a lovely little church, a two-thirds-scale replica of the one that existed in the settlers' day. Displays give visitors insight into how farm families lived, with everything from old Victrolas and early kitchen equipment, to a corner filled with the attire of a 1923 wedding. The place is huge. In the wings of Grand Prairie, a minitheater, you can feel the modern-day thrill of a "crop duster turn" riding in the cockpit of a crop duster's plane. A display of antique musical instruments and fine needleware fills much of a recent 20,000-square-foot addition.

Because ducks are the other half of the economy hereabouts, it is no surprise that one of the more popular exhibits is the Waterfowl Wing, which houses a re-creation of a morning duck hunt, complete with circling birds, duck blind, cypress boat, and backgrounds painted by artist Don Edwards. All of the world-champion duck callers from the

Catfish—Anyway You Like It

You may have figured out by now that more catfish is eaten in Arkansas than in any other state of the Union. The fish is almost always dipped in egg and cornmeal and fried to a crispy finish on the outside with a soft, flaky moist interior. Of course,

you may also have noticed that everything else in Arkansas is fried, too—unless it's barbecued. This is not California. Even former president Clinton takes a lot of ribbing (pun intended) about his love of barbecue and fried foods.

Wings Over the Prairie Festival held each Thanksgiving weekend are represented here, and visitors can listen to the thirty-seven varieties of ducks that come through the Mississippi flyway each year. Spotlights highlight each bird.

Famed wildlife artist William D. Gaither created realistic scenes for wildlife in its natural habitat, and the museum offers taped information on the flora and fauna of the Grand Prairie. Arkansas has one of the largest fish farming industries in the country, and the exhibit of live catfish is one children enjoy. The museum is open Tuesday through Saturday from 10:00 A.M. to noon and from 1:00 to 4:00 P.M.; Sunday hours are from 1:30 to 4:30 P.M. There is no admission fee, but donations are accepted. Call (870) 673–7001 for information.

The *Arts Center of the Grand Prairie,* at 108 West Twelfth Street, Stuttgart 72160, features rotating exhibits of local and state artists' paintings, sculptures, and other artwork. Not only is it a year-round exhibit, but other art-related activities are going on here all the time. Performing arts are presented, too. The Art Center Thespians, a community theater group, has several productions a year. A musical production runs in conjunction with the Grand Prairie Art Council's annual Grand Prairie Festival of the Arts. There is no admission charge to the center, and it's open from 9:00 A.M. to 5:00 P.M. Monday through Friday. Call (870) 673–1781 for information.

You can find a number of good eating places in Stuttgart. One of the more unique spots is the *Cajun Hideaway* at 942 West Washington Extended (²/₁₀ of a mile off of Highway 79 South), Stuttgart 72160. Robbie and Bud Borman have added a renovated Memphis tour bus to the restaurant and those are the first fifty seats to be taken. The bus is built like a paddle wheeler with a pilothouse on the upper deck. The unique pilothouse has seats arranged so that they face each other around a new, large dining table seating ten, ideal for a large party. A recently added bar with big screen TV and bands on Friday and Saturday night keep the place packed. The restaurant was established in 1980 and all of the *sac-or-liat* (fish) prepared by the Bormans is either grilled, blackened, stuffed, or fried with their secret Cajun seasoning. They make their own boudin links or boulettes, crawfish étoufée, alligator, gumbo d'jour, and famous crab stuffed mushrooms. Bud and Robbie have added the *Cajun Chateau,* a bed-and-breakfast for up to five duck hunters. Call (870) 673–7460 or 673–2819 for reservations for dinner, served only between 5:00 and 10:00 P.M. or for the Chateau. You can buy an authentic Cajun cookbook.

American Legion games are played on a fine baseball field in Pine Bluff. Taylor Field was originally built for professional baseball with a grandstand, a press box, and regulation 90-foot base paths. The field now hosts national and regional tournaments.

Something a little more down home would be the Readers' Choice award-winning **Little Chef** (best desserts, best catfish, best atmosphere, and a bunch of others) at 1103 East Michigan Street, Stuttgart 72160. Owner Kathy Nichols turns out fine food from 6:00 A.M. until 9:00 P.M. Monday through Saturday. Call (870) 673–7372.

South of Stuttgart on Highway 79, **Pine Bluff,** the second-oldest city in the state, was founded in 1819 by Joseph Bonne, a French-Quapaw Indian, who built a log cabin on a pine-covered bluff overlooking a bend in the Arkansas River. Pine Bluff is now a trade center of the southeastern part of the state. It's a pretty town, with big old houses and wide streets. The University of Arkansas at Pine Bluff is here, and those interested in Black history will enjoy the *Persistence of the Spirit* exhibit in the campus Fine Arts Center, which chronicles the lives of Black Arkansans from pioneer days to the present. Call (870) 547–8236 for information.

Highway 65 intersects with Highway 79 at Pine Bluff. **Mrs. Jones' Cafe,** on Highway 65 South, has been a favorite spot for years. Could it be the cornbread? Or perhaps the homemade pie? Or maybe it's because the cafe feels so comfortable, with its small tables covered with bright red-and-white cloths and with its white curtains letting sunlight through the square, white-trimmed panes of glass. Ruby Jones is now ninety-nine years old and just recently stopped coming to the restaurant on a regular basis. A white basket on each table is filled with Ruby's homemade apple relish and apple jam, and the list of the current day's pies is on a chalkboard on the wall. The *Best of Ruby Jones* cookbooks are best-sellers here in the new gift shop, as are the well-loved relish and jam. The managers are Ruby's son, W. R. Jones, and his wife, Jan. Ruby's is open Monday through Saturday from 6:00 A.M. to 9:00 P.M. and Sunday from 11:00 A.M. to 2:00 P.M. for specials as tempting as chicken and dumplings, pot roast, fried chicken, and the daily turnout of some eighteen dozen rolls and biscuits to go with forty to fifty pies. All the vegetables are garden fresh, and the pies are, well, unique and wonderful: lemon pecan, egg custard, coconut cream, and sweet potato pie. The blackberry cobbler is a favorite, too. Call (870) 534–6678 for information.

The Razorback wing of the Confederate Air Force, where everyone is a colonel (there is no other rank), has an annual affair the last week of August or first week of September. World War II trainers, fighters, bombers, and liaison planes are all there; it is like stepping back in time, and the public is invited to take close-up looks at the planes. The air show is full of action, explosions, and fast-moving aircraft diving, turning, and smoking. Solo acrobatic acts, wing riders, parachute jumpers, and formation flights fill the skies. Call the Pine Bluff Visitor Information Center at (870) 536–7606.

The *Arkansas Railroad Museum,* 1700 Port Road, Pine Bluff 71601, at the Cotton Belt Railway Shops, re-creates railroading in the 1940s. The sixty-year-old engine was the last 4-8-4 steam locomotive ever built and was donated to the city by the railroad. This major restoration project, called "The Pride of Pine Bluff," utilized all-volunteer labor. Several cabooses and passenger cars have recently been added. Call (870) 535–8819 for more information. The museum's hours are 8:30 A.M. to 3:00 P.M. Monday through Saturday.

The *childhood home of Martha Mitchell,* wife of former Attorney General John Mitchell and media darling of the Nixon years, is a stately blue Victorian house built in 1887. Martha's old homeplace, at 902 West Fourth Street, Pine Bluff 71601, is open for tours. It has been restored and has several pieces of the original furniture dating from 1900 to 1930. Wallpaper was duplicated from scraps of original wallpaper for the renovation. The upstairs porch is decked in white gingerbread.

Photographs of Martha and clippings about her time in the capital— including a framed *Life* cover—adorn the walls of one bedroom. Bob Abbott bought the house from Martha before she died in 1979 at age fifty-seven after battling cancer.

Tours are free but by appointment. Call Bob at (870) 535–4973 or the Pine Bluff Visitors Bureau at (800) 536–7660, extension 2145.

There is a cluster of lovely B&Bs on Second Avenue in Pine Bluff.

Margland II, at 703 West Second Avenue, Pine Bluff 71601, is one of four homes owned by innkeepers Wanda Bateman and Ed Thompson. All three have been restored and decorated in an elegant fashion and serve as B&Bs. This one, a 1903 Colonial Revival house, is a Bermuda cottage of "shingle style" architecture and done in pastels—blue, mauve, and pink. The detailed beauty is filled with Victorian antiques and touches of the nearest holiday—Christmas offers particularly outstanding decorations. Three of the bedrooms have lofts. A large, modern kitchen at the back of the house overlooks the brick-paved yard, which has a gazebo and small wrought-iron tables scattered about. The first floor and yard are used for private parties and wedding receptions. Rooms are $110, with "anything you want," states Wanda, for breakfast. It's a popular wedding and honeymoon spot.

Margland III is next door, at 705 West Second Avenue, Pine Bluff 71601, and is done in a bold wine color scheme inside. Even the bathrooms are done in lovely detail. This structure was built as a duplex in 1894, and guests have use of the kitchen if they desire. Rooms are $90. Breakfast is included.

Margland IV, at 709 West Second Avenue, Pine Bluff 71601, is a 1907 home with chambered projecting bays, round corners, and a porch with round corner turns. An exercise room, a whirlpool bath in each suite, and three loft bedrooms at the top of spiral staircases are part of the six suites, which all have private baths. Each is decorated with its own theme—country, art nouveau, Pennsylvania Dutch. A full breakfast is included, and other meals may be had by reservation. Rooms are $90.

The newest, *Margland V,* is at 704 West Barraque, Pine Bluff 71601, and it is, of course, as beautiful as the others. Rooms there are $90.

And where is Margland I, you might ask? It's in the town of Earle and was called Margland Farm. It's where Wanda Bateman's husband grew up. Call Wanda at (870) 536–6000, 534–8400 or (800) 545–5383 for reservations at any of the homes.

A Pine Bluff tradition has long been *Sissy's Log Cabin,* 2319 Camden Road, Pine Bluff 71601, for gift shopping. For more than thirty-one years, it has been an international gathering spot for people who love fine jewelry and good service. Sissy Jones is justifiably proud of her custom-designed jewelry. Her trademark "slide bracelets" were born of her antiques business in the log cabin off Highway 65 on Highway 79. She used antique Victorian clasps and mounted them on two 14-karat-gold rope chains, and because they seemed to be an instant hit, she found herself in the jewelry business. Now the store designs its own clasps. But there are many other original pieces to admire, too. Former First Lady Hillary Rodham Clinton owns several pieces of Sissy's jewelry.

Sissy's is open 10:00 A.M. to 5:30 P.M. Monday through Saturday, and, during May and December, it's open Sunday, too. Call (870) 879–3040 for information.

Other places to check out in Pine Bluff include the *Arkansas Entertainers Hall of Fame* at the Pine Bluff Convention Center, 1 Convention Center Plaza, where you can see an "animatronic" Johnny Cash sing five songs when you punch his buttons. The museum chronicles the many entertainment stars who called Arkansas home: Glen Campbell, Allan Ladd, Tracy Lawrence, Al Green, Charley Rich, Mary Steenburgen, Conway Twitty, Billy Bob Thornton, Dick Powell, Floyd Cramer, Harry Thomason (producer of *Designing Women* and *Evening Shade,* as well as many other well-known television shows). Recent inductees include Jerry Van Dyke, K.T. Oslin, Bronco Billy Anderson, and William Warfield. Call (870) 536–7600 for more information. The Hall is open Monday through Friday from 9:00 a.m until 4:30 P.M. It's open on weekends seasonally.

The *Jefferson County Historical Museum* is at 201 East 4th Avenue, Pine Bluff 71601. It has displays of items from 1830 to the present time. There are tools, dolls, cotton farming implements, Victorian and Civil War clothing, and an interesting display of water fowl, as well as a multitude of other things to see. A large collection of WWI and WWII items has recently been added. The building itself is on the National Register of Historic Places. Since it served as a Union train depot during the Civil War. Call (870) 541–5402 for more information. Hours are 9:00 A.M. to 5:00 P.M. every day but Sunday.

Jerry Horne is his name (it really is), and he loves old band instruments. So much, in fact, that he used his vintage band instruments collection, which was taking up too much space in his music store (Wallick Music Company nearby), to open *The Band Museum* in a circa 1890 building at 423-425 Main Street, Pine Bluff 71601. Jerry, who looks a lot like Mitch Miller, says his collection was a "semiretirement project," and he enjoys showing visitors the sousaphones, piccolos, trumpets, double-bell euphonium (remember it from "76 Trombones" in *The Music Man?*), and a double-bell trumpet, an odd instrument that has a bell at either end and no mouthpiece. Many of the 700 instruments date from the 1700s, and all are from bands—marching bands, swing bands, symphonic bands, and jazz bands. Jerry, a former band director, not only is an accomplished trombone player, but he can play the slide trumpet or something as simple as a carved whistle.

The museum features history exhibits on circus bands and a history of the Smiles Girls Band, a group of girls from Fort Smith who traveled around the country in the 1930s playing signal horns made in Germany for the Hitler Youth movement. There is the Arkansas Heritage Hall of Fame in the museum, which pays tribute to jazz musicians like the late Art Porter and Louie Jordan. Unusual instruments, such as a trumpet made of plastic because of the World War II brass shortage, are displayed in the History of Trumpets section. Visitors will also see such instruments as those made by the Holton Company, which have highly engraved, gold-plated bells, and a folding brass drum made in 1917.

This is more than just a museum, though. There is a 1950s-style soda fountain where you can sit and sip a cherry phosphate and listen to the rockin' jukebox, which is filled with songs from the 1950s and 1960s. Jerry says he can fix just about anything you could buy at a soda fountain in the 1950s. In fact, he used to be a soda jerk, so the festive black-and-white checkered floor and the antique-oak bar make him, and a lot of people, feel right at home.

Vintage orchestra posters, old photographs, and sheet music decorate the walls. A colorful Chinese drum, antique percussion instruments, flutes, and saxophones will keep your interest, as will Jerry, who is a virtual one-man band. Admission is free, and hours are 10:00 A.M. to 5:00 P.M. Monday through Friday and by appointment on Saturday. Call (870) 534–HORN (4676) for more information. A gift shop features items related to music, and exhibits change periodically.

After you have browsed the museum and had a phosphate, you can explore the history of the town, beginning in the early 1700s, through a series of impressive outdoor murals. Start on Main Street at Barraque Street.

The town has a colorful history. Legend has it that a Quapaw hero named Saracen, born about 1735, rescued two pioneer children from marauding Chickasaws. When the Quapaws were sent into Indian territory in

It's a Grand Ole Flag!

*T*he people of Arkansas trace their state flag to Miss Willie Hocker, a member of the Pine Bluff chapter of the D.A.R. It was this group, in 1913, that became concerned when the USS Arkansas *was about to christened that the state had no flag. A statewide contest ensued with sixty-five entries, some designed by school children with crayons, others designed by accomplished seamstresses.*

The twenty-five stars on the blue diamond border of the flag signify that Arkansas is the twenty-fifth state in the Union, which is represented by the

color selection of red, white, and blue. The diamond shape is because Arkansas is the only diamond producer in the Union. The single star above the name Arkansas represents the state's role in the Confederacy and the three stars below represent the three countries that have owned the region: France, Spain, and the United States.

Miss Hocker's design was officially adopted by the state legislature on February 26, 1913, and the Pine Bluff D.A.R. chapter commissioned her to make the first flag for the USS Arkansas *battleship.*

Oklahoma, Saracen was allowed to stay on land along the river at today's Port of Pine Bluff. His remains lie in the Catholic cemetery.

World-famous archer and bow hunter Ben Pearson lived in the home at 714 West Fourth Avenue. The 1860 home served as Union army headquarters during the Civil War. The first shots in the war may actually have been fired at Pine Bluff in April 1861, before Confederate gunners opened fire on Fort Sumter, South Carolina. The Jefferson Guards fired warning shots and halted federal boats headed upriver with garrison supplies, which the guards seized for the Confederate army. A real battle happened here later, when, in 1863, Confederate General John S. Marmaduke was unsuccessful in taking the city from Union General Powell Clayton.

Digging Southeast Arkansas

*M*odern archaeology buffs will make the drive to Sheridan, on Highway 270 west of Pine Bluff, because literally digging up the past is what Elwin Goolsby, the county historian and the founder and director of the **Grant County Museum,** is famous for. The museum, at 521 Shackleford Road, looks like an old mercantile store but is packed with things that preserve the history of the area. The retired history teacher has gathered thousands of historical items using a metal detector and a shovel. He and his team of amateur archaeologists— his students—have uncovered gas pumps made of solid iron dating from 1919; a rusted-out moonshine still, whiskey barrel hoops, and a lantern apparently smashed by ax-swinging feds in the 1930s; abandoned farming equipment; and 200 roadside signs. There are also musket balls, pistols, and scabbards from the Civil War. But probably the favorite items are the remains of a B-17 bomber that crashed in a swampy area north of town while on a training mission. The

plane was left to sink into the bog, but when a road grader turned up a rusty pistol, Goolsby and his gang grabbed shovels and uncovered a machine gun, canteens, oxygen masks, and the dog tags of some of the nine crew members who died there.

The museum area contains not only photographs and microfilm genealogical records, but also log cabins, barns, corncribs, and a depression-era church on the grounds. Each is filled with small items that tell a story—a tiny shoe from a little girl named Leola, who died in a house fire; a slave's tombstone—reflecting the history of Grant County. An acre of ground about 1 mile from the site, now called Heritage Square, is being used to save historic buildings scheduled for demolition. So far a Victorian folk house, circa 1904, and a small 1927 cafe, complete with kitchen utensils and dishes of food, have been restored. The museum is open from 9:00 A.M. to 5:00 P.M. Tuesday through Saturday. Call (870) 942–4496 for information.

The mural at Second Avenue and Main Street portrays the story of the oldest public institution in the state with a Black heritage, today's University of Arkansas at Pine Bluff, which was formed as Branch Normal College. Among the dignitaries on the mural are Joseph C. Corbin, first principal of that school. Another mural at Third Avenue and Main Street shows the 1892 fire station and other handsome structures from the turn of the century. The murals—eleven so far with eleven more planned—brighten downtown.

Lybrand's Bakery & Deli, at 2900 Hazel Street, Pine Bluff 71601, was voted best bakery in southeast Arkansas, and it has been cooking since 1946. It offers delicious sandwiches, soups, salads, quiche, and lasagna. Open 6:00 A.M. to 5:30 P.M. Monday through Friday, 6:00 A.M. to 2:00 P.M. on Saturday. Call (870) 534–4607 for information or 535–SOUP for daily lunch specials.

The search for the great burger continues in Pine Bluff. You would not believe where great burgers can be found. Here in Pine Bluff one of the best is in the back room of a liquor store, *L. V. Rogers Package Store,* at 4712 Highway 65 South (at Highway 425) just east of town. These big, juicy burgers are made from meat that's ground fresh daily. Be sure to try the creamy, light Velveeta fudge, which is served in cupcake cups. Hours for burgers are 9:30 A.M. to 6:00 P.M. Thursday, Friday, and Saturday only. Strictly carryout. Call (870) 534–9569 for information.

Pine Bluff is full of surprises. Who would expect a town of 58,000 people to raise $4.35 million for the *Arts and Science Center*? The 22,000-square-foot facility, at 2701 South Main, Pine Bluff 71601 is the first new downtown building in several years. The three spacious art galleries display exhibitions and selections from the Center's 1,400-piece permanent collection as well as traveling exhibits. A fourth gallery is Adventure Space, a hands-on science center. The theater is filled for performances of Broadway musicals. Call (870) 536–3375 for information.

Pioneer Village, on Highway 35 in *Rison,* south of Pine Bluff, is a growing restoration of a village as it would have been during the last half of the nineteenth century. It includes Mount Olivet Methodist Episcopal Church, built in 1867, containing handmade pews and many original windows; a 1902 country mercantile store, selling handmade crafts, as well as homemade lemonade, two-cent cookies, old-fashioned hoop cheese, and crackers; a doctor's simple Victorian home, built in 1892;

Lois's Cottage, a two-room shotgun dwelling with a wraparound porch; and a one-room circa-1900 log cabin with a fireplace for cooking and a handmade table for meals. A ladder on the cabin wall leads to the loft where settlers slept on straw mats. To the right of the cabin is the smokehouse and to the left a small herb garden. A fully stocked blacksmith shop, complete with anvil, bellows, and tools of the trade, is here as well, as is a barn with wagons and plows of the same time period.

The third weekend in March sees the dogwoods and daffodils in full bloom and so is the ideal time for the Pioneer Crafts Festival, when demonstrations of old-time crafts and string music fill the village. Original, handmade, quality items composed of native materials are for sale. (There is a small admission charge to the festival.) And on a Wednesday in the middle of December, a pioneer Christmas exhibit begins with carols in the church and ends, after dark, with an old-fashioned prayer meeting. The village Christmas tree, a tea table, and often a country supper fill the village with delightful sounds and scents. The mercantile is usually open from December 1 to 15 for Christmas shopping. For more information contact Rison City Hall at (870) 325–7444.

About 9 miles southwest of **Sheridan** on Highway 46 is the **Jenkins' Ferry Battlefield,** one of three sites in the state commemorating the Union Army's Red River Campaign. The point where the Union Army escaped the pursuing Confederates by crossing the rain-swollen Saline River on April 30, 1864, is now a National Historic Landmark. For more information, call (501) 682–1191.

Drive south of Sheridan on Highway 167 to **Fordyce,** which each spring celebrates its railroad industry with the popular, weeklong Fordyce on the Cotton Belt Festival. Ole Number 819, one of the few remaining steam locomotives in operation, rolls into town from Pine Bluff for rides. The childhood home of Paul "Bear" Bryant is a short drive from downtown on Highway 8; the Alabama football coaching legend grew up here and played football for the Fordyce Redbugs.

Smell the aroma of fresh bread in the air? You must be near the **Klappenbach Bakery,** at 108 West Fourth Street, Fordya 74712. The bakery turns out French, pumpernickel, rye, sourdough, cinnamon-raisin, and cheese breads, as well as oatmeal cookies, brownies, and muffins, all

> ### Trivia
>
> *Why is a county that lies in the heart of cotton country named Grant? Why is the county seat named Sheridan? They are named for two U.S. Army generals, Ulysses S. Grant (commander in chief of the Union army) and Philip Sheridan (infamous Union cavalry leader), because the county was formed during Reconstruction. Local folks blame the Yankee carpetbaggers.*

made from scratch by Norm and Lee Klappenbach. The bakery's reputation is so well known—all by word of mouth—that treats are shipped all over the country to people who came, saw, and were conquered by the huge selection of baked goods.

The bakery opens into a sandwich shop, where the proprietors' son Paul creates such mouthwatering sandwiches as the pepper steak cheese sandwich—grilled green peppers and onions, marinated beef sliced real thin, and melted Swiss cheese, all on a poor boy bun fresh and warm from the bakery. There is always something hot—soup or quiche—and tempting desserts, such as cheesecake, meringue pie, pastry, or chocolate chip cookies. The two dining rooms are quite large and filled with the Klappenbachs' eclectic collection of antique tables and cupboards in assorted sizes. The bakery and shop are open from 6:00 A.M. (for the doughnut crowd) to 5:00 P.M. Tuesday through Saturday and are closed Sunday and Monday. Call (870) 352–7771 to see what's cooking or ask for a mail-order brochure so that you can have goodies sent.

If you are staying the night in Fordyce, the **Wynne Phyllips House Bed and Breakfast Inn,** at 412 West Fourth Street, Fordyce 74712, is one of the state's newest B&Bs. Agnes Wynne Phyllips and her husband, James, are the daughter and son-in-law of the original builder of this 1905 Classical Revival house. The large, tree-shaded lot has grape arbors for strolling, a lap pool for swimming, and lots of flowers. The house is furnished with family antiques and touches (like Oriental rugs) from the couple's travels all over the world. The four bedrooms with private baths on the second floor all have original furnishings. A mint julep on the front porch at night, if the mood strikes you, and a full southern breakfast, complete with grits and family-recipe biscuits, are part of the hospitality, and Agnes sends you to bed with a platter of homemade cookies, too. It doesn't get any better than this—and all for between $55 and $75. Call (870) 352–7202 for reservations.

There is a new **Dallas County Museum** in a 1907 building at 221 North Main Street, Fordyce 74712. Agnes Wynne Phyllips chairs the board of the museum. Agnes is quite excited about the new children's museum that is now open on the second floor with more than 3,500 square feet of hands-on historical activities for kids. Also on the second floor is a communications exhibit. The building that houses the museum was once the Fordyce Telephone Company, so much of the exhibit was already in place. Hours are Tuesday through Friday from 11:00 A.M. to 4:00 P.M. and Saturday from 11:00 A.M. to 3:00 P.M. There's an antiques mall next door full of real bargains.

MORE PLACES TO STAY IN SOUTHEAST ARKANSAS

OIL AND TIMBER COUNTRY
Camden Holiday Inn,
950 South
California Avenue, 71701;
(870) 836–8822

Crossett The
Lakewood Inn,
1400 South Florida Street,
71635;
(870) 364–4101,
(800) 870–1182

El Dorado Holiday Inn,
1925 Junction City Road,
71730;
(800) HOLIDAY

Lake Village Ramada Inn,
912 Highway 65/82 South,
71653,
(870) 265–4545

Magnolia Best Western
Coachman's Inn,
420 East Main Street,
71753;
(501) 234–6122,
(800) 237–6122

RICE AND DUCK COUNTRY
Dumas Days Inn,
501 Highway 65 South,
71639;
(870) 382–5880

Pine Bluff Holiday Inn,
2 Convention Center Plaza,
71601;
(870) 535–3111

Stuttgart Stuttgart Best
Western Duck Inn,
704 West Michigan, 72160;
(870) 673–2575

West Helena Best Western,
1053 West Highway 49,
72390;
(870) 572–2592

Chambers of Commerce in Southeast Arkansas

Oil and Timber Country
Camden Chamber of Commerce;
P.O. Box 99, Camden 71701;
(870) 836–6426

Crossett Chamber of Commerce;
101 West First Avenue, Crossett 71635;
(870) 364–6591;
crosset@cei.net

El Dorado Chamber of Commerce;
201 North Jackson, El Dorado 71730;
(870) 863–6113;
www.boomtown.org

Helena Chamber of Commerce;
111 Hickory Hills Drive, Helena 72843;
(870) 338–8327

Magnolia Chamber of Commerce;
P.O. Box 866, Magnolia 71753;
(800) 482–3330

Pine Bluff Chamber of Commerce;
510 South Main, Pine Bluff 71601;
(870) 535–0110;
www.pinebluff.com

Rice and Duck Country
Brinkley Chamber of Commerce;
1501 Weatherby Drive, Brinkley 72021;
(870) 734–2262;
chamber@brinkley.grsc.k12.ar.us

Stuttgart Chamber of Commerce;
507 South Main, Stuttgart 72160;
(870) 673–1602, (800) 810–2241;
www.stuttgart.ar.us

MORE PLACES TO EAT IN SOUTHEAST ARKANSAS

OIL AND TIMBER COUNTRY
Camden Boiling Pot,
950 South
California Avenue, 71701;
(870) 836–8822

Crossett The Woodlands
Restaurant,
1400 South Florida Street,
71635;
(870) 364–8870

El Dorado Al's,
200 East Main, 71730;
(870) 863–0404

Lake Village The Cowpen,
5198 East Highway 82,
71635;
(870) 265–9992

Magnolia Legends Cafe,
800 East Main, 71753;
(870) 234–8310

Miller's Cafeteria,
2402 North Vine, 71753;
(870) 234–2181

Sheridan The Ice House,
108 East Bell, 72150; (870)
942–3712

Central Arkansas

The hub of the state is its central region. Here the capital, Little Rock, and its sister city across the river, North Little Rock, are the core of the state's government, cultural, and financial life. Cosmopolitan and urban, the city and its surrounding suburbs offer sophisticated shopping, fine dining, and big-city nightlife.

Several state parks are nearby, too. Toltec Mounds, an archaeological site to the east; Pinnacle Mountain, an environmental education park—and trailhead to the challenging Ouachita Trail—to the west; and Woolly Hollow State Park, north of Conway, can be part of your travel plans when you are based in the capital city.

Towns with names such as Pickles Gap, Toad Suck, and Romance dot the heart of the state, and there are surprises everywhere. There's a thirty-three-room mansion on a plantation that is still growing cotton and even an elephant breeding farm hidden away near this metropolitan center.

The Heart of Arkansas

Start in *Little Rock.* It's called the City of Roses because of the abundance of the lovely flowers planted all over the city. Little Rock sits on a rocky bluff overlooking the Arkansas River. The best view of the river is from the walkways and terraces of seventeen-acre Riverfront Park at the foot of Rock Street. There the little rock for which the city is named is marked by a bronze plaque.

Little Rock will be the home of President Bill Clinton's presidential library—beating out Hot Springs and Hope. It's an interesting city for history buffs, for it houses three state capitols, making Arkansas unique in this respect. The first is the *Historic Arkansas Museum,* formerly known as the Arkansas Territorial Restoration. On these grounds, located at 200 East Third Street, Little Rock 72201 (park at the intersection of Third and Cumberland Streets), are some of the oldest buildings in the state on their original sites. Among them are the 1830s Hinderliter

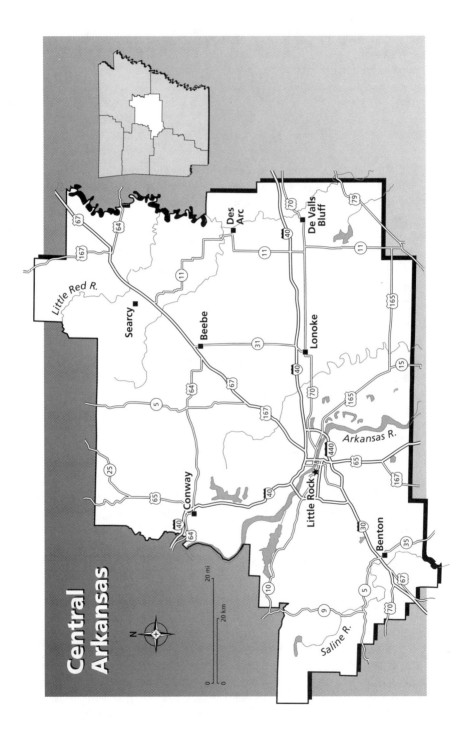

Grog Shop, the 1840s McVicar and Brownlee Houses, and the 1820s *Arkansas Gazette* Print Shop. Huge old magnolia trees shade the area, and there is a feeling of leaving the modern world and returning to a different time. The houses are held together by white oak pegs and are graced by original hand-carved mantels and doors and costumed interpreters heighten the sense of originality in the tour. Tours are offered on the hour Monday through Saturday from 9:00 A.M. to 5:00 P.M. and on Sunday from 1:00 to 5:00 P.M.

An important component of the museum is Arkansas Made, an area devoted to the best of Arkansas' decorative, mechanical, and fine arts. A permanent collection includes the state's premier paintings, silver, pottery, textiles, and furniture made by Arkansas artists over the past 200 years.

Admission is $2.00 for adults and 50 cents for children. Call (501) 324–9351 to learn about traveling exhibits and special programs for children and families.

The second capitol, the circa-1836 **Old State House,** at 300 West Markham Street, Little Rock 72201, is a perfect example of Greek Revival architecture. It is one of the most beautiful buildings in the South and the oldest standing state capitol building west of the Mississippi. The museum inside covers the political and social history of Arkansas, but many come to see the beautiful display of thirty-one gubernatorial inaugural gowns worn by Arkansas First Ladies. Hours are 9:00 A.M. to 5:00 P.M., Monday through Saturday and 1:00 to 5:00 P.M. on Sunday. There's no admission charge. Call (501) 324–9685 or visit their Web site at www.oldstatehouse.com.

And, of course, the new capitol, circa 1900—a downscaled model of the nation's capitol that is made of Batesville marble quarried in the state— finishes the list. This, of course, is where former President Clinton was Governor Clinton, and more and more tourists want to see the building—built, by the way, by convict labor where the old walled penitentiary stood. A two-ton brass chandelier hangs in the rotunda. Six massive brass doors from Tiffany's reflect the morning light on the eastern facade—doors so sensitive to fingerprints that they are roped off except on Inauguration Day. Sunlight pours into the chambers of the

House and Senate through stained-glass domes and into the central halls through barrel-vaulted ceilings. Here the "Dash" bus sprints from the capitol to downtown for 25 cents, making lunch and shopping easy for both tourists and politicians. For information on tours of the building, call (501) 682–1010.

Follow Seventh Street from the capitol to the **Quapaw Quarter** with its renovated Victorian homes and buildings. It extends from the capitol to I–30 and from the Arkansas River to Roosevelt Road and is an interesting place to spend the whole day. In fact, if you want to stay the night, there are two B&Bs in the Quarter.

<table>
<tr><td>

Trivia

The Little Rock Zoo (off I–630 exit 4 at 1 Jonesboro Drive) has more than 500 native and exotic animals. There is a tropical rain forest and a fine big cat exhibit. It is open daily 9:30 A.M. to 5:00 P.M.

</td></tr>
</table>

Villa Marre, at 1321 South Scott Street in the Quarter, is an elegantly restored Victorian built in 1881 by a saloonkeeper who wanted a little respect and had plenty of money to spend. He envisioned an elegant house that would impress people with the refinement that seemed to be lacking in his profession. Combining Italianate and Second Empire elements and topped with a French mansard roof, the house had indoor plumbing; its parquet floors of oak and mahogany quilt the floor with flowers, squares, fans, and zigzags. You may have already seen the arched windows and wrought-iron fence of this lovely old home, for it appeared on the television show *Designing Women*. Villa Marre is open Monday through Friday from 9:00 A.M. to 1:00 P.M. and Sunday from 1:00 to 5:00 P.M., but appointments are recommended for tours. The phone number of the Quapaw Quarter Association is (501) 371–0075, and their Web site is www.quapaw.com. The organization offers a walking-tour brochure on other buildings in the historic district.

The Quapaw Quarter contains some magnificent houses, such as the fabulous Gothic Queen Anne mansion at 2120 Louisiana Street, Little Rock 72206, which is now *The Empress of Little Rock Bed & Breakfast Inn.* It is a tour house, too. Owners Sharon Welch-Blair and her husband, Bob, share the history and beauty of their home with everyone. Dressed in period costumes to lead the tours, Sharon acknowledges that Bob is the resident, and very accurate, historian. The beautiful structure was finished in 1888 by a Mr. Hornibrook, who owned a bar. Because of his occupation, he was blackballed from the then prestigious Scott Street. He got his revenge by building the most magnificent mansion in Little Rock. The home is made of native materials. Beyond the curved front doors—with a stained-glass transom—rises a dramatic double staircase. There are

CENTRAL ARKANSAS

five fireplaces, four with their original Eastlake mantels, on the first floor. The woodwork alone is worth seeing. There are three different styles of parquet wood floors. The tower is octagonal, as are many of the rooms. Legend has it that Mr. Hornibrook held illegal poker games in the tower. In fact, during renovation, one of the workers encountered a ghost in the attic. Bob insists he has seen a gentleman in a homburg hat descending the staircase. Ask him to tell the story.

There are five rooms, each with a private bath and telephone. Rates are $125 to $200. They would rather not have children under ten years old. If you just want to see this stunning home, tours are at 11:30 A.M. and 3:00 P.M. Tuesday and Thursday for $5.00 a person. Call (501) 374-7966 for reservations and information, e-mail to hostess@theempress.com, or log on at www.theempress.com.

MacArthur Park, also part of the Quapaw Quarter, was the site of the Little Rock Arsenal, built in 1836. Here, in the arsenal, General Douglas MacArthur was born in 1880. His father, Captain Arthur MacArthur, with Mrs. MacArthur, came to the arsenal as commandant during the Reconstruction after the Civil War. There are a couple of interesting places in the park. One is the **Arkansas Arts Center,** at Ninth and Commerce Streets, where you can be an active participant in the arts. You can develop your talents in many creative areas, such as photography, pottery, woodworking, painting, and drawing. The spacious halls are filled with contemporary crafts by Arkansas artists and works by Picasso, Cézanne, and Degas. Handcrafted jewelry and toys are also available. Call them at (501) 372-4000.

Drawings restaurant is a project of the Fine Arts Club, the center's volunteer organization. Daily specials include grilled chicken or chicken salad and are only $7.50. The arts center is open 10:00 A.M. to 5:00 P.M. Monday through Saturday and noon to 5:00 P.M. on Sunday. Lunch is served from 11:15 A.M. to 2:30 P.M. Monday through Friday. Call (501) 372-4000 for information.

BEST ANNUAL EVENTS IN CENTRAL ARKANSAS

Riverfest, Little Rock, Memorial Day Weekend; (501) 255-3378

Toadsuck Daze, Conway, first weekend in May; (501) 327-7788

Annual Kid Fest, Greenbrier (Woolly Hollow State Park), first weekend in August; (501) 679-2098; free admission

Annual Summer Bluegrass Show, Adona (Cypress Creek Park), (501) 327-4214; all-acoustic bluegrass show, no alcohol or drugs allowed; admission $7.00 Thursday, $8.00 Friday, $9.00 Saturday

Annual Summerset, North Little Rock; first weekend in September; (501) 834-0731; admission $1.00 ages 16 and up

Annual Waterfowl USA National Celebrity Duck Hunt and Banquet, North Little Rock (Sherwood Forrest), December; contact Elizabeth Parten (501) 758-1424; celebrities and bird-hunters come from across the country to hunt the Grand Prairie, opens with a Celebrity Hunt Banquet and auction open to the public: bid on hunts, prints, guns, plus meet celebrities; admission $85.

The Arkansas Arts Center's *Decorative Arts Museum,* housed in the Pike-Fletcher-Terry Mansion at Seventh and Rock Streets in the Quarter, is a three-story beauty full of mirrors, silver services, and carved wooden decorative items used in homes over the years. The museum has both permanent collections and changing exhibits. The Crystal Room is a mirrored area filled with crystal and glass displays, almost resulting in a fun-house effect. Each room has its own fireplace. In 1839 the original house—a seven-room brick home—was built on grounds large enough to make it self-sufficient, including slave quarters, a smokehouse, and a detached kitchen. It was occupied by federal troops during the Civil War. In 1916 it was remodeled into its present Colonial Revival style, complete with a leaded glass skylight opened by a pulley in the attic. The museum is open Monday through Thursday and Saturday from 10:00 A.M. to 5:00 P.M., Friday until 8:30 P.M., and Sunday from 2:00 to 5:00 P.M. Admission is free. Call (501) 372–4000 for more information.

Turn your children loose to run and play and touch and enjoy in the *Children's Museum of Arkansas,* at 1400 West Markham Street, Little Rock 72201, in the lobby of the old Union Station downtown. They can make soap bubbles the size of an elephant, squeeze plastic veggies in the farmer's market as they pretend to buy or sell, or build wonderfully huge forts from gigantic interlocking blocks. A full-size house done in the style of the 1930s becomes an enclosed backyard exhibition where parents with toddlers can watch the older children work the computers or visit the kids' gallery where the artwork they do is displayed. Hours are 10:00 A.M. to 5:00 P.M. Monday through Saturday and from 1:00 to 5:00 P.M. on Sundays. Admission is $4.00 ($2.00 for seniors) and absolutely free the first and third Friday of the month. Call (501) 374–6655 for information.

Cantrell Gallery, at 8206 Cantrell Road, Little Rock 72201, has more than 3,500 square feet of gallery area, featuring an eclectic group of art by artists from around the state. It is the largest commercial gallery in Arkansas. The gallery is open from 10:00 A.M. to 5:00 P.M. Monday through Saturday. Call (501) 224–1335 for information.

The *Aerospace Education Center,* at 3301 Roosevelt Road, Little Rock 72201, is another kid-friendly museum, near the Little Rock airport (if you have a couple of hours to kill between flights, this is perfect). Take exit 3 off I–440 and drive toward the airport, turn left at the light onto East Roosevelt Road (if you are coming from the airport, turn right). The center is ½ mile on the left.

The children can see a mock-up of the *Mercury* space capsule (the first space vehicle to carry an American into space) and compare it with the Soviet *Vostok* space capsule right next to it. If you are old enough to remember the launches from Cape Canaveral, you will be fascinated with the information in the exhibit. For example, remember Laika, the Soviet space dog on *Sputnik II* in 1957? She was the first living creature launched into space, but the Soviets didn't tell us that she died shortly after launch because her compartment overheated. Along with the vintage spacecraft (who would think we would ever be talking about *vintage* spacecraft?) and airplanes, there is an IMAX theater with stunning big-screen space movies and a gift shop with plenty of science toys. There is an exhibit of Russian and American space art, too. Hours are 9:00 A.M. to 9:00 P.M. Monday through Thursday, 9:00 A.M. to 11:00 P.M. Friday and Saturday, and 11:00 A.M. to 5:00 P.M. on Sunday. Admission is free. The IMAX theater is $6.00 for adults and $4.75 for children ages three to fourteen. Call (501) 376–4629 for information.

After walking the gallery you might want some food or perhaps a cappuccino. Well, you are in luck, because nearby, at 8026 Cantrell Road, is the **Purple Cow,** where you can get a juicy cheddar cheeseburger for $3.85 and polish off a thick, hand-dipped butterscotch or strawberry milkshake to rejuvenate yourself. In fact, they serve "adult shakes" with a shot of liquor. You will recognize the place right away by the purple doors. *Southern Living* magazine described it as "charmingly odd," but the corrugated metal siding isn't the reason, it's the Alka-Seltzer on the menu, which may, indeed, be necessary after woofing down a cheeseburger with hot pepper cheese and jalapeños. Hours are 11:00 A.M. to 9:00 P.M. Monday through Thursday and 11:00 A.M. to 10:00 P.M. Friday (they serve breakfast on Saturday and Sunday from 8:30 to 10:30 A.M.). The Cow closes at 10:00 P.M. on Saturday and 9:00 P.M. on Sunday. Call (501) 221–3555 for more information.

Cantrell Road features other places nominated for having the best burgers in Little Rock, too. The **Buffalo Grill,** for example, is a perennial winner of the *Arkansas Times* poll for favorite burgers. It is off Cantrell Road, at 1611 Rebsamen Park Road, Little Rock 72201. Munch into a thick, grilled hamburger that is crisp on the outside and juicy on the inside. The square-cut French fries are superb. Hours are 11:00 A.M. to 10:00 P.M. Monday through Saturday and noon to 9:00 P.M. on Sunday. Call (501) 224–0012 for information.

The River Market area is fun to spend a day in. There is a fine collection of eating places in the cantina—Middle Eastern, Japanese, Spanish, and barbecue restaurants, a bakery—and a meat market as well. An art gallery and a great shop filled with eclectic decorative accessories and furniture and the area will soon be the home of the *William Jefferson Clinton Presidential Library.*

The *Soho on Grant* shop, at 101 South Commerce, Little Rock 72201, is filled with early- and mid-twentieth century designs and furniture. Remember Danish Modern, lava lamps, and things our parents thought were too cool? They were handed off to us for our first apartment, and we hated them. (Of course, this depends on your age. Maybe you were sent off with the blond limed-oak furniture of the 1950s.) What goes around comes around, according to Becca Hayley, and what is ultramodern to one generation becomes hideously old-fashioned to another. But then along comes a new crop of young adults, and suddenly it's hot. Deco, retro, mahogany—you name it, she has it. Cat's-eye-shaped glasses and things kitschy or made of chrome or vinyl are here in this small shop in the neighborhood known as Hillcrest. Becca studied design in Los Angeles and once performed in a techno-funk band. Now she is an interior decorator who can work with any style. (She and her husband live in a pyramid-shaped house.) The smooth lines of these home-decorating pieces appeal to her. Their unadorned curves and angles blend into any decor. Becca works with and supports local artists. She also has a bargain basement in addition to the two floors of furniture and accessories, featuring Herman Miller for the home and mid-century classics. Hours are 11:00 A.M. to 7:00 P.M. Monday through Saturday. Call (501) 372–4884 or fax (501) 372–5125 for information.

The River Market area is an amazing renovation in Little Rock, and it is booming. A must-see attraction is *River Market Art Space,* at 301 President Clinton Avenue, Little Rock 72201, where Suzan Strous has taken a circa-1850s building with 25-foot ceilings and 3,000 square feet and filled it with art. There is art on the walls and even more walls hang from pipes in the ceiling and display even more art. Eighty percent of the work is by Arkansas artists; more than one hundred artists exhibit here in every medium—oils, pastels, watercolors, water sculptures in clay, and other sculptures in wood and stone. There is raku pottery, stoneware, and art glass, too. Hours are from 10:00 A.M. until 6:00 P.M. Tuesday through

Saturday. In November and December it is open Sunday from 1:00 to 5:00 P.M. and also by appointment. Call Susan at (501) 324–ARTS or see some of the fine works on display at www.rivermarketartspace.com.

You can wander around this wonderful part of town for days and not see or get a taste of it all. Next door to Susan is **Afrajamex,** at 305 President Clinton Avenue (501–372–3460), which features imports from Africa, Jamaica, and Mexico. Next is **Starr Guitars,** at 303 President Clinton Avenue (501–372–1234), where you can see the largest assortment of collectible guitars in the state. Next door to that is the **Flying Saucer Beer Emporium** (501–372–7468), just what it sounds like, a good spot to rest and have a brew and think about what you are going to do next. On the river side of the Museum of Discovery is the **Underground Pub,** at 500 President Clinton Avenue (501–707–2537), with British food right here in Arkansas. Keep exploring and find the **Pyramid Gallery** (also called Hearne Fine Arts) for a collection of African-American art. Call (501) 372–6822.

Hillcrest is just before the neighborhood known as the Heights. Keep going and find **Cheers!,** a tiny place on Van Buren just north of Cantrell Road. This lovely little spot serves burgers and fries similar to those at the Buffalo Grill, because the restaurants once shared ownership. Hours are 11:00 A.M. to 9:00 P.M. Monday through Saturday. Call (501) 663–5937 for information.

Once you have reached the Kroger store at 1816 Polk, Little Rock 72207, look inside for **Silvek's European Bakery,** which specializes in Eastern European baked goods. A sign reads SILVEK'S WILL BAKE POPPY STOLLEN THE LAST FRIDAY OF EACH MONTH, FOR SPECIAL ORDERS ONLY. If you plan to be in Little Rock a while, it is worth the *weight.* (Sadly, pun intended.) Hours are 7:00 A.M. to 8:00 P.M. Monday through Saturday and 7:00 A.M. to 7:00 P.M. on Sunday. Call (501) 661–9699 to order a stollen.

Just west of Little Rock is the forty-one-acre **Oasis Renewal Center,** a nonprofit ecumenical retreat; nestled within it is a small lunchroom staffed with volunteers who give all their tips to the center. The **Oasis Restaurant,** at 14913 Cooper Orbet Road, Little Rock 72223, is where Wilma Crowder and Judith Hale create meals that make you think of home. Everything is made from scratch every day, using homegrown herbs and served in huge portions. Softball-size rolls are served in this quiet little corner of central Arkansas. A wall of windows open onto a pond inhabited by wild birds, ducks, and geese. A swan dips in the water near her nest of eggs. The restaurant is open to the public and lunch is served Monday through Saturday from 11:00 A.M. until 2:00 P.M.

Call (501) 225–6890. The center also has a great bookstore and a log cabin for rent for either a night or a week at a time. Cabins rent for $50 a night. Walking trails through the grounds are highlighted by large rocks with Bible scriptures carved upon them. Numerous workshops offered throughout the year provide spiritual insight and motivational direction. Visit their Web site at www.oasisrenewalcenter.org.

With Little Rock as the hub, explore some surrounding towns.

But if you just happen to be headed west on Highway 70, you will pass through the tiny, one-store town of *Nance* (6 miles west of I–30), and there you will see the gravel parking lot of *Rural Dale Antiques.* Old service-station signs lean up against the front of what was a school gym. A very old fire engine is parked in the playground. The classrooms are filled with vendors.

Bee Oxford has recently remodeled and added lots of new vendors. She can show you an 8 x 10-foot steel-plated jail from Lonsdale, the next town down the highway. No electricity? She can find you a kerosene refrigerator. Want an antique tractor? There are plenty of old farm implements. A Victrola? And how about some records to play on it? There are more than a thousand LPs. Okay, to some it's a lot of junk. But you know what they say about someone else's junk. . . . This enormous flea market is open from 8:00 A.M. until 5:00 P.M. Call (501) 939–2454 for information.

Benton is southwest of Little Rock on I–30. The small *Gann Museum* on Market Street is the former office of Dr. Dewell Gann Sr., built in 1883 by patients who could not afford to pay for their medical care. These amateurs sawed out porous blocks of bauxite by hand, allowed them to dry, then cemented them together. It is the only known building anywhere made of bauxite. The museum has a collection of the unique multicolored swirl patterned Niloak pottery (Niloak is "kaolin" spelled backwards, the high-quality clay found nearby and used in making Eagle Pottery in the early nineteenth century). Next door is Dr. Gann's Victorian home, which had the first telephone and indoor bathroom in town. The home has been restored to its original elegance but is not open to the public. The museum is open 10:00 A.M. until 4:00 P.M. Tuesday and Thursday, 11:00 A.M. to 1:00 P.M. Saturday. Call (501) 778–5513.

At *Jerry's Soda Shoppe,* a couple of blocks north of the museum at 107 South Market Street, Benton 72015, you can choose between a round cafe table or a booth and admire the white, embossed tin ceiling and dark-wood soda fountain with its high stools and brass rail. A large cigar store Indian guards the front of the shop, and a grand Wurlitzer jukebox cheers up the back, blasting out oldies. The sponged yellow walls are covered in movie posters and photos, and a one-man-band player piano with a large sculpture of Jerry playing a banjo on top. You can have a generous burger for $3.50 with cheese, bacon, or chili topping for 25 cents extra, or a huge banana split or a malted. You might just recognize Jerry Van Dyke. He had a role as Luther Van Dam on the ABC sitcom *Coach*. He also appeared on the *Dick Van Dyke Show* and *Diagnosis Murder* (you may notice the family resemblance, Dick's his brother.) Jerry is in the Pine Bluff Entertainer's Hall of Fame, even though he is not originally from Arkansas. He and his wife, Shirley, bought the complete downtown block and renovated the soda shop along with a movie theater, candy shop and antiques store. The Soda Shoppe's hours are 11:00 A.M. to 4:00 P.M. Monday through Thursday and until 9:00 P.M. on Friday and Saturday. Call (501) 860–5500 for more information.

Here is a special note for serious hikers: The **Ouachita Trail** begins at Pinnacle Mountain State Park, just across the Arkansas River from **Maumelle** on Highway 30. The mountain rises more than a thousand feet into the sky above the Arkansas River Valley, a wedge of rock jutting abruptly from the flat valley. Surrounded by heavily wooded hillsides, bright waterways, and rich lowlands, the summit offers a panoramic view of the eastern slopes of the Ouachita Mountain range. There are hiking trails for everyone in this day-use park, from the gentle $1/2$ mile loop for the physically limited to the day trip for birders and wildflower hunters, to the infamous Ouachita Trail that extends more than 250 miles into eastern Oklahoma for really serious hikers. The starting point of this awesome trail is just west of the visitors center and is marked with blue blazes. So, if you are headed for Oklahoma, and not in a hurry, call (501) 868–9150 for trail information.

If it happens that you are driving through this area in the spring when the daffodils bloom, slip through the tiny community on **Wye Mountain** and see and smell seven rolling acres of daffodils. You won't be alone; thousands of others will be doing the same thing. More than thirty different types of daffodils—ranging from light to dark yellow or orange—nod in the sunshine. Flowers usually bloom in mid-March. The local Homemakers' Club offers barbecue and homemade cobbler at their annual arts and crafts fair then. To reach Wye Mountain from Little Rock, take exit 9 from I–430, drive west on Highway 10 past Lake Maumelle, turn right on Highway 113, and drive 7 miles north until you see a small Methodist church surrounded by thousands of bright flowers.

Driving north on I–40 from Little Rock, you'll find the city of **Conway** between the towns of Pickles Gap and Toad Suck. Lake Conway is a nearby 6,700-acre fishing lake, and Lake Beaverfork offers not only fishing, but swimming and waterskiing. Toad Suck Park is at a historic ferry site on the Arkansas River, and the Cherokee Trail of Tears Memorial can be found at **Cadron Settlement Park.**

The Cadron Settlement blockhouse, a two-story log structure, is in the final stages of its third life. There is probably more history here—the geographical center of the state—than anywhere else. This settlement dates back two centuries. Spanish explorer Hernando de Soto's expedition passed by looking for riches, and the French explorers Marquette and Jolliet made their way here. After the French and Indian War, the British stripped France of its North American possessions. No one knows whether it was the French or the Spanish who made the first settlement here, but all recognized the juncture of a broad creek made an excellent landing site for a trading post to trade in the beaver pelts found here. There was fresh water in a free-flowing spring, lots of timber and game, and the site was on a rocky bluff that would be safe from the flood waters and easy to defend should the Quapaw become hostile. It was set to be the capital of the new territory, but somehow Little Rock won the prize. Cadron was a stopping point of the Trail of Tears—the Cherokee were forced to land here due to low water. Many died and the dead are identified on a marker. The Civil War saw brutal and bloody guerilla warfare here.

Rosalie and Paul Revis are good source of information about what's going on in Conway. They are the innkeepers at the **Olde Towne Bed and Breakfast** at 567 Locust Street, Conway 72032. This 1922 Colonial Revival is listed on the National Register of Historic Places and has two guest rooms and two suites all with private baths (one has a Jacuzzi), television, and private phones. The common area includes the dining room and a lovely sunroom. It is walking distance from downtown. Rates are from $75 to $95 per night. Call (501) 329–5989 or see the inn at www.oldetownebb.com.

Rosalie recommends **The Mean Bean Cafe,** at 2501 Dave Ward Drive, Conway 72032 (Highway 286 West), for an afternoon latte or cappuccino and for its spinach burrito. There is a daily lunch special, as well as the sandwiches and soup that Trisha Cooper and Susie Schwarznau turn out. Hours are Monday through Thursday from 11:00 A.M. to 8:00 P.M., Friday until 9:00 P.M. You have to get there early on Saturday because they are only open until 3:00 P.M. Call (501) 336–9957 for more.

Conway has a nice downtown area full of shops, all neatly topped with awnings. Probably the most interesting place in town is **Antiques Mall,** which comprises an antiques mall and a "previously owned" designer clothing shop, at 713 Oak Street. Call (501) 327–4044 for information. Hours are 10:00 A.M. to 5:00 P.M. Monday through Saturday. But there is an even bigger surprise tucked inside: the *Oak Street Bistro.*

Begin by inspecting the deli called *Rollin' in the Dough,* where gourmet sauces and all manner of edible goodies line the shelves. Carry-out salads, a pastry case filled with homemade desserts, and even frozen casseroles are stocked in the refrigerator cases. Call (501) 450–9908 for information.

In the restaurant the woman responsible for both eateries, Pam Ferguson, creates a cool and comfortable atmosphere. The dining room is a cool yellow-peach with green-and-white cloth napkins and fresh flowers on white tablecloths. There is a variety of salads, at least six different ones daily (ask for the salad sampler plate with three of them), along with huge, fresh croissant sandwiches, oozing smoked turkey, cheese, sprouts, and guacamole, and a good selection of other entrees. And there are, of course, desserts: carrot cake, a creation called Chocolate in Excess with orange liqueur, five different cheesecakes that change daily (the key lime cheesecake is great). Hours are Monday through Saturday 11:00 A.M. to 2:00 P.M.

People come in to stroll around and shop, not just to eat. The boutique of previously owned designer clothing shares the front half of the building with the restaurant, while the back half comprises 15,000 square feet of antique furniture. The consignment shop is *Perfect Expressions* (501–329–7343), and while you are strolling around the mall, peek into *Interiors by Ivo* where interior decorators Charles or Ivo wait to help you create elegance with the antiques you buy. To reach the mall take exit 127 off I–40 and go south on Highway 64, which is Oak Street. Hours are Tuesday through Saturday from 8:00 A.M. to 9:00 P.M. Call (501) 327–2185 for information.

If you leave Conway northbound on Highway 65, then it might be fun to look for the town of *Greenbrier.* A good Samaritan deed on a very hot Kansas City, Missouri, day was the beginning of the *Safaripark* conservatory at 394 Highway 65 North in Greenbrier. Steven Henning tells the story of finding his first lioness, Christy, in a truck. She was hot and without water and very stressed. Steven let his feelings be known to the truck driver, and the driver told him that if he could do better, he could just buy the animal. He did.

His plan was to donate her to the Kansas City Zoo, but the zoo didn't want her. So Steven took Christy home to his tree farm and began to study lions. He discovered that they need companionship of their own kind, and soon he bought Clarence as a mate for her. He took them along when he moved to Arkansas. There he purchased twenty-eight acres only twelve minutes north of Conway, near Greenbrier, and developed twelve of those acres into animal habitats measuring 100 feet by 300 feet; each enclosure has fresh water and food. They also have mounds for draping on, platforms for leaping from, trees for crouching in, and water bogs for cooling off in.

The park now has conservatory status, and more cats have found a home in the Ozarks. Ruth Clayton is the park manager and oversees the volunteers who work there. She is also in charge of ordering supplies and cuddling newborn lion cubs. The lions are big eaters, consuming between three and six hundred pounds of chicken or beef a day.

Of course, a favorite attraction is newborn cubs, when they are available. Visitors are allowed to pet and hold the babies, who live in a large cage in the back of the gift shop. Lion young are allowed the run of the gift shop, and trained volunteers are on hand to keep an eye on things. The lions are bred when they are three years old, and other blood lines are brought into the park to avoid inbreeding. A large sign outside the park lets visitors know when there are new arrivals to cuddle. A nine-week-old cub is the size of a large house cat, but when they stop nursing and begin eating, they grow fast.

The park is home to 400-pound twin Bengal tigers—Romeo and Rajah—who have been declawed and can wrestle with Steven. Tyson, a Siberian tiger, is already a member of the animal kingdom no longer in existence in the wild due to poachers. Tyson and his mate, Tia, have had cubs here in the park. Henning's dream is someday to return lion cubs to their natural environment.

But for now he provides a home and breeding ground for the cats and an area where children can come and see these beautiful creatures without bars or hot dog vendors. The park is open every day except Monday and some holidays. There are plenty of other animals for children to see here as well. It is home to pigs, ducks, llamas, lemurs (primates from Madagascar), emus, rheas, a couple of pythons, and some black bears.

Hours are 10:00 A.M. until 6:00 P.M. every day but Monday April through October. Abbreviated hours occur in fall or spring. Call (501) 679–3455 for more information. Look for a big billboard just before the Heber Springs exit on Highway 65 North.

Mike Smith began making furniture in 1974 while working in his dad's shop. Now he has his own shop, *Mike Smith Furniture,* in his home in a rustic setting near Round Mountain, at 283 Round Mountain Road. His post-and-rung chairs are custom pieces in oak, cherry, or walnut, and each is signed. He begins with rough, hand-chosen pieces of green lumber from saw mills in the northwestern part of the state. He then air dries or kiln dries them and begins the process of sculpting with an old-fashioned wood lathe and handheld chisels and gouges to make spindles, posts, and stretcher rungs. Rocker runners are cut with a band saw, and the parts are carefully assembled. The combination of green wood and kiln-dried wood creates shrinkage that clamps, giving the joints a tight fit. The chairs are then stained and hand-rubbed to show off the natural grain. Mike's wife, Susie, now hand-weaves the rush, a durable, twisted paper cord, for chair seats, taking over the task from Mike. Rocking chairs are available in many sizes, from a child's chair to an impressive 44-inch man-size rocker. Stools, benches, and tables are also available in different sizes and may be custom ordered. Prices range from $25 to $300. Take the Mayflower exit from I–40, and call ahead for directions (501–327–0385). "We're off in the country on a dirt road," Mike says.

Riddle: What does someone do with a baby elephant when it reaches 6,000 pounds? The answer is a Riddle, too—Scott Riddle, to be exact. *Riddle's Elephant Breeding Farm and Wildlife Sanctuary* is where Scott Riddle and his wife, Heidi, care for elephants from all over the world that are no longer wanted by the places that were once their homes. Elephants too old, too cranky, or injured in some way are routinely destroyed every year. Because they are almost extinct, because there are so few places left to support elephants in their natural environment, and because the Riddles wanted to do something for this endangered animal, the couple bought 330 acres off Pumpkin Center Circle between Guy and Quitman (on Highway 25) and took them in. The farm contains a spring-fed creek, a waterfall, a pasture, and forest-land. The Riddles have recently completed a 2,000-yard swimming hole for their eight jumbo guests.

Trivia
Did you know that the bottom of an elephant's foot is not hard like a hoof, but rather a shock-absorbing pad that is able to contract, expand, and adapt to the terrain, allowing elephants to move quietly and with agility? Elephants walk on tiptoe. The bones of the toe point toward the ground but are protected by a thick fatty pad inside the sole of the foot.

Two such guests are Solomon and Mugsy (called "the little guys"), ten-year-old African elephants that were to be killed in a culling, or herd-thinning operation, in their native land. A wealthy man who bought them as calves and then watched them grow to 6,000 pounds soon tired of caring for them (a full-grown male can weigh six tons and stand 12 feet tall). African elephant Willie (from the Nashville Zoo, hence his name) joined Toby, a seventeen-year-old male, and Tonga, a nineteen-year-old female from a small Indiana zoo. Asian elephants Kate and Betty Boop came from a circus, where they were injured by an over-wrought male (females weigh only half as much as males and are shorter by 4 feet; they are no match in a domestic dispute).

Scott Riddle's most famous elephant is Mary, a twenty-two-year-old Asian elephant with an artistic bent. Her paintings hang in galleries around the country, where they bring in as much as $350. (Asian elephants, a separate species, are smaller—if you can call it that—and often lack tusks.) Riddle, who is also an artist, calls Mary's style "impressionist." One gallery owner sees it as "abstract." But whether in the style of Monet or Picasso, Mary likes primary colors, "with red her favorite," Riddle says. Mary's talents don't stop there. She also plays the drum, the bell, the tambourine, and, believe it or not, the harmonica. She travels to Pickles Gap with "the little guys" for $5.00 elephant rides and does her share to support her $100-a-week food habit. Mary is the primary fund-raiser. In the wild elephants eat 500 to 600 pounds of food a day—that's a lot of groceries—and even with high-nutrition elephant chow, 100 pounds a day is average. The nonprofit operation is constantly searching for ways to bring in funds.

The Riddles are even active on the world scene. In 1991 the nation of Zimbabwe began destroying elephants, and the Riddles sent protests through their congressman to try to stop the killing. "We would take them all if we could find the money to move them," Scott says. Long-range plans include massive, pachyderm-size barns; medical facilities; and the corralling of a large pasture to allow all the elephants to roam unchained, as Boop and Kate do now. Scott also wants to open an elephant museum with his collection of more than 1,500 elephant items—ancient temple rubbings, figurines, and prints—and a large assortment of books on the subject.

The farm is home to a collection of geese, goats, dogs, cats, and chickens right now, but the designation "wildlife sanctuary" entitles the Riddles to take in any zoo or circus animal that might otherwise be destroyed. Most funding comes from individual memberships ($25) and corporate sponsorship of the farm. "This is not a job; it's a life," Riddle says. Call (501) 589–3291 for directions to the farm and a chance to hear the incredible vocabulary of sounds these gentle creatures use to communicate—twenty-five different sounds, ranging from high-frequency whistles to deep rumbles, two octaves below human range—and an unbeatable

Riddle's Elephant Breeding Farm and Wildlife Sanctuary

photo opportunity. Tours are conducted on the first Saturday of every month between 11:00 A.M. and 3:00 P.M. or by appointment.

Riddle puts out a newsletter called *The Elephants Trunk Nose News*. Volunteers are always needed to help with these wonderful creatures. Call Gordon McIntyre, the volunteer coordinator, at (501) 589–3291 if you want to offer a helping hand.

Heading back to Little Rock on Highway 70, which parallels I–40, will take you through the little town of *DeVall's Bluff* and a chance to try a couple of interesting eating places.

Since Highway 70 runs right smack through the middle of DeVall's Bluff, *Craig's Bar-B-Q* at the west end of town on Highway 70 will be easy to find if you're not in the mood for catfish. The sauce here makes the ribs or pork sandwich something to remember. But be careful. The mild is like the prelaunch rocket fire at NASA, the medium is launch-incendiary, and the hot: We have ignition! You can take home some sauce if you want the fire next time, too. Hours are 9:00 A.M. to 9:00 P.M. every day except Friday and Saturday, when it is open until 10:00 P.M. Call (870) 998–2616 for information.

Across the street the words **Family Pie Shop** are hand-scrawled on an unpretentious white concrete block shop. But a cooling dessert waits inside. Mary Thomas's handmade creations are simply great. Try the Karo-nut pie—it's Mary's rendition of the classic southern pecan pie. If she doesn't have the kind of pie you like, just tell her and she'll bake one special for you. Hours are 9:00 A.M. to 5:00 P.M. Monday through Saturday. Sunday is her day of rest, Mary says. Call (870) 998–2279 for information.

The **Prairie County Museum** is in the town of **Des Arc.** The museum shows a hundred years of hard river life from 1831 to 1931. The diverse history of this life, when men fished with nets and dived for mussels, is in these three small rooms. Fish were brought up in seines, tammel nets, and hoop nets, one of which is in the museum. Stringers with metal hooks called crow's feet were dragged across the river bottom, and the mussels with shells open to feed closed on the hooks and were hauled aboard. A drag, a device that dredged the bottom and pushed mussels into a net, was also used. Catfish and buffalofish were caught and carried by rail from the White River to the rest of the country. Houseboats were owned by river workers. Meat of mussels was popular, and shells were used for buttons. Native Americans (Quapaw to the south, Osage to the north) used them for tools and jewelry, and newcomers built button factories at Claredon and DeVall's Bluff. The museum has an early button-making machine.

Safari

*T*he day began in Fairfield Bay at the home of friends. My mom and dad had driven to Arkansas with us to do some exploring. Actually, my dad and my husband had golf in mind, and my mom and her friend Terry had shopping in mind. I was thinking about elephants.

I had heard about a man who took in neglected pachyderms—somewhere between Guy and Quitman on the map—and who was open to seeing visitors. The men vetoed the elephant safari and headed for the golf course. Mom and Terry, always good sports in these matters, jumped into the car and we headed out.

We arrived at Riddle's Elephant Farm in a cloud of gravel dust. Scott Riddle met us at the gate and took us on tour. I learned more about my mom than about elephants that day. She is fearless. She walked up to huge elephants and rubbed their trunks. She fed them handfuls of hay and even asked about riding one. She was fascinated with the sounds the elephants made—the high sounds and deep rumbles—when they communicated with each other.

I now have a great photo on my desk of my mom—smiling sweetly—with her arm around an elephant's trunk. It is one of my favorite pictures of her.

Divers groped in the murky waters for the shells of creatures called bankclimber, hill splitter, hogshell, washboard, Wabash pigtoe, monkey-face, and purple pimpleback mussels. They often improvised, making diving helmets from things like the gas tank of a Ford Model T.

The river was the lifeline of the area and the highway for products grown in the region. Everything from canoes to steam-powered boats cruised the river. Then the Civil War brought thousands of riverboats along the Mississippi and its tributaries.

Artist George Caleb Bingham's paintings, showing river life from 1811 to 1879, are on display. Admission is $2.50, $1.25 for children six to twelve years old. The museum is open from 8:00 A.M. to 5:00 P.M. Tuesday through Saturday and 1:00 to 5:00 P.M. on Sunday. Call (870) 256–3711 for information.

If you are looking for a place to spend the night, find the **Palaver Place Bed and Breakfast,** at **Loomis Landing,** 7 miles south of DeValls Bluff off Highway 302, on the White River, where Charles Spellmann offers five guest rooms with private baths and a gourmet or country breakfast served in the dining room or on the porch. This rustic-looking inn will fool you, because it has a hot tub, swimming pool, and canoe rides. It also has a computer and fax, *and* you can take painting lessons or be hypnotized. Charles will serve lunch or dinner, too, with advance notice. Room rates range from $55 to $85. Call (870) 998–7206 or visit their Web site at www.palaver-place.com. On the Web site, you'll see a picture of a large bell. The bell, which Chuck has in a safe place, once belonged to Willie Nelson, but when the famous country music singer ran into a little trouble with the IRS a few years back, this was one of the items auctioned off to pay his debts. Apparently, Willie would like to have it back and Chuck says he'll be glad to give it to him, but Willie has to come to DeValls Bluff himself to pick it up.

An impressive archaeological site, even though misnamed, **Toltec Mounds** lies southeast of Little Rock off Highway 165. An early owner thought these were the mounds of the Toltec Indians of Mexico, but the people who built the mounds and lived in the central part of the state had a culture different from that of other contemporary groups in the Mississippi Valley. They were not nomads but lived in permanent villages where they built sturdy houses and farmed the rich soil. For more than fifteen years now, the Arkansas Archaeological Survey and volunteers from the Arkansas Archaeological Society have been digging for answers about the lives of a culture named Plum Bayou who lived here about A.D. 700 to 950. Self-guided tours take visitors through areas of the central plaza and five of the original eighteen mounds. The nearby Arkansas River was used for transportation and fishing, and clay was used for pottery; the soil was fertile, and the surrounding uplands supported an abundance of animals for hunting. A dugout canoe measuring 24 feet was found in the Saline River, miraculously preserved, perhaps because of being quickly buried in mud. This and other artifacts are on display at the park. One of the mounds is thought to have been a religious site, another was a burial mound. Others were platforms for leaders' homes. Building the mounds took tremendous effort (250,000 basket loads of dirt were required for the largest one). In June you can watch digs under way by the Arkansas Archaeological Survey. The mounds are arranged to mark solstices and equinoxes as the sun's rays change with the seasons to time crop planting and hunting. They are covered with grass and trees now, but when they were used by the Plum Bayou they were bare. There are storytelling sessions featuring myths and legends, and during workshops visitors can learn "flintknapping"—chipping arrowheads from stones. The mounds are on Highway 386, 9 miles northwest of the town of England, off Highway 165. The park is open Tuesday through Saturday from 8:00 A.M. to 5:00 P.M. and Sunday from noon to 5:00 P.M. Admission is $2.50, $1.50 for children. Call (501) 961–9442 for information.

The city of **Scott** is at the junction of Highways 161 and 165, and in an old store and post office built in 1912 is the **Plantation Agriculture Museum,** which focuses on the massive cotton plantations of the 1800s and the turn of the century—and the small farms that surrounded them. These plantations ranged from 1,000 acres to 7,000 acres, and most had

Romance in Arkansas

Arkansas has a place where "Romance" is never missing, but it is Nancy Bryant's job to cancel it every day. She is postmaster in a little town that has been called by that name ever since pre–Civil War settlers from Kentucky came in covered wagons and did a lot of courting by the creek there. Romance (72136) got its fifteen minutes of fame when the United States Postal Service selected the office to host the inaugural introduction of the 25-cent "Love" stamp in 1990. One of the best collections of Love stamps and stationery is housed here to accommodate the high volume of business around St. Valentine's Day. If you are seeking romance in Searcy on Highway 5, go west on Pleasure Street about 10 miles until you reach Joy, Arkansas; Joy will lead to Romance. Any letter can be sent to the post office with a request to cancel the letter there and forward it to someone.

huge homes. Many of the plantations were like small towns, with housing for workers, a church, school, blacksmith shop, and cotton gin.

This is a constantly changing exhibit with live demonstrations often on the agenda: demonstrations on Wash Day (everything from washboards to a gas-engine Maytag operating); Homespun Day with spinning, weaving, and dyeing; or Hay Harvest Day. The most popular is Antique Power Days, featuring steam engines and draft animals. Admission is $2.50 for adults and $1.50 for children (six and under get in free). Hours are Tuesday through Saturday from 8:00 A.M. to 5:00 P.M. and Sunday from 1:00 to 5:00 P.M. The museum is closed Monday. Call (501) 961–1409 for information on the demonstrations.

You might want to grab a "Hubcap" Hamburger (that got your attention, didn't it?): three-quarter pounds of beef on a 6-inch bun, with lettuce, tomato, pickle, and onion at *Cotham's Country Store and Restaurant.* The country store has been in business since 1919 and the restaurant was added in 1984. Owners Larry and Linda Griffin have added lots of antiques to the store's merchandise. To find the hamburger the fast-food places can't match, leave Highway 165 and go to Highway 161. Turn right and drive 1/4 mile past the museum and post office. Hours are 11:00 A.M. to 2:00 P.M. Tuesday through Saturday for lunch, and dinner is served from 5:00 to 8:30 P.M. on Friday and Saturday. Ask for a table in the back with a view of the Horseshoe Bayou. But be prepared to wait. Call (501) 961–9284 for information.

Sixteen miles southeast of Little Rock on old Highway 165, which parallels I–40, is *Marlsgate Plantation,* a working plantation with 2,000 acres of cotton and a beautiful, thirty-three-room mansion on Bearskin Lake, an oxbow lake, in the center of it. This wooded setting is where David Garner lives. The plantation, a lovingly maintained beauty, is a picture of Victorian elegance, and the ties between Arkansas and the Deep South are plain to see. This mansion, with its four Ionic capital square brick columns, was built in 1904 and is shaded by pecan trees. The interior features a stairway landing with stained-glass windows, 14-foot ceilings of pressed tin, each in a different design, oak woodwork, and a fireplace in every room. David serves lunches to groups of sixteen or more and has an antiques, flower, and gift shop in the carriage house. The mansion is 5 miles off the road and not visible from the highway, but tours of this private home can be arranged on an individual basis by appointment. Call (501) 961–1307.

Keo is fifteen minutes southeast of Little Rock. Dean Morris has turned the Morris farm into an antiques wonderland. *Morris Antiques* fills five buildings, and you will need all day to see everything. Buildings number 3 and 4 contain mantelpieces, old pipe organs, Victorian sofas and chairs, Tiffany-type lamps, beautiful old clocks, and French furniture. There are glass bowls and jars of all kinds. Dean and Becky Morris have warehouses in Chester, England, where an Englishman buys antiques as a hobby at garage sale-type events. They have another warehouse in Paris (not Paris, Arkansas, but the other place across the pond). To find Keo take Highway 165 Southeast. It is 13 miles from exit 7 off I–440. Turn right on Highway 232. Morris Antiques is on the right, behind the Methodist church. Hours are 9:00 A.M. to 5:00 P.M. Tuesday through Saturday and noon to 5:00 P.M. on Sunday. Call (501) 842–3531 for information.

If you get tired and need a lunch break, look for **Charlotte's Eats & Sweets,** in a lovely old drugstore at 290 Main Street, Keo 72083, where Charlotte Bowls will fix you a sandwich or dessert at the soda fountain (the pies here are beautiful). Ask about the Keo Classic, which is Charlotte's favorite. She also prefers the coconut cream pie. Hours are 11:00 A.M. to 2:00 P.M. Tuesday through Friday and 11:00 A.M. to 3:00 P.M. on Saturday. From 3:00 to 5:00 P.M. only dessert is available so they can prepare for the catfish and chicken dinner served from 5:00 to 8:00 P.M. Sorry, but it is closed on Sunday and Monday. Call (501) 842–2123 for information.

Just across the Arkansas River from Little Rock is the city of **North Little Rock,** which actually started out as the town of Argenta, until the city of Little Rock annexed Argenta in the early 1900s. You will find several businesses and other information in the city that reflect the name Argenta. You can find much of the history of North Little Rock in **Burns Park** at exit 150 off I–40. This is one of the largest city parks in the country, and includes a log cabin dating from the 1850s, a covered bridge, fishing access for the disabled, and a thirty-six-hole golf course.

Another nice park is the **Riverfront Park,** which includes a pleasant, paved one-mile walking path along the banks of the Arkansas River. While in this part of town, you may want to stop for lunch or dinner or some other refreshment at **Gators on the River.** Gators is actually on the river, on a barge, and you can float up to the restaurant in your own boat after a day of fishing, swimming, or skiing. Gators is obviously a very casual place and serves great Cajun food and drinks. Call them at (501) 372–7678.

There is a familiar sight in T. R. Pugh Memorial Park in North Little Rock if you have seen *Gone with the Wind* as many times as some people. It is what appears to be an abandoned gristmill tucked away in a grove of pine and oak trees.

The Old Mill's shingled roof overlooks a lazy stream gurgling around a rusted waterwheel. Bent persimmon trees form a natural bridge across the water. It looks authentic, but on closer inspection you will see that the "wooden" bridge, rain barrels, benches, and everything right down to the downspouts are made of concrete. Sculptor Dionicio Rodriguez created all of it in the tradition of *el trabajo rustico,* a Mexican folk art. Rodriguez sculpted painted concrete over copper forms, using lamp-black and chemicals to give it the texture of weathered wood. It took four years to create and had its fifteen minutes of fame as the background for the opening credits of *Gone with the Wind.* Time took its toll on the mill, and it became dilapidated and was deeded over to the city in 1979. A major restoration project has returned the mill to its original appearance, and new walking trails and picnic areas have been added. The Old Mill is in the T. R. Pugh Memorial Park at the corner of Fairway Avenue and Lakeshore Drive off Highway 107. Call (501) 758–1424 or (800) 643–4690 outside Arkansas.

Want more than a dip in a pool? Learn to find underwater splendors at *Rick's Dive 'N Travel Center,* at 2323 North Poplar, North Little Rock 72113, where you can start diving in a specially designed indoor pool in North Little Rock. The courses range from private lessons to group classes and cost about $200 to $350. The most popular class lasts three weeks and has its final day at a lake. If you are a little nervous about it, come over on a Saturday morning; they'll put you in the pool for forty-five minutes of free instruction to see if scuba is your thing. You can use their equipment for the lessons and buy your own after you are qualified. Hours are Monday through Thursday from 9:00 A.M. to 6:00 P.M., Friday until 7:00 P.M., and until 5:00 P.M. on Saturday. Call (501) 753–6004. The Web site is simply www.ricksdivecenter.com.

Argenta Antiques Mall, at 201 East Broadway, is in a big old building that was a stationery store in the 1940s and now has forty booths with everything from small glassware, old tools, pocket watches, and toys to a German sideboard of oak and beveled curved glass. Collectors seek out places like this for kitschy 1950s items, which are once again hot. Hours are 10:00 A.M. to 5:00 P.M. Monday through Saturday and 1:00 to 5:00 P.M. on Sunday. Call (501) 372–7750 for information.

A great place to stay in North Little Rock, particularly if you appreciate African-American history, is *Baker House Bed and Breakfast* at 109 West 5th Street, North Little Rock 72114. The house was built in 1898 by

A.E. Colburn, a Black man who had achieved his wealth in England. But after the grandiose Queen Anne was complete, racial unrest in the South discouraged Colburn from making it his home. Nearly one hundred years later, Colburn's home became the first bed-and-breakfast in North Little Rock, welcoming guests of all races. The five guest rooms range from $88 to $140. Call (501) 372–1268 or (888) 298–0255 or learn more about the history and the inn at www.thebakerhouse.com.

MORE PLACES TO STAY IN CENTRAL ARKANSAS

Little Rock Best Western Inn Towne, I–30 at Sixth and Ninth Streets, 72202; (501) 375–2100

Days Inn, 2600 West Sixty-fifth Street, 72209; (501) 562–1122

Excelsior Hotel, 3 Statehouse Plaza, 72201; (501) 375–5000 www.arkexcelsiorhotel.com

Holiday Inn, 617 South Broadway (Capitol area), 72201; (501) 376–4000

La Quinta Inn, 200 Shakleford Road, 72211; (501) 224–0900

North Little Rock Baker House Bed & Breakfast, 109 West 5th Street, 72114; (501) 372–1268

Country Inn & Suites, Poplar & Persing Streets; (501) 758–2002

MORE PLACES TO EAT IN CENTRAL ARKANSAS

Conway Stoby's, 805 Donaghey, 72032; (501) 327–5447

Little Rock Club Room Restaurant, 617 South Broadway, 72201; (501) 376–4380

The Dixie Cafe, 1220 Rebsamen Park, 72211; (501) 224–3728

Graffiti's, 7811 Cantrell, Little Rock 72211; (501) 224–9079

Chambers of Commerce in Central Arkansas

Conway Chamber of Commerce; *P.O. Box 1492, Conway 72032; (501) 327–7788*

Little Rock Chamber of Commerce; *101 South Spring Street, Little Rock 72203; (501) 374–4871*

Little Rock Convention & Visitors' Bureau; *P.O. Box 3232, Little Rock 72203; (501) 376–4781; E-mail: lrcvb@littlerock.com; www.littlerock.com/lrcvb/*

North Little Rock Convention & Visitors' Bureau; *P.O. Box 5311, North Little Rock 72119; (501) 758–1424 or (800) 643–4690; www.northlittlerock.org*

Index

INDEX

INDEX

INDEX

INDEX